The No-Growth Imperative

More than two decades of mounting evidence confirms that the existing scale of the human enterprise has surpassed global ecological limits to growth. Based on such limits, *The No-Growth Imperative* discounts current efforts to maintain growth through eco-efficiency initiatives and smart-growth programs, and argues that growth is inherently unsustainable and that the true nature of the challenge confronting us now is one of replacing the current growth imperative with a no-growth imperative.

Gabor Zovanyi asserts that anything less than stopping growth would merely slow today's dramatic degradation and destruction of ecosystems and their critical life-support services. Zovanyi makes the case that local communities must take action to stop their unsustainable demographic, economic, and urban increases, as an essential prerequisite to the realization of sustainable states.

The book presents rationales and legally defensible strategies for stopping growth in local jurisdictions, and portrays the viability of no-growth communities by outlining their likely economic, social, political, and physical features. It will serve as a resource for those interested in shifting the focus of planning from growth accommodation to the creation of stable, sustainable communities. While conceding the challenges associated with transforming communities into no-growth entities, Zovanyi concludes by presenting evidence that suggests that prospects for realizing states of no growth are greater than might be assumed.

Gabor Zovanyi is a Professor of Urban Planning at Eastern Washington University, USA. He has degrees from UCLA, San Diego State University, and the University of Washington. His research specializes in growth management, sustainable communities, and land-use law, he is also the author of *Growth Management for a Sustainable Future*.

'Gabor Zovanyi, an urban planner, persuasively demolishes the temporizing evasions of managed growth, balanced growth, smart growth, green growth, etc., and logically demonstrates the imperative of no-growth. Many ideas and strategies for implementing no-growth at the local level are insightfully discussed. Well referenced and highly recommended!'

Herman Daly

'Humans are endowed with several unique qualities of which perhaps none are more important than our capacity for logical, evidence-based analysis and our ability to engage in forward planning. In short, humankind is the only species able to act deliberately to change its future for the better. We even have a whole 'Planning' profession founded on this singular reality. That said, the evidence today suggests that the sheer scale of the human enterprise, and our seemingly unthinking dedication to continued material growth, are undermining global life support systems and with them, the human prospect. Change is coming; the end of growth is inevitable. The only question is whether the end will be dominated by chaotic disorder or inspired vision. But where are the planners? At last with "The No-Growth Imperative: Creating Sustainable Communities under Ecological Limits to Growth", we have a 'de-growth' book for community planners and social activists that should let them confront society's growth demons head on. Let us begin the transition to an equitable stable steady-state within the means of nature and, in the doing of it, rise to our full human potential.'

William Rees

'This book is an outstanding resource for community leaders and activists seeking to move beyond the endless growth model and towards greater stability and sustainability.'

Eben Fodor

'As the era of exponential economic growth comes to its end, societies are experiencing extraordinary levels of stress. Planners should be at the forefront of this inevitable historic shift, and this clear, well-argued book points the way. It could hardly be more timely.'

Richard Heinberg

'Gabor Zovanyi is a professor on a practical mission who makes a crucial contribution by describing in detail the characteristics of sustainable communities. *The No-Growth Imperative* will be read by sustainability scholars and students far and wide, but it is a must-read for the mayors, city councils, county commissioners, and other civic leaders of the 21st Century.'

Brian Czech

The No-Growth Imperative

Creating Sustainable Communities under
Ecological Limits to Growth

Gabor Zovanyi

Routledge
Taylor & Francis Group

LONDON AND NEW YORK

from Routledge

First published 2013
by Routledge
2 Park Square, Milton Park, Abingdon, Oxon, OX14 4RN

Simultaneously published in the USA and Canada
by Routledge
711 Third Avenue, New York, NY 10017

Routledge is an imprint of the Taylor & Francis Group, an informa business

British Library Cataloguing in Publication Data
A catalogue record for this book is available from the British Library

Library of Congress Cataloging in Publication Data
Zovanyi, Gabor, 1943-
The no-growth imperative : creating sustainable communities under ecological
limits to growth / Gabor Zovanyi.
p. cm.
Includes bibliographical references and index.
1. Sustainable development--United States. 2. Economic development--
Environmental aspects--United States. 3. Communities--United States. 4. Land
use--United States--Planning. I. Title.
HC110.E5Z686 2013
338.973'07--dc23
2012023431

ISBN13: 978-0-415-63014-6 (hbk)
ISBN13: 978-0-415-63015-3 (pbk)
ISBN13: 978-0-203-08401-4 (ebk)

Typeset in Garamond
by Taylor and Francis Books Ltd

Printed and bound in Great Britain by the MPG Books Group

To Herman E. Daly, Paul R. Ehrlich, and William E. Rees for providing both the foundation and inspiration for this work on the no-growth imperative.

Contents

Preface

By the beginning of the twenty-first century diverse cultures across the globe had incorporated the growth imperative into their national social paradigms. A legacy of viewing demographic, economic, and urban growth as expressions of social progress had produced a worldwide cultural network committed to an unending pursuit of growth. This pro-growth posture did not change in response to the transition from linear growth to exponential growth that occurred more than 200 years ago. Population growth and economic growth began to demonstrate exponential increases with the advent of the industrial revolution in the mid-1700s, while urban increases took on decidedly exponential characteristics during the twentieth century. With the defining characteristic of exponential growth being its surprising ability to generate large numbers quickly under the ongoing application of a percentage growth rate to a rapidly growing base, the exponential demographic, economic, and urban increases being recorded by the latter half of the twentieth century came under significant scrutiny. Critics pointed out that while it had taken the entire history of our species to reach a population of 2.5 billion in 1950, our numbers exploded to 6 billion by the year 2000, an increase of 3.5 billion in a mere 50 years. During the same time period the global economy expanded from $6 trillion of goods and services to $43 trillion, a 7-fold increase, with the annual increase in the value of goods and services in the 12 months of 2000 exceeding that during the entire nineteenth century. The dramatic magnitude of urban growth from 1950 to 2000 was capable of being illustrated in multiple ways, as with data indicating the number of cities with populations in excess of 5 million jumped from 1 in 1950 to 46 in 2000.

By the beginning of the new millennium these significant demographic, economic, and urban increases had come to be associated with dire consequences for the ecosystems needed to support life on earth. Ecologists argued that exponential growth had already taken the scale of the human enterprise to a level that was degrading and dismantling the planet's ecological life-support systems. Rather than endorsing the popular view of growth as progress, they drew attention to the role of exponential growth in bringing about a global ecological crisis. From an ecological perspective it is possible to argue that the historical idealization of physical growth under current ecological realities represents an obsolete and lethal ideology. If that iconoclastic argument can come to be accepted, it will be possible to consider the necessity of having to abandon the growth imperative as part of any survival strategy for human-kind. This book advances the premise that we have no alternative but to relinquish the growth imperative that drives the human enterprise, and in its place adopt a no-growth imperative that will serve to stop the physical growth that represents inherently unsustainable behavior and threatens the ecological underpinnings of civilization.

The opening chapter of this book surveys the traditional reasoning that has been used to support positive views of demographic, economic, and urban growth. That survey illustrates how rationales that have evolved to support growth in each of these terms have elevated growth to the status of a social imperative across the globe. Socioeconomic systems have universally accepted the idea of growth as a social good, and have, as a result, awarded the growth imperative favored status within the dominant social paradigms of nation states. The chapter then explores the nature of exponential growth and the absurd challenges it presents to any attempts to sustain growth rates in light of the dramatic quantities generated to date. Following the portrayal of the pernicious nature of exponential growth, the chapter reviews some two dec-ades of mounting evidence that the existing scale of the human enterprise has surpassed global ecological limits to growth. That review is followed by arguments in support of the inherently unsustainable nature of material increases and the assertion that the term "sustainable growth" represents a fatuous, moronic oxymoron that impedes recognition of the urgent need to quickly transition to a sustainable state of no growth. Based on mounting evidence that ecological sustainability is being undermined by continued growth, the chapter concludes with the assertion that any progress toward ecological sustainability must be predicated on the replacement of the growth imperative with a no-growth imperative.

The second chapter portrays the historical pro-growth bias of American communities and the associated role of state and federal governments in supporting the growth-promotion function of local jurisdictions. That review documents the extent to which the pursuit of growth has been the most consistent theme in local governance throughout American history. The chapter illustrates the degree to which it is possible to think of local govern-ments as "growth machines" serving the interests of land-based elites seeking to increase their land values through the ongoing intensification of local land use. Under this line of reasoning local politicians are seen as members of "growth coalitions" backing the consensual objective of continued land development. Depictions of these "growth machines" and their associated "growth coalitions" are provided to illustrate likely sources of opposition to any attempts to shut down growth in local jurisdictions. An accompanying overview of the planning profession's pro-growth bias over time is intended to shed light on another potential obstacle to any prospective strategies to stop growth in America's communities. That portrayal reveals the ongoing growth-accommodation orientation of the planning profession over time, and the impediment that this orientation might pose to any local no-growth initiatives. In a related vein, the chapter describes the pro-growth stance of the growth-management movement in the United States, and the obstacle that existing growth-management programs are therefore apt to present to local efforts to stop growth. Observations on urban growth machines, state and federal support of these machines, and the pro-growth biases of the planning profession and the growth-management movement are all intended to illustrate the magnitude of challenges inherent in devising and implementing a strategy for stopping growth within local political jurisdictions.

Chapter 3 of this work addresses possible rationales and strategies for stopping growth in America's communities. The focus on stopping growth in local jurisdictions is based on the belief that efforts to merely *oppose* development or *slow* growth represent insufficient responses to the mounting evidence that global ecological limits have been surpassed. Simply retarding ongoing growth by defeating some development proposals, slowing continued growth, or realizing more efficient forms of growth, would only serve to delay an inevitable ecological catastrophe. The true challenge is represented as one of shutting down growth and undertaking the process of transitioning to stable, sustainable communities. Most of the *rationales* for implementing local no-growth programs surveyed in the chapter derive from a set of discounted pro-growth myths, with the exercise of debunking those myths revealing that ongoing growth represents more in the way of costs than benefits for local communities. The subsequent treatment of political, economic, and planning and regulatory *strategies* for stopping growth in local settings is intended to provide jurisdictions with tactics to shut down unsustainable demographic, economic, and urban increases. With the understanding that any implementation of local no-growth programs would certainly prompt litigation, the chapter addresses potential constitutional, statutory, and case-law barriers to implementing local no-growth programs, and concludes that none of these legal considerations represent insurmountable obstacles to stopping growth in America's communities. Legal challenges associated with crafting a defensible no-growth program may be significant, but the treatment of those challenges concludes that local no-growth initiatives are capable of being fashioned to survive litigation.

Chapter 4 explores the extent to which continued support for the growth imperative outside of local jurisdictions can be expected to impede efforts to stop growth. While some growth advocates still extol the virtues of demographic and urban increases, the greatest challenge to local no-growth initiatives is assumed to come from having to counter the pro-growth mythology associated with economic growth. The chapter addresses the current international and national obsession with continued economic expansion, identifying that fixation as a form of "growthmania." That obsession is attributed to dogma presently championed by neoclassical growth economists who demonstrate faith in perpetual economic growth. The chapter surveys the concepts in support of the infinitude of economic growth that have served to underpin the idea of extending free-market capitalism across the globe as part of an economic globalization effort capable of yielding a material paradise. While offering counterarguments to the merit of economic globalization, the review concedes the stranglehold that positive views of economic growth exert in international and national contexts, with the admission that support for local no-growth programs is unlikely to come from these arenas. In a similar vein, the chapter portrays the persistent pro-growth stances of state and regional jurisdictions, suggesting additional support for the idea that local communities are unlikely to realize support for no-growth initiatives from outside their own locales. However, an alternative growth orientation demonstrated by a few regional entities suggests that regional bodies might play a role in helping local communities transition to states of no growth. In particular, the chapter reviews the principles and tenets of the bioregionalism movement to illustrate the guidance they might provide in initiating a societal rejection of the growth imperative and the associated adoption of a no-growth imperative. The chapter concludes with an overview of the role that no-growth communities might serve in advancing societal sustainability. With the growing dominance of urban places across the American landscape, realizing national sustainability will clearly require achieving sustainable states in urban settings. The chapter restates the earlier argument that merely realizing more efficient future growth is an insufficient response to the reality of having surpassed the planet's ecological limits to growth, and that America's communities will be unable to achieve true sustainability if they cannot let go of the growth that represents inherently unsustainable behavior.

Chapter 5 outlines likely economic, social, political, and physical features of stable, sustainable, no-growth communities, under the assumption that no-growth advocates will have to provide a plausible conceptualization of such communities if local residents are to be expected to abandon their historical support for the pro-growth mindset that still dominates most local jurisdictions. Likely economic features of no-growth communities are portrayed by comparing and contrasting neoclassical growth economics with community no-growth economics. Proponents of community economics are shown to favor diverse, needs-based, import-substitution businesses that would enable local communities to realize relative self-reliance based on stability rather than growth. In terms of likely social features of no-growth communities, the chapter suggests a need to forgo some of the current emphasis on individualism in favor of communitarian values as a necessary antidote to evidence of an ongoing erosion of social connections, under the argument that personal well-being ultimately depends on the social connections of family, friends, and community. As for likely political features of no-growth communities, it is suggested local politicians in these settings might be expected to abandon their current focus on the *exchange* values of land in favor of its *use* values to residents. It is also noted that politicians in these no-growth communities could be expected to develop reciprocal relationships with the counties that house them in order to protect the sustainable productive capacities of their bioregions as no-growth communities pursued the end of self-sufficiency. On the topic of likely physical features of communities that have undergone a transition to sustainable states of no-growth, the chapter makes the case for a radical restructuring of today's communities so as to bring them in line with the ecological capabilities of their bioregions. It is suggested that these communities would be diametrically opposed to today's dominant suburban landscape, being characterized by higher-density, mixed-use, pedestrian-oriented environments. The chapter concludes with observations on prospects for realizing no-growth communities in light of the dramatic changes required to realize sustainable, no-growth states. Those prospects are said to be more likely than might initially be assumed in light of evidence that has been building for decades of a new attitude toward growth and an increasing interest in an alternative to continued adherence to the growth imperative. That evidence is presented both in terms of survey results and the emergence of the following movements since the 1970s: the Bioregionalism Movement, a Voluntary Simplicity Movement, a Slow Food Movement, an Ecovillages Movement, a Take Back Your Time Movement, a Transition Town Movement, and most recently the appearance of a Degrowth Movement in Europe. Those survey results and these movements suggest that the shift from a cultural allegiance to the growth imperative toward a no-growth imperative is already underway. Prospects for realizing no-growth communities in America would appear to hinge on little else than the willingness of progressive communities to implement the political, economic, and planning and regulatory no-growth strategies laid out in this work.

The epilogue to this book identifies "ten difficult personal actions needed to save the world." This list is intended to serve as a counterpoint to lists of recent decades that have suggested "ten easy personal actions to save the world." These lists typically call on individuals to do such things as recycling cans, changing out incandescent light bulbs, switching to cloth grocery bags, and turning down their thermostats, whereas the changes required to stop ecological deterioration will be much more significant and challenging. Stopping the inherently unsustainable demographic, economic, and urban increases that are destroying the ecological life-support structures on earth will not be easy, but shutting down these forms of growth represent essential first steps in transitioning to a state of ecological sustainability.

1 Requiem for the growth imperative

The roots of our current dilemma lie in the enormous growth of the human enterprise over the last century.

Lester R. Brown[1]

In a physically constrained world, material growth cannot continue indefinitely, and when that growth is exponential—and involves mega-countries like China and India—the limits are reached more abruptly and catastrophically than even the best scientists are able to predict.

Christopher Flavin[2]

Growth has represented the central defining characteristic of the human enterprise since its inception. While growth of human populations and their associated socioeconomic activities has a history extending back to the earliest communities formed by our species, for most of human history our demographic and economic growth exhibited linear growth characteristics. The resulting material increases never came to represent quantities that threatened to exceed the planet's carrying capacity. However, with the advent of the Industrial Revolution in the mid-1700s, both population growth and economic growth based on industrial capital began to expand exponentially. The exponentially growing population and economy have been described as "engines of growth" in the industrialized world, driving other exponential increases, such as those associated with resource consumption and pollution generation.[3] "Because of their potential for self-reproduction, population and industrial capital are the driving forces behind exponential growth in the world system."[4]

With more than 250 years of exponential growth of population and industrial capital, it is still not widely understood that "exponential growth has been a dominant behavior of the human socioeconomic system since the industrial revolution."[5] And with the surprising ability of exponential growth to generate huge numbers quickly, there has been even less public understanding of "the causes and consequences of a population and economy that have growth past the support capacities of the earth" during the last decades of the twentieth century.[6] "There is pervasive and convincing evidence that the global society is now above its carrying capacity."[7] The era of exponential growth has taken the human enterprise into the unsustainable realm of having already overshot the biophysical limits of the planet's support capacity. "Human use of many essential resources and generation of many kinds of pollutants have already surpassed rates that are physically sustainable."[8]

More importantly, the existing scale of the human enterprise is also disrupting the essential ecological life-support services of nature. During the latter half of the twentieth century "humanity has become a truly planetary ecological force"[9] capable of affecting the ability of ecosystems to regulate climate, regenerate biomass, turn wastes into nutrients, purify air and water, generate and preserve biodiversity, and so on. In terms of what is arguably the greatest threat to civilization, the exponential growth of the human enterprise has produced "a significant disequilibrium in the global atmosphere, and it is getting exponentially worse."[10] Emissions of greenhouse gases have risen to levels that threaten the global ecosystem's ability to provide climate control in the form of moderation of weather extremes. Scientific meetings and international negotiations are now addressing the topic of a possible ecological collapse on a global scale due to changes in the benign mix of atmospheric gases that enabled civilization.[11]

If exponential growth has already expanded the human enterprise to a scale where it threatens the ecological underpinnings of civilization, the merit of further demographic and economic growth must be called into question in all political contexts. However, challenges to either of these forms of growth can be expected to meet considerable resistance, because positive views of both population growth and economic growth have ancient historical origins. During the exponential growth era those positive views were extended to the point of identifying demographic and economic increases with societal progress. For generations both population growth and economic growth were classified as an unmitigated good and seen as cause for celebration. Over time these attitudes produced a global outcome where the "[e]xponential growth of population and industrial production is built into the self-generating structure of the 'real world' socioeconomic system."[12] With synonyms for growth extending beyond progress to include terms like development, improvement, and advancement, widespread acceptance of growth as a social good spread rapidly during the twentieth century. "Especially over the past few decades, the expanding industrial culture has instilled into nearly every community on earth the desire for and expectation of ever-increasing material growth."[13] Under this line of reasoning, to cease to grow would represent the end of progress; as a result, growth was elevated to the status of a social imperative across the globe. This growth imperative has progressed to a point where the "political and economic systems of the globe are dedicated to achieving the highest possible growth rates."[14] Diverse cultures around the world have incorporated the growth imperative into their own dominant social paradigms. As a consequence we now have what may be described as a worldwide cultural network united in its pursuit of growth.

Pursuit of growth on a global basis has had dramatic consequences since it took on exponential characteristics some 250 years ago. When that growth began to demonstrate hyperactive or superexponential features during the 1970s, quantities being generated suggested both dire consequences for the natural world and impending limits to material growth.[15] By the early 1990s evidence of existent ecological limits began to surface, and over the subsequent 20 years mounting documentation confirmed the human enterprise had already surpassed ecological limits to growth on earth. A forthcoming review of those existent ecological limits is intended to illustrate the magnitude of the human predicament early in the twenty-first century.

With the existing scale of the human enterprise already serving to degrade and dismantle the ecological life-support systems needed to sustain life on earth, it is time to recognize that the idealization of physical growth has now become an obsolete and lethal ideology, and that we are at a point of having to abandon the growth imperative if we are to survive.[16] Abandoning the growth imperative will certainly encounter serious challenges at all levels of government, because the view of growth as a social good has come to represent a central tenet of a dominant global paradigm. While some of those challenges at governmental levels beyond local governments will be acknowledged and addressed in this work, the central focus here will be on local political jurisdictions and associated rationales and strategies for stopping growth in America's communities.

The historical pro-growth paradigm

The world's dominant social paradigm—the collection of beliefs, values, norms, and ideals that form a worldview representative of an emerging global culture—has as one of its central tenets an unquestioning allegiance to the growth imperative. Other tenets of that paradigm serve to support the growth imperative, such as an unwavering faith in science and technology, a focused belief in the industrialism development model, and a strong conviction in the merit of consumerism and materialism. While all these tenets play a role in explaining our troubled relationship to the natural world, the growth imperative and the pro-growth legacy it continues to leave in its wake are at the core of the current dilemma confronting humankind. If the ongoing demographic and economic growth at exponential rates is being linked to impending global ecological collapse, it becomes necessary to understand why the growth imperative continues to demonstrate such tremendous staying power in light of mounting evidence of the magnitude of the threat we collectively face. In order to understand the holding power of the growth imperative on our collective imaginations, one needs to consider the historical reasoning that has been employed to support positive views of population, economic, and urban growth.[17]

Origins of favorable views toward population growth may be surmised to derive from familial or small-group settings where, out of necessity, attention centered on survival. With high infant and child death rates, and famine and pestilence frequently decimating populations, large numbers of children were essential to ensure survival. Beyond biological survival, numerous offspring were also perceived to ensure economic survival by contributing to the family economy from an early age, in addition to representing a form of old-age insurance. With biological and economic survival having early associations with high levels of reproduction, these positive views of population came to find expression in, and formal support from, the dictates of numerous religions. It has been noted, "the laws of the Hindus, the Jews, the Zoroastrians, and many other ancient religious groups revere fertility and regard procreation as both a blessing and a duty."[18] Pronatalist pronouncements in the sacred writings of religions are common, as those in the Judeo-Christian camp would recognize in the form of the biblical directive endorsing procreation: "Be fruitful, and multiply."[19]

The previously noted association between childbearing and the concern with economic survival illustrates the difficulty of disassociating supportive rationales for population growth from economic considerations. Population growth has been credited with promoting economic growth and has also been linked to the pace of potential economic growth. These associations mainly derive from the production and consumption potential of additional numbers of people. However, there have been a host of other economic-based rationales for supporting population growth. There have been those who have emphasized the prospects for "economies of scale" or "increased returns to scale" with the large-scale production processes made possible by large numbers of people. Others have stressed the "economies of mass production" that large populations make possible by facilitating specialization of function and the division of labor. Then there have been those who have focused on the role of large populations in reducing the per capita burdens in funding the cost of social overheads like transportation and communication improvements. Yet another economic-based rationale in support of population growth derives from the favorable impact that population increases are assumed to exert on the promotion of a bullish investment psychology. Without population growth driving adequate investments this line of reasoning raises the specter of large-scale, persistent unemployment. In the current American context attention has recently turned to population increases in the form of additional workers being absolutely necessary to support the cost of entitlement programs for retiring baby boomers.

All the noted rationales make it easy to understand why population growth has long been considered a social good. These positive perceptions toward demographic increases have existed long enough to be incorporated into the values and norms of many present-day societies. Those values and norms have, in turn, found expression in laws, such as tax credits that reward the addition of each child. In this respect, the United States has been described as a setting where "fertility has always occurred in the context of massive collective intervention of a pronatalist type" that has "encouraged parenthood and discouraged nonparenthood using virtually the entire spectrum of available pressures to induce conformity."[20] When taken together, all of the noted rationales supportive of population growth have served as powerful inducements to a continued pro-growth posture regarding population increases.

A review of the historical reasoning that has been employed to argue the desirability of economic growth would reveal a similarly extensive set of rationales utilized to support ongoing economic expansion. Economic thought as developed in the West has assumed a close correlation between economic welfare and general welfare.[21] Increased economic welfare has in turn been equated with increased levels of individual affluence and consumption. Increased affluence is valued under this line of reasoning because it is believed to increase the range of individual and collective choice. This expanded choice has typically come to be expressed principally in terms of increased prospects for consumption. In the American context this consumption focus has been elevated to a sort of ideological status referred to as "consumerism."[22] In this conceptual framework increased consumer choices are made dependent on the prior state of realized affluence, as evidenced by high per capita incomes, which in turn are assumed to require economic growth in the form of an increasing Gross National Product (GNP). In the American context a fixation on growing the total size of the economy as measured by GNP took hold after the Second World War, and "[f]rom that point on, growth [of GNP] became America's mantra, and then the world's."[23] During the latter half of the twentieth century an evolving global economic culture came to view "development," "modernization," and "progress" in terms of the single economic index of an expanding GNP, which in the mid-1980s was quietly transformed into the new Gross Domestic Product (GDP) as the revised indicator of economic progress.[24]

While GDP records the total annual value of both goods and services in national contexts, the main emphasis of "consumerism" has been on the increased consumption of material goods. The focus of virtually all national economies has been on increasing the material standards of citizens.[25] In the United States and elsewhere, there has been a tendency to define prosperity in a materialistic way, to associate materialism with happiness, and even to identify material well-being with spiritual well-being.[26] This value placed on increased material consumption goes a long way in explaining the widespread endorsement of technology in an increasingly industrial world. Technology assumes a pivotal role in increasing material output for consumption, and is embraced for its contribution to advancing the goal of realizing a state of universal material affluence.

Rationales used to support the merit of economic growth have also equated it with reduced prospects for a host of social ills. Economic growth has been linked to the avoidance of unemployment, recession, and depression. It has additionally been common to associate economic growth with the reduction of poverty and economic disparities among countries. The future outlook for social expenditures has been directly tied to economic growth. It has been suggested that the future availability of natural resources, or the derivation of suitable substitutes, is directly linked to the higher prices capable of being absorbed under further growth. It has even been argued that growth is necessary to pay for pollution abatement without acknowledging the role growth itself plays in generating additional pollution. In more sweeping terms, economic growth has been linked to such disparate factors as peace, security, increased likelihood of greater exercise of compassion, forestallment of social tension, and resolution of an array of societal problems. Taken together, these rationales are capable of instilling the belief that a viable future without economic growth is simply unattainable. As a result, most of the world's people now deify economic growth in much the same fashion they have traditionally deified population growth.

After population growth itself, urbanization has been referred to as the second dominant demographic trend of our time.[27] With population growth and economic growth viewed as desirable phenomena and identified with societal progress, the assumed need for growth of urban places to house demographic and economic increases also translated into a positive view of urban growth. To the extent that development has been equated with industrialization during the exponential growth era, a similar association evolved with regard to industrialization and urbanization. Both industrialization and urbanization have been expressed as preconditions for, and results of, each other, as well as in terms of mutually reinforcing links that appear to preclude consideration of one without at the same time considering the other. Scarcity of investment capital produced a natural bias in favor of pursuing development in a limited number of urban centers over attempts to initiate development simultaneously over an entire countryside. In a similar vein, urban places have been credited with making possible a more rational deployment of scarce facilities and personnel than could be possible under a scattered arrangement of villages and small towns. Urban places have also been credited with inducing new ways of thinking and acting necessary to advancing industrialization, to the point where they came to be viewed as essential environments for the creation of economic capacities. With the widespread acceptance of the theory of "urban growth poles" as communicators of growth,[28] urban growth additionally came to be viewed favorably for its ability to spread economic development to areas beyond urban centers themselves.

The prior reasoning has produced a positive view of an increase in both the number of urban places and the growth of specific urban centers. However, under the industrialism development model large urban centers have been credited with being better suited for advancing economic growth than either small or intermediate centers. Large centers are favored on multiple grounds under such reasoning, including the advantages of a large and concentrated labor and consumer market, their economies of scale and their juxtaposition of industries and specialists, and their alleged advantages in instilling the skills and values of an industrial system. Such views have led to the conclusion that the largest cities provide the best physical setting for effective industrialization and economic growth, and that large metropolitan centers are necessary environments for advanced industrialization. From this perspective, urban growth is seen in such a favorable light that there is little willingness to entertain the possibility that any urban center may be too large. When the noted reasoning is viewed collectively, one has an elaborate set of rationales to support urban growth that are a natural consequence of the rationales that have evolved to support population growth and economic growth.

In the end, it is easy to understand how supportive rationales for population growth and economic growth lead to a natural endorsement both of urbanization in general and the growth of specific urban places in particular. With the dominant social paradigm's growth imperative reinforcing population increases on a massive scale during the exponential growth era, it was inevitable that urban places should be assigned a positive role in accepting that growth. In a similar fashion, the social paradigm that equates development and progress with economic growth, credits industrialization with providing the greatest impetus to furthering such growth, and argues that industrialization presupposes conditions that tend to produce agglomeration of population, would also inevitably produce a positive view of urban growth. When taken together, rationales that have evolved to support population, economic, and urban growth comprise a pro-growth legacy that has played a key role in generating the growth called for by the dominant social paradigm's growth imperative. The growth imperative's success in generating large demographic, economic, and urban increases during the exponential growth era, and the huge subsequent increases during the superexponential growth period of the latter half of the twentieth century, served to illustrate the absurd nature of attempting to maintain exponential growth into the future. The demographic, economic, and urban quantities being generated by exponential growth at the close of the last millennium, and the associated ecological dilemma emerging as a direct result of those quantities, clearly revealed that exponential growth could not be part of any viable future development strategy. Any attempt to formulate a sustainable development path in the twenty-first century will of necessity require a better understanding of the nature of exponential growth. That understanding will make it possible to comprehend why it must be rejected in a finite world where prior exponential growth has already exceeded the ecological capacity of the planet to support even the current scale of the human enterprise.

The exponential growth era

In 1972 the authors of *The Limits to Growth* presented readers with the incontrovertible axiom that infinite growth is impossible in a finite system.[29] The authors of that work examined exponential growth trends in world population, industrialization, resource depletion, pollution, and food production by using a computer model and concluded that under existing trends limits to growth would be reached within 100 years. Under the standard run of the model it collapsed because of nonrenewable resource depletion. When that constraint was assumed away the model collapsed due to levels of pollution generated by growth. In a subsequent run resource and pollution constraints were both relaxed and the collapse occurred because of food shortages. Even with the most optimistic assumptions introduced into the model regarding impending constraints, the basic behavioral mode of the modeled world system under ongoing exponential growth of population and industrial capital was consistently one of sudden and uncontrollable collapse of both population and industrial capacity.[30] The authors attributed the overshoot of limits to growth and the subsequent collapse to what they referred to as the fundamental or essential problem of exponential growth in a finite system.[31] Examining exponential growth trends they concluded that the short doubling times of many human activities, combined with the immense quantities being doubled, would bring us close to the limits to growth of those activities surprisingly soon.

With a view of exponential growth in a finite system as the fundamental problem driving the world system toward the limits of the earth and ultimate collapse, the authors of *Limits to Growth* attempted to convey the nature of exponential growth and why in their view it represents the central threat to a viable future for humankind. In comparing linear growth (increases of a constant amount in constant time periods) with exponential growth (increases of a constant percentage of the whole in constant time periods), they pointed out the surprising ability of exponential growth to generate large numbers quickly under the ongoing application of a percentage growth rate to a rapidly growing base. When linear growth is portrayed on a graph, where the amount is represented on the vertical axis and time on the horizontal axis, it demonstrates growth in the form of a straight line that does not have the capability of producing large numbers quickly. Exponential growth, on the other hand, demonstrates growth in the form of a J-shaped curve that generates large numbers rapidly as the percentage growth rate is applied to an ever-larger base. "Exponential increase is deceptive because it generates immense numbers very quickly."[32] As pointed out in *Limits to Growth*, the rub lies in the fact that most people are accustomed to thinking of growth as a *linear* process, and thus have little or no appreciation of the absurd amounts capable of being generated under an *exponential* growth process.

The authors of *Limits to Growth* went further in attempting to convey an understanding of the dangerous potential outcomes of exponential growth by treating the *doubling time*, or the time it takes a growing quantity to double in size, under different percentage growth rates. They pointed out that doubling time is approximately equal to 70 divided by the growth rate expressed in terms of percent per year. A growth rate of 10 percent per year would therefore yield a doubling time of 7 years (70 ÷ 10% = 7 years), while a growth rate of 1 percent per year would yield a doubling time of 70 years (70 ÷ 1% = 70 years). The shorter time periods associated with higher percentage growth rates readily demonstrate the ability of exponential growth to generate immense numbers in relatively short periods of time. The capability of successive doublings to produce large numbers quickly may be illustrated by pointing out that the number 1 becomes 1,000 times larger after 10 doublings, and then becomes 1,000,000 times larger after another 10 doublings. China's annual economic growth of some 10 percent over two decades prior to the onset of the global recession in 2008 meant the country's economy was doubling in size every 7 years. Had it been maintained, that growth trajectory after 10 doublings in 70 years would have generated an economy 1,000 times its size in the late 1980s. After another 10 doublings in a subsequent 70 years China would have had an economy a million times larger than its starting size 140 years earlier. Clearly, such absurd numerical outcomes illustrate the impossibility of maintaining exponential growth rates on a finite planet. The American economy, with its average annual growth rate of some 3.5 percent over the last 75 years, which represents a doubling time of 20 years, would likewise generate an economy a million times larger after 20 doublings, it would just take a little less than 3 times as long to reach that absurd number than the more rapidly growing Chinese economy.

It is instructive to examine some of the quantities that have been generated to date under exponential growth rates. In terms of demographic increases over time, until about 10,000 years ago it took some 35,000 years for the global population to double.[33] With the advent of agriculture around 8,000 B.C. that changed dramatically, instituting a progressive reduction in doubling times. From a population of 5 million in 8,000 B.C. the population increased to 500 million by 1650 A.D., with that 100-fold increase representing between 6 and 7 doublings, and each of those doublings taking about 1,500 years on average. Between 1650 and 1850 the global population doubled from 500 million to 1 billion in 200 years under the influence of the emerging exponential growth era. The next doubling from 1 billion to 2 billion by 1930 required just 80 years, and the subsequent doubling to 4 billion by 1975 took a mere 45 years. A 2006 revision of global population prospects by the United Nations revealed that even under the low variant projection the planet would have to contend with 8 billion residents before population could be expected to begin leveling off.[34] In 2011 the United Nations released a medium variant population projection of 8 billion by 2025, reflecting a slight slowing in the doubling time to 50 years from the former doubling that occurred in 45 years, but nevertheless adding a 4 billion increase in just 50 years. Exponential growth of population clearly continued to demonstrate its ability to generate large numbers quickly over the last decades of the twentieth century and the initial decades of the new millennium.

Another way to illustrate the dramatic demographic effects of exponential growth is the change that has occurred over time in annual increases to the total global population.[35] In 1650 the global population of 500 million was growing by about 0.3 percent per year, which translated into an annual addition of only 1.5 million a year. By 1900 the growth rate had increased to 0.5 percent per year, which when applied to 1.5 billion people on the planet at that time yielded an annual increase of 7.5 million. In 1950 the annual growth rate increased to 1.7 percent, which applied to 2.5 billion produced an annual increase of 42.5 million. The increase in the annual growth rate to 2.1 percent by 1970 clearly illustrated the occurrence of superexponential growth, with the rate of growth itself growing, which applied to a global population of 3.6 billion yielded an annual increase of 75.6 million. By 1990 the annual rate of growth had fallen back to 1.7 percent, but when applied to the larger base of 5.3 billion it yielded an annual increase of 90.1 million. In 2000 a decline in the growth rate to 1.3 percent applied to a base of 6 billion produced an annual increase of some 78 million. The subsequent decline in the annual rate to around 1.2 percent at present yields an annual increase of about 84 million when applied to a total global population that reached 7 billion at the end of 2011. Clearly, exponential growth produced dramatic outcomes during the last half of the twentieth century. It had taken all the previous history of our species to attain the level of 2.5 billion by 1950, but in expanding to 6 billion by 2000 exponential growth had added 3.5 billion in a mere 50 years. That exponential demographic expansion continued during the opening decades of the twenty-first century, with the seventh billion added between 2000 and 2012.

Exponential demographic growth during the latter half of the twentieth century accelerated to the unprecedented point of adding an additional 1 billion people to the planet in just 12 years. Part of the inherent problem in attempting to convey the significance of an additional billion people lies in the difficulty of comprehending the meaning of a billion. While many are aware that a billion represents 1,000 million, that knowledge still fails to impart a meaningful idea of the actual nature of an additional billion individuals. As Palos pointed out in his 1980 book *Innumeracy*, there can be as great a societal danger associated with a poor understanding of numbers as that posed by illiteracy.[36] One way to illustrate the magnitude of the difference between 1 million and 1 billion is to point out that it would take only 11.5 days for a million individuals transported on a conveyor belt to pass by a fixed point at the rate of one each second, whereas it would take 31.5 years for a billion to pass by at that same rate. To add that many individuals to the planet in just 12 years, as occurred with the addition of each of the fifth, sixth, and seventh billions, clearly represents the antithesis of sustainable behavior. "A population that is growing, however slowly, will eventually overwhelm its life-support systems."[37] Even the apparently innocuous current demographic growth rate of around 1.2 percent is increasing the total number of people on the planet by some 80 million each year and is clearly unsustainable.

Exponential demographic growth during the twentieth century also left its mark on the United States. America increased from a population of 76 million in 1900 to 150 million in 1950, adding 74 million during the first half of the century. Between 1950 and 2000 the country grew by 131 million, reaching a total population of 281 million and nearly doubling the increase realized during the prior 50 years. In the single decade of the 1990s America added 33 million to its population, surpassing the previous single decade record of 28 million added in the post-Second World War decade that produced the baby boom generation. That growth rate of approximately 3 million new Americans each year continued during the first decade of the twenty-first century, taking the country to 300 million by 2006. At that growth rate the United States would add almost 100 million every 30 years to its population, which again obviously fails to constitute sustainable behavior.

The economic growth generated by exponential growth rates has demonstrated even more dramatic outcomes than those realized under exponential demographic increases. While global population expanded more than 6-fold since 1800, the gross world product increased more than 58-fold during the same time period.[38] Between 1900 and 2000 global population increased 4-fold, while global economic output surged some 18-fold as it was expanding from a much larger base than the one that existed in 1800. During the second half of the twentieth century global population increased 2.4-fold as it jumped from 2.5 billion to 6 billion, while the global economy expanded 7-fold, raising output from $6 trillion of goods and services in 1950 to $43 trillion in 2000.[39] By 2006 global output was reported to have jumped to $66 trillion,[40] with the American economy representing about $14 trillion of that total output. This meant that the global economy grew by the equivalent of almost 2 American economies from 2000 until the onset of the global recession in 2008. The quest to reestablish and then maintain an economic growth rate of at least 3 percent in the United States in response to the nation's recession that began during the last quarter of 2007 would mean a doubling time for the national economy of about 23 years. Two doublings within 46 years at that growth rate would take the country's former $14 trillion economy to $56 trillion, surpassing the size of the total global economy of $43 trillion in 2000. Prospects for such economic increases are already being negated by rapidly emerging ecological realities.

Further insights into the nature of exponential economic increases during the latter half of the twentieth century may be gained by a review of the changes in global motor vehicle production during that period.[41] In 1950 total annual production of motor vehicles (cars and light trucks) stood at 10.5 million units, and there were some 70 million registered vehicles worldwide at that time. By 2000 annual global production had increased to 57.2 million units, and registered vehicles to over 500 million. In 2007, before the onset of the global recession in 2008, the respective numbers were 74.1 million and 806 million. This 7-fold increase in production between 1950 and 2007, and the almost 11.5-fold increase in the number of registered vehicles during that period, paralleled the 10-fold increase in the global economy between 1950 and 2007. In the United States motor vehicle sales jumped from 6.7 million in 1950 to 17.4 million in 2000, illustrating the exponential growth trends associated with the American love affair with motor vehicles and mobility. If the 6.76 billion people on the planet in 2008 were to own motor vehicles at the ratio exhibited by Americans, where in 2008 there were over 250 million vehicles for just over 300 million people, the total number of motor vehicles globally would have to increase from the 2007 level of 806 million to 5.6 billion, a 7-fold increase. The prospect of realizing that number seems highly unlikely under rapidly emerging ecological limits to growth.

The era of exponential growth has also demonstrated dramatic outcomes with respect to urban growth. It has been noted that "until 1900, urbanization was, with a few exceptions, a slow, barely perceptible process."[42] In 1900, 150 million people lived in cities, whereas by 2000 some 2.8 billion lived in urban places, a 19-fold increase.[43] Between 1950 and 2000 the urban population increased from 732 million to 2.8 billion, a nearly 4-fold increase over a time span that global population increased only 2.4-fold. At the beginning of the last century there were only 6 urban agglomerations with a million people, but by 2000 there were nearly 400 cities that had at least that many inhabitants.[44] As part of the ongoing urbanization process that ended up placing 50 percent of the planet's 6.8 billion inhabitants in cities by 2008, the number of megacities of over 10 million increased from just 2 in 1950 to 21 such centers by 2010. The exponential increases recorded by some of these megalopolises between 1950 and 2000 were exceptionally striking: Mexico City exploded from 3.1 million to 26.3 million, Sao Paulo from 2.8 million to 24 million, Mumbai from 2.9 million to 16 million. It took superexponential growth rates during the latter half of the twentieth century to record some of these astounding increases. In developing countries their urban populations increased by an average of 58 million per year between 2000 and 2010.[45] With the United Nations projecting an additional 3.3 billion people between 2000 and 2050, and nearly all of that increase projected to take place in cities in developing countries, such a doubling of urban population would require building as much additional urban habitat as exists today. The implications for increased material and energy use to accomplish that end also raises serious questions about being able to create such a monumental new level of urban habitat in an era of mounting ecological constraints.

While urban growth in the United States during the exponential growth era has not been as striking as that recorded globally, it has nonetheless been significant. The 33 million people added to America during the 1990s represented an average annual increase of 3.3 million a year, or the equivalent of 33 cities of 100,000 people every 12 months. This rate of exponential urban growth translated into rather dramatic implications for ongoing land development in the United States during the 1990s, with the rate of development having increased to 2.2 million acres per year from a figure of 1.4 million acres per year in the previous decade.[46] The development of 2.2 million acres each year represents the conversion of an area the size of Vermont about every 2.5 years. Clearly, such ongoing development of rural land would not constitute sustainable land-use practices.

The prior portrayal of outcomes associated with exponential demographic, economic, and urban growth clearly illustrates the ability of exponential growth to generate huge numbers quickly. Under the superexponential growth exhibited by population, economic, and urban increases during the latter half of the twentieth century, ecological limits to such ongoing increases began to surface by the early 1990s. Mounting evidence of existent ecological limits to growth over the last two decades represents the ultimate challenge to the continued legitimacy of the growth imperative guiding social behavior at all levels of government. An understanding and acceptance of those ecological limits is vital to any hope of being able to abandon the growth imperative and develop an alternative imperative to guide social behavior toward a sustainable future.

Existent ecological limits to growth

Since the early 1980s multiple considerations of possible limits to growth have addressed the unsustainable exploitation of renewable resources.[47] These assessments have uniformly documented the unsustainable demands already being placed on the renewable resources of fertile topsoils, rangelands, forests, fisheries, groundwater deposits, and biodiversity. These sources point out that all these renewable resources represent natural capital that is being progressively damaged and depleted. Rather than living off the annual sustainable income of these resources, the sources document the extent to which the current scale of the human enterprise is consuming the capital base of each of these forms of natural capital. The cited research points to diminished fertility on existing agricultural lands, overgrazed grasslands, truncated natural forests, overharvested fisheries, depleted and polluted groundwater sources, and reduced biodiversity. A single example can serve to illustrate the extreme pressures that are already being placed on renewable resources across the globe. Research findings published in 2003 revealed that industrial fishing had already eliminated 90 percent of the large predatory fish like marlin, sharks, and blue fin tuna over the last 50 years.[48] At present 75 percent of fisheries are being fished at or beyond their sustainable capacity, pushing many into a state of decline and others to total collapse.[49] Similarly distressing data have been reported across all of the cited categories of renewable resources. The fact that even the present scale of the human enterprise is depleting the planet's natural capital across all renewable resources, rather than living on the annual sustainable income of those resources, suggests limits to physical growth have already been surpassed. However, even more disturbing evidence of current limits to growth has emerged from research indicating the present scale of the human enterprise is threatening the planet's ecological life-support systems.

The planet's ecosystems constitute what may be thought of as a life-support apparatus. All life is utterly dependent on these ecosystems to support it, and the continued existence of our species and civilization is not exempt from such dependency. These natural ecosystems provide a wide variety of essential life-support services that are delivered at no cost. Descriptions of these free life-support services illustrate the vital roles ecosystems play.[50] These services include:

- Maintenance of a benign mix of atmospheric gases essential to life as we know it.

- Climate control in the form of moderation of wind and temperature extremes.
- Regulation of the hydrologic cycle through water absorption and storage in a manner that mitigates droughts and floods.
- Purification of air and water.
- Decomposition, detoxification, and sequestering of wastes.
- Regeneration of soil nutrients that build up soil structures essential for agriculture and forestry.
- Pollination and pest control.
- Seed and nutrient dispersal.
- Provision of forest products and food from the world's oceans.
- Provision of a wide variety of agricultural, medicinal, and industrial products.
- Creation and maintenance of the biodiversity that performs all of the above tasks and represents the "genetic library" from which humans were able to fashion civilization.
- Lessons in survival, resilience, evolution, and diversification strategies that have proved themselves over millions of years.
- Aesthetic, spiritual, and intellectual rewards.

Such a list of life-support services provided by the planet's ecosystems reveals how completely dependent humans are on the life-support functions of ecosystems. As our species impairs or destroys ecosystems we threaten the very life-support functions on which we depend. Unrelenting expansion of the human enterprise serves to expropriate ever more of the natural landscapes of which ecosystems are comprised, and in the process, the services performed by those ecosystems are impaired or lost. Widespread ecological illiteracy represents a monumental challenge in this regard, because there is little public understanding of the vital functions carried out by ecosystems, or of the impossibility of successfully or cost effectively replacing any lost life-support services provided by ecosystems across the globe due to their scope and complexity. "Civilization can't persist without ecosystem services, and these are threatened in innumerable ways by the expanding scale of human activities."[51] Since we are utterly dependent on such services, it is imperative to understand the degree to which continued adherence to the growth imperative is unraveling the ecological framework that provides those services. That understanding may be furthered by reviewing the mounting evidence that has been amassing since the early 1990s of material growth having already surpassed the ecological limits to growth on the planet.

In 1991 the Ecological Society of America endorsed the view that the existing scale of the human enterprise was "threatening the sustainability of Earth's life-support systems."[52] A year later some 1,700 of the world's leading scientists issued a warning stating: "Human beings and the natural world are on a collision course."[53] As members of the Union of Concerned Scientists they expressed the view that many current practices threaten to "so alter the living world that it will be unable to sustain life in the manner that we know."[54]

Their warning stated that our "massive tampering with the world's inter-dependent web of life ... could trigger widespread adverse effects, including unpredictable collapses of critical biological systems."[55] In terms of the challenge confronting humankind, they asserted great change was required "if vast human misery is to be avoided and our global home on this planet is not to be irretrievably mutilated."[56]

In 1991 and 1992, noted ecologists Paul Ehrlich and Edward O. Wilson warned that under current and accelerating trends fully 50 percent of the remaining species on the planet could be eliminated by 2050.[57] The extinction of other species has direct implications for the ability of ecosystems to provide their vital life-support services since other life forms are intimately involved in the delivery of those services. To diminish the complexity of ecosystems through extinctions is a threat to our own future, because living organisms in natural ecosystems play enormous roles in the provision of life-support services critical to our own well-being. Estimates of the current species extinction rate place it at as much as 1,000 times higher than background rates typical over the planet's history.[58] This high extinction rate threatens humankind because "[b]iodiversity loss can cause ecosystems to become stressed or degraded, and even eventually to collapse."[59] Any degradation or loss of ecosystems "threatens the continued provision of ecosystem services, which in turn further threatens biodiversity and ecosystem health."[60] In the end, the dependency of human society on ecosystem services makes any loss of those services a serious threat to the future well-being of humans. To eliminate other life forms must therefore come to be recognized as a direct assault on future prospects for our species. The growth of the human enterprise is directly implicated in the sixth great extinction on our planet, and the absence of ecological literacy largely explains the poor public understanding of the threat this poses to our own species.

By 1997 research on per capita ecological footprints revealed an average ecological footprint of some 5.7 acres (2.31 hectares), whereas the planet was found to contain only about 4.2 acres (1.7 hectares) of ecologically productive space per capita.[61] This global deficit of 1.5 acres (0.6 hectares) indicated that the ecological footprint of humanity had already exceeded the planet's ecological capacity to sustain the human enterprise prior to 2000, and that the existent scale of the human enterprise was living off the capital base of ecological resources rather than from their sustainable annual incomes. A subsequent analysis of the ecological footprint of humanity in 2002 concluded that collective demands on global ecosystems first surpassed the earth's regenerative capacity around 1980, and a more recent assessment of global demands on natural systems concluded they exceeded the sustainable yield capacity of those systems by an estimated 25 percent.[62] These findings indicate that for the last two decades of the twentieth century humanity was meeting its demands by consuming the planet's natural assets, rather than living off the annual renewable productive capacities of those ecological assets.

In 2002 an international team of ecologists, economists, and conservation biologists published a study indicating that nearly all ecosystems on the planet are shrinking in response to expanding human demands on the natural world.[63] In 2004 the World Wildlife Fund issued a fifth *Living Planet Report* with its index of average trends in populations of terrestrial, freshwater, and marine species, which noted that the index had declined by about 30 percent from 1970 to 2000.[64] In 2005 a 4-year assessment of the state of global ecosystems carried out by some 1,360 experts from 95 countries reported that approximately 60 percent of the ecosystem services that support life on the planet were being degraded or used unsustainably.[65] That *Millennium Ecosystem Assessment* pointed out that 15 of 24 primary ecosystem services were being degraded or pushed beyond their limits. The authors of that assessment issued what they called a stark warning, asserting: "Human activity is putting such strain on the natural functions of Earth that the ability of the planet's ecosystems to sustain future generations can no longer be taken for granted."[66] In 2005 additional troubling information on the state of global ecosystems was released by the organization Conservation International. In an update on the status of 34 "biodiversity hotspots" noted for their especially high numbers of endemic species, the assessment reported that 86 percent of the hotspots' habitats had already been destroyed, and that whereas they once covered nearly 16 percent of the earth's land surface they now cover less than 3 percent.[67] By 2008 the World Wildlife Fund's seventh *Living Planet Report* concluded the planet's natural ecosystems were being degraded at a rate unprecedented in human history. This escalating degradation and destruction of ecosystems in the twenty-first century represents an extremely dangerous trend because it constitutes an accelerating dismantling of the planet's life-support apparatus. In 2009 a group of eminent scientists shed new light on the matter of ecological limits to growth with a publication warning that human activity had already pushed 3 of Earth's 9 biophysical processes beyond the planet's ability to self-regulate.[68] The scientists identified 9 Earth-system processes and associated thresholds or "planetary boundaries" that define the safe operating space for humanity within the Earth system. They concluded that the boundaries for 3 of those processes (rate of biodiversity loss, climate change, and human interference with the nitrogen cycle) had already been exceeded, and that humanity appeared to be quickly approaching boundaries for global freshwater use, change in land use, ocean acidification, and interference with the global phosphorous cycle. They warned that exceeding any of these planetary boundaries could produce potentially disastrous consequences for humanity, with some of those consequences being "detrimental or even catastrophic for large parts of the world."[69] In 2010 the World Wildlife Fund's 8th edition of the *Living Planet Report* provided further evidence of humankind's troubled relationship to the planet's ecosystems with the claim that our collective ecological footprint in 2007 "exceeded the Earth's biocapacity—the area actually available to produce renewable resources and absorb CO_2—by 50 per cent."[70] The authors of that report referred to this assault on the planet's biocapacity as a state of "ecological overshoot." William Rees, who introduced the ecological footprint as an accounting tool to measure sustainability, interpreted the findings in similar terms, writing "the world is well into a state of ecological 'overshoot'—the human enterprise is using about 50% more bio-productive and waste sink capacity annually than the ecosphere can regenerate."[71] Rees sees this as evidence the "world community is living, in part by depleting natural capital and degrading ecosystems essential for survival—the very definition of unsustainability."[72] Taken together, the findings from the noted studies carried out since the early 1990s confirm that exponential growth has already taken the human enterprise beyond ecological limits to growth on the planet. However, the most threatening evidence of having surpassed existent ecological limits to growth only surfaced during the latter years of the first decade of the twenty-first century. During that period scientific consensus coalesced around the view that anthropogenic changes in atmospheric gases were threatening to change the planet's climate to an extent that would be catastrophic for ecosystems and civilization.

In 2007 the Intergovernmental Panel on Climate Change (IPCC) issued its Fourth Assessment Report, announcing the "unequivocal" warming of the climate system, and stating it was more than 90 percent likely to be attributable to human causes.[73] That consensus report affirming humanity's role in climate change represented another step in the evolution of a process that began with the United Nations Framework Convention on Climate Change (UNFCCC) that came into existence in 1992. It would take another 5 years for the convention to agree to an implementation agreement in the form of the Kyoto Protocol, and that agreement would not be ratified until 2005. The Kyoto Protocol represented an agreement on the part of participating industrial countries to reduce their greenhouse gas emissions by an average of 5 percent of their 1990 levels by 2012. That modest reduction target provides a sad form of commentary on the importance the global community had accorded the threat of global warming in the opening decade of the twenty-first century. The IPCC Reports had, after all, consistently reported similar projections of possible temperature increases during this century, with the 2007 Report concluding the earth's average temperature will rise in the range of 1.1–6.4 degrees Celsius (2.0–11.5 degrees Fahrenheit) above the average in the 1980–99 period by 2100. With the IPCC estimating the world needs to reduce global emissions by as much as 80 percent of 1990 levels by 2050 to avert "dangerous anthropogenic climate change,"[74] the 5 percent Kyoto reductions are clearly but a small fraction of what scientists believe will be necessary to limit average global temperature increases to levels that avoid crossing potentially catastrophic thresholds in Earth's climate system.

When the UNFCCC set its main objective of stabilizing greenhouse gases at a level that would prevent dangerous anthropogenic interference with Earth's climate systems in 1992, there was a poor understanding of what emission level would actually be dangerous. Much of the subsequent debate has centered on the level of CO_2 that would be "safe" in the sense of avoiding large-scale adverse changes in the climate system often called "tipping points." At these points climate change acquires a momentum that makes it irreversible. Noted elements of the climate system susceptible to "tipping" include the complete loss of Arctic summer sea ice, a meltdown of the Greenland ice sheet (resulting in a sea level rise of 7 meters or 23 feet), a disintegration of the West Antarctic ice sheet (resulting in a sea level rise of 5 meters or 16 feet), a complete shutdown of the major Atlantic Ocean currents, and a collapse of the Amazon rainforest due to warming and rainfall reductions.[75] Considerable attention has focused on the level of atmospheric CO_2 that could be attained without triggering such tipping points, with potential increases related to the pre-industrial level of 278 parts per million (ppm) and the 2007 level of 382 ppm. These considerations of a safe level of atmospheric CO_2 have taken place in the context of an understanding that the average global temperature has already warmed by 0.75 degrees Celsius (1.35 degrees Fahrenheit) above the pre-industrial level, and that there is at least an additional 0.5 degrees Celsius (0.9 degrees Fahrenheit) implicit in current atmospheric concentrations of greenhouse gases because of the lag time in the buildup of heat.[76] The considerations of a safe level of atmospheric CO_2 have also been carried out under an awareness that they have continued to rise significantly over the course of the transition to a new millennium. For example, global emissions of CO_2 from fossil fuel combustion and cement production increased by 37 percent between 1990 and 2007, and the annual rate of increase in those emissions shot from 1 percent a year in the 1990s to 3.5 percent a year from 2000 to 2007.[77] In 2006 researchers reported that annual global CO_2 emissions, including those from deforestation and agricultural practices, had more than doubled since 1990 and the rate of increase was accelerating.[78] Clearly, the continued increase in ppm of CO_2 in the atmosphere and associated temperature increases have yet to evidence any movement toward stabilization.

In 2004 an ecologist and an engineer paired up to identify 15 technological approaches for preventing atmospheric CO_2 concentrations from rising above 500 ppm.[79] Some sense of the average global temperature increase associated with that level of atmospheric CO_2 may be inferred from an assessment of the increase associated with 450 ppm carried out by James Hansen of NASA and others in 2007.[80] They reported that a level of 450 ppm coupled with an effective concentration (including methane and trace gases) of 500 ppm would limit the temperature increase to 2.4–2.8 degrees Celsius (4.3–5.1 degrees Fahrenheit) above pre-industrial levels. Such a warming of almost 3 degrees Celsius (5.4 degrees Fahrenheit) represents a troubling increase, since a significant number of dangerous tipping points have been linked to warming of more than 3 degrees Celsius.[81] Recognizing this danger, Lester Brown's Plan B calls for cutting existing CO_2 emissions 80 percent by 2020 to prevent concentrations from exceeding 400 ppm and producing unacceptable temperature increases. The findings of the IPCC's Fourth Assessment Report and more recent studies strongly reinforce the conclusion that "safe" levels of warming lie at 2 degrees Celsius (3.6 degrees Fahrenheit) or below.[82] These findings suggest that even a 1 degree Celsius warming (1.8 degrees Fahrenheit) represents significant risks in the form of ongoing loss of ice from the ice sheets and large disruptions to vulnerable ecosystems. In 2008 Hansen and his colleagues called for an "initial" CO_2 stabilization level of 350 ppm, significantly below the 2007 level of 382, because they believed the current level was already too high to maintain the climate to which humanity and the rest of life are adapted.[83] They noted this would keep warming in the 1 degree Celsius range, but that even this level might have to be lowered further to reduce the risks of large-scale loss of ice from the ice sheets. The threats associated with even the warming of less than 1 degree Celsius to date continue to surprise researchers. The ability of the planet to absorb greenhouse gases now appears to be lower than was initially assumed, the potential temperature increases due to rising gas concentrations seem higher than once believed, and the physical impacts of a warming planet are appearing at a faster rate than many expected.[84]

Although a 1 degree Celsius increase may not appear to be threatening, it must be remembered this figure represents an average global increase, and that the rise will be very uneven across different geographical areas. The increase will be much greater over land than over oceans, in high northern latitudes than over the equator, and in continental interiors than in coastal regions.[85] Arctic regions have, for example, already seen winter temperatures climb by 3–4 degrees Celsius (4–7 degrees Fahrenheit) over the last half century.[86] In terms of the rate of increase, the Arctic and U.S. West are warming about twice as fast as the rest of the planet.[87] Under existing trends global climate models project a 70-percent reduction in snow pack for the Western United States by 2050,[88] with obvious implications for water supplies that support tens of millions in an arid zone. Recent projections suggest that extreme surface temperatures will rise faster than global warming, with prospects for dangerously high surface temperatures over 48 degrees Celsius (118 degrees Fahrenheit) every decade in much of the world by 2100 if the average global increase exceeds 4 degrees Celsius (7.2 degrees Fahrenheit) above the pre-industrial level.[89] Such prospective high temperatures evoke memories of the record-breaking heatwave across Europe in 2003 that claimed more than 52,000 lives in 9 countries. Many other threatening outcomes associated with global warming are addressed in Lester Brown's 2008 book *Plan 3.0*.[90] Over the long term, a sea level rise of 12 meters (39 feet) would create more than 600 million climate refugees. According to the IPCC a rise in average global temperature of 1 degree Celsius (1.8 degrees Fahrenheit) will put up to 30 percent of all species at risk of extinction. For each 1 degree Celsius increase ecologists estimate there will be a 10 percent decline in grain yields. At 40 degrees Celsius (104 degrees Fahrenheit) photosynthesis ceases entirely, with implications for grain yields and the global food supply being obvious. As Brown aptly opined: "We need to stop this dangerous experiment that humankind is conducting on the Earth's atmosphere."[91]

Global ecological threats associated with continued CO_2 emissions are not limited to dangerous atmospheric changes. Emissions are also leading to the acidification of oceans as they take up CO_2 and convert a portion of it to carbonic acid. The oceans now contain more acid by a factor of 0.1 pH unit than in the pre-industrial era, which may seem inconsequential but is actually dangerous due to the fact that the pH reading is on a logarithmic scale and the current level is 30 percent more acidic.[92] This represents an extreme threat to tens of thousands of marine species that rely on a calcium carbonate equilibrium to build shells and skeletons from calcium carbonate, including tiny planktonic organisms that exist in huge numbers at the base of marine food chains. Change is already being detected at the base of food chains off Alaska and in the North Atlantic.[93] Phytoplankton in the world's oceans are being threatened by more than the acidification attributable to rising carbon dioxide emissions. In 2010 researchers published findings indicating an ongoing decline in phytoplankton over the past century in 8 of 10 ocean basins.[94] Those researchers reported a global rate of decline of approximately 1 percent of the global median per year during the twentieth century, and with more reliable data for recent decades they concluded there had been a 40-percent decline since 1950. They found the decline to be negatively correlated with a rise in ocean sea surface temperatures attributable to global warming, pointing out that warming ocean surfaces result in increased stratification of ocean layers, characterized by a warmer layer sitting on colder layers of water, which serves to inhibit the cycling of nutrients from deeper waters and thus deprives phytoplankton of their food source. The researchers pointed out that phytoplankton account for approximately half the production of organic matter on Earth, affect prospects for other life forms in the sea due to their critical role at the base of the marine food web, and ultimately set upper limits to yields from the world's fisheries. The function of phytoplankton as microscopic marine organisms capable of photosynthesis also establishes the role they play in oxygen production and carbon sequestration. They produce around 50 percent of the world's oxygen and draw down atmospheric carbon dioxide at a rate that has played a part in taking up some 30 percent of carbon that human activities have put into the air since the advent of the Industrial Revolution.[95] Clearly phytoplankton represents a critical part of our planetary life-support system. The ongoing reduction in this life form in the seas suggests the threat to life in the oceans is both real and serious.

The threat to life on land associated with global warming is equally grave, which can be illustrated by the nature of expected changes in agricultural production and biodiversity associated with rising temperatures. In October of 2009 the United Nations Food and Agriculture Organization (FAO) sponsored a High-Level Expert Forum titled "How to Feed the World in 2050."[96] The report issued by that Forum concluded global food production would have to increase 70 percent by 2050 to meet the needs of the 9.1 billion people expected by that date, with this increase attributable to population growth, rising incomes, and growing consumption of meat. With most arable land already being farmed, the FAO report suggested fully 90 percent of the growth in crop production would end up having to come from intensification of agricultural productivity on existing farmland. Challenges of realizing such an increase through higher yields and increased cropping intensity were acknowledged, considering that past efforts to increase yields had already produced significant problems stemming from soil erosion, topsoil compaction, salinization, soil pollution, nutrient loss, and water resources depletion. Attempts to meet the increasing global food needs of a growing population from 1961 to 1999 entailed increases in nitrogenous and phosphate fertilizers of 638 percent and 203 percent, respectively, and an increase of 854 percent in the production of pesticides.[97] In spite of those massive increases in artificial fertilizers and pesticides as part of former efforts to realize intensification of yields, the global rate of growth in yields of major cereal crops has been steadily declining, dropping from 3.2 percent per year in 1960 to 1.5 percent in 2000.[98] That decline has been attributed to ongoing land degradation associated with past farming practices, with the intensive applications of fertilizers and pesticides exacerbating the problem.

In 2011 the FAO released a report representing the first global assessment of the state of the planet's land resources.[99] That report revealed that 25 percent of the world's farmland was "highly degraded," and another 8 percent was "moderately degraded," with part of the degradation attributable to biodiversity loss. In spite of the noted scale of degradation, the report held out prospects for being able to realize the needed 70-percent increase in food production under innovative farming practices based on "sustainable intensification." But the quest for such a dramatic increase in food production would certainly come at a cost for the planet's biodiversity, because "agriculture remains the largest driver of genetic erosion, species loss, and conversion of natural habitats."[100] At present, "[h]abitat modification through agriculture ... is, in general, the most important factor in increasing species' risk of extinction."[101] The scale of that increasing risk may be illustrated by the recent expansion of large-scale agricultural practices in tropical regions. In the World Wildlife Fund's 2010 *Living Planet Report* references to a growing global demand for palm oil indicate such demand has doubled over the last decade, with new plantations to meet that demand converting an estimated 7.8 million hectares of tropical forests over the last 20 years.[102] With oil palm cultivation having increased nearly 8-fold over that 20-year period, and projected to double again by 2020, implications for habitat and biodiversity loss in the tropics have been significant. When considered in conjunction with other agricultural operations in the tropics the costs in tropical biodiversity losses have been staggering.

The 2010 *Report* on the status of nearly 8,000 populations of vertebrate species worldwide revealed a decline of about 30 percent of tracked species between 1970 and 2007, but in the tropics tracked species declined by 60 percent during the same period. The impacts of agriculture on biodiversity extend to coastal seas, where chemical fertilizers from farming make their way to oceans and serve as nutrients that produce algal blooms, which in turn are consumed by bacteria when the algae die, a process that uses up available oxygen and produces "dead zones" incapable of supporting marine life. Threats to biodiversity stemming from intensive agricultural practices are obviously varied, but as noted previously habitat modifications associated with industrial agriculture have historically been the principle force driving habitat losses and associated biodiversity declines worldwide. However, in the current era there has been a growing awareness that global warming associated with the "speed of climate change will become a more important driver of change in biodiversity this century, leading to an accelerating rate of species loss."[103] As the authors of the 2005 *Millennium Ecosystem Assessment* noted, we have reached a point where in this century "climate change and its impacts may be the dominant direct driver of biodiversity loss and changes in ecosystems globally."[104] Potential impacts of rising temperatures on agricultural production have also been acknowledged, with the aggregate negative impact on agricultural output in some regions during this century calculated to be between 15 and 30 percent.[105] In the end, the extent of impacts that increasing temperatures might be expected to exhibit on biodiversity and agriculture will ultimately be determined by how much warming actually occurs under anthropogenic climate change. Consideration of what possible temperature increases might be expected during this century has largely taken place within various explorations of likely temperatures associated with a doubling of the concentration of atmospheric CO_2. Economic projections from the Intergovernmental Panel on Climate Change suggest that under a "business as usual" burning of fossil fuels, that doubling can be expected around 2060.

During the first decade of the twenty-first century noted climate scientist James Hansen and his collaborators suggested we may have only a decade to cap CO_2 emissions and begin dramatic reductions if we are to avoid dangerous climate tipping points.[106] The challenge lies in the fact that many of those dangerous tipping points end up being associated with temperature increases well below those associated with a doubling of the concentration of CO_2 in Earth's atmosphere. "Most models suggest that a doubling in atmospheric CO_2 will lead to a global temperature rise of about 3°C [5.4°F] (with a probable uncertainty range of 2–4.5°C) [3.6–8.1°F] once the climate has regained equilibrium."[107] However, these models "do not include long-term reinforcing feedback processes that further warm the climate, such as decreases in the surface area of ice cover," and when these feedbacks are included "doubling CO_2 levels gives an eventual temperature increase of 6°C [10.8°F] (with a probable uncertainty range of 4–8°C [7.2–14.4°F])."[108] Even without consideration of feedback influences, all of the noted prospective temperatures stand in stark contrast to the reality that the "balance of scientific evidence suggests that there will be a significant net harmful impact on ecosystem services worldwide if global mean surface temperature increases more than 2°C [3.6° F] above preindustrial levels."[109] Multiple assessments of possible temperature increases associated with a doubling of CO_2 levels suggest prospects for temperatures going up by a number of factors greater than 2°C. In 2006 the British chemist James Lovelock, who played a key role in alerting the world to the threat posed by atmospheric chlorofluorocarbons to the planet's ozone layer, expressed the view that it is already too late to avoid catastrophic changes associated with inevitable warming.[110] He believes that as the twenty-first century progresses the temperature will rise 8 degrees Celsius (14.4 degrees Fahrenheit) in temperate regions and 5 degrees Celsius (9 degrees Fahrenheit) in the tropics, producing intolerable conditions everywhere except in the Arctic, and as a result billions will die. Lovelock is not alone in suggesting the possibility of dangerous levels of warming under a doubling of CO_2 levels. Published research findings in 2010 based on paleoclimate data and consideration of the feedback influences of short-term greenhouse warming being amplified by changes in ice sheets concluded a doubling of CO_2 could produce possible temperature increases in the 7.1° to 9.6°C [12.8–17.3°F] range.[111] In 2011 another research undertaking utilizing an improved carbon-cycle model and an expanded data set, and incorporating the influence of glacial amplification associated with the waxing and waning of ice sheets, suggested possible temperature increases of 6° to 8°C [10.8–14.4°F] under a doubling of CO_2.[112] It is the upper end of such possible increases that evoke apocalyptic predictions of massive ice sheet collapses, catastrophic coastal flooding, continental crop failures, mass extinctions, dead oceans, large-scale desertification, and billions of human deaths. Even under low probabilities of reaching the noted extreme temperatures and experiencing the cited apocalyptic outcomes, the potential threats to all life on the planet and human civilization are such that a dramatic response is long overdue.

Rapidly emerging threats to the ecosystems that represent the planet's life-support apparatus demand an immediate mobilization to stabilize the planet's climate, "for if we cannot stabilize climate, there is not an ecosystem on earth that we can save."[113] It follows that if ecosystems cannot be saved there can be no hope for saving civilization because of its utter dependence on the life-support services ecosystems provide. Stabilizing the planet's climate will obviously require a rapid transition from fossil fuels to renewable energy sources because of the role fossil fuels have played in creating the current climate crisis. The explosive exponential demographic, economic, and urban growth of the twentieth century was made possible by cheap oil, which ballooned from a production rate of 150 million barrels a year in 1900 to 28 billion barrels in 2000, an increase of more than 180-fold. With world reserves of some 2 trillion barrels, of which half have been extracted and combusted to date, it turns out the world has run out of atmosphere to hold CO_2 emissions before it has run out of oil. Coupled with the use of other fossil fuels the effect has altered the atmosphere to a degree that the global ecosystem's life-support service of climate moderation has been compromised. But the challenge that lies ahead is much greater than just making the transition from fossil fuels to renewables. For even if the continued exponential expansion of the human enterprise were to be fueled by renewable energy sources, and the threat to the planet's atmosphere thereby largely negated, other threats to earth's ecological life-support services would escalate as the natural world continued to be displaced by a rapidly expanding human enterprise. Continued exponential demographic, economic, and urban increases of the current era are driving the ongoing degradation of the planet's ecosystems and their critically important life-support services. None of these forms of growth show any sign of abating in the near term, and it is this continued demographic, economic, and urban growth that ultimately represents the greatest challenge and threat confronting humankind.

The magnitude of projected population increases over coming decades was portrayed in a 2011 United Nation's document that revised a former assessment of world population prospects.[114] That revision abandoned the long-held expectation that the population of the world would stabilize at just over 9 billion by the middle of the century, in favor of a new medium variant that projects a population that reaches 9.3 billion in 2050 and then continues to grow to 10.1 billion by 2100. Expected declines in fertility in the former projection had failed to materialize, and that put the planet on a path of adding another 3 billion plus to the 7-billion mark reached in 2011 before global population was projected to peak at just over 10 billion at the end of the century. In the United States the nation's population increased by 60 million over the two decades from 1990 to 2010, taking the country from 248.7 million to 308.7 million. The average annual increase of 3 million over those 20 years showed little sign of diminishing over the first years of the subsequent decade. In spite of two decades of mounting evidence by 2010 of ecological limits to growth having already been exceeded globally, the planet's population in the post-2010 period continued to grow by some 80 million each year, while America's population continued to expand by around 3 million annually during that same period. With the scientific community asserting that the 7 billion individuals present in 2011 were already exerting unsustainable demands on the planet's ecosystems, the wisdom of such demographic increases globally and in the United States certainly ought to be questioned, if not aggressively challenged. However, with the exception of China's controversial one-child policy, there has been no concerted effort to confront these unsustainable population increases.

Global economic increases have continued on the same upward trajectory as global population increases. While the global 2008–09 recession caused the first global economic downturn since 1946, the hundreds of billions of dollars of stimulus spending by multiple nation states across the globe succeeded in bringing about an economic recovery that yielded a 5 percent growth rate in global GDP in 2010. While that growth rate fell back to 3.7 percent in 2011,[115] the ongoing momentum of globalization initiatives suggests prospects for continued growth into the foreseeable future. In 2009 the World Bank released baseline projections of global economic growth extending to 2050, suggesting an average rate of GDP growth of 2.9 percent annually until 2050, with that growth breaking out into 1.6 percent for high-income countries and 5.2 percent for developing countries.[116] The difference in doubling times for the global economy between the 5 percent growth rate in 2010 and the projected annual rate of 2.9 percent forecast by the World Bank is significant, because the former would double the 2010 GDP of some 63 trillion dollars in a mere 14 years while the latter would entail a doubling time of 24 years. So a 5 percent growth rate would result in almost 3 doublings by 2050, taking the global GDP to around 500 trillion dollars, while the 2.9 percent rate would produce just under 2 doublings, taking the global GDP to around 250 trillion dollars in 2050. The 2005 *Millennium Ecosystem Assessment* report acknowledged the direct link between such economic expansion and the ongoing degradation of ecosystems, noting this degradation was apt to grow significantly worse in coming decades "as a consequence of a likely three-to six-fold increase in global GDP by 2050."[117] In the United States strong political pressures are at work to produce an annual growth rate of at least 3 percent, both to recover from the high unemployment rate resulting from the national recession of 2007–09 and to create jobs for a rapidly growing population. A 3 percent growth rate would double the 15 trillion dollar American economy in about 23 years, while the 1.6 percent growth rate projected by the World Bank would represent a doubling time of around 44 years. So a 3 percent rate would produce an American GDP quickly approaching 60 trillion dollars by 2050, while a 1.6 percent rate would yield a national GDP of close to 30 trillion by that same date. The possibility of the American economy becoming almost as large as the 63 trillion dollar global economy of 2010 by 2050, or the possibility of a global economy expanding to something like 250 trillion or 500 trillion by 2050, clearly illustrate the absurdity of attempting to keep economic growth going on a finite planet. With mounting evidence that a global economy of over 60 trillion dollars is dismantling the planet's ecological life-support structures, the absence of prospects for continued economic growth needs to be quickly conceded. Any attempt to replicate the American economy across other nation states has been shown to be impossible by ecological footprint analysis, which has determined that "[t]o raise just the present global population to North American material standards using existing technologies would require the biocapacity of 4–5 Earth-like planets."[118] Continued economic growth will only exacerbate the problems that prior growth has demonstrated, such as the record CO_2 emissions associated with the 5 percent global economic growth rate reported for 2010. In that year global emissions rose 5.9 percent, with more than 9 billion tons of carbon entering the atmosphere, representing both the largest absolute jump in any year since the Industrial Revolution, and the largest percentage increase since 2003.[119] Such ecological effects clearly illustrate an inherent conflict between economic growth and the maintenance of ecological integrity across the planet. On ecological grounds humankind will have to concede the inherent unsustainability of continued growth and devise an alternative economic system if there is to be any hope of an extended human future.

Urban growth in the current era ends up demonstrating equally absurd outcomes to those associated with continued demographic and economic growth. The 2009 United Nations update of its *World Urbanization Prospects* publication projected that the population living in urban areas would grow from 3.5 billion in 2010 to 6.3 billion in 2050.[120] According to the United

Nations projections, virtually all of the world's population growth up to 2050 will be concentrated in urban areas, taking the world from 50 percent urban in 2008 to 70 percent urban by midcentury. In the process those projections predict dramatic increases in the number of large urban centers, with the number of megacities of at least 10 million inhabitants expected to increase from 21 in 2010 to 29 in 2025, the number of centers ranging from 5 to 10 million in size expected to jump from 33 to 46 during the same time period, and the number between 1 and 5 million projected to explode from 388 centers in 2010 to 506 in 2025. Optimists are not troubled by such increases because they see prospects for these dense urban environments evolving into the most efficient and sustainable settlement options available to humankind. But it is also possible to consider such giant cities in a negative light, since "ecological footprint analysis shows that they act as entropic black holes, sweeping up the output of whole regions of the ecosphere vastly larger than themselves."[121] Under such an analysis, cities are shown to be responsible for at least 70 percent of current levels of resource depletion and pollution, and thereby "causally linked to accelerating global ecological decline."[122] With explosive projected growth in urban populations the threat to ecosystems can only be expected to increase. The nature of projected urban increases in developing countries vividly provides an example of such increasing threats to ecosystems. According to the United Nations the urban population in developing countries increased by an average of 58 million per year between 2000 and 2010, and during the same period the absolute number of urban slum dwellers increased by nearly half that number (28 million) each year.[123] That increase in so-called informal or slum populations is adding to the more than 2.6 billion people globally who lack access to improved sanitation,[124] which represents an ongoing increase in poorly treated sewage discharged into oceans that combined with the runoff of nitrogen-rich fertilizers is driving the dramatic growth of "dead zones" globally. Another threat to ecosystems associated with ongoing urban growth stems from the role of cities in fueling ongoing increases in global CO_2 emissions. Cities are already the source of almost 80 percent of global CO_2 emissions, and with the projected growth of cities that percentage seems destined to keep increasing.[125] Such increases represent clear threats to ecosystems worldwide. In the end, continuation of urban growth at an average annual percentage rate of nearly double the rate for population growth is just as unsustainable as ongoing demographic and economic increases. All three forms of growth are driving the ongoing ecological degradation that scientists are documenting with a wide array of research initiatives.

A particularly troubling aspect of the ecological threats associated with continued demographic, economic, and urban growth derives from the fact that an increasing number of the changes in ecosystems resulting from ongoing growth of the human enterprise are evidencing nonlinear characteristics. As the 2005 *Millennium Ecosystem Assessment* report noted, there is established evidence that changes being made in ecosystems are increasing the likelihood of accelerating, abrupt, and potentially irreversible subsequent shifts in eco-systems.[126] The report pointed to disease emergence, the creation of "dead zones" in coastal waters, the collapse of fisheries, and shifts in regional climate as examples of nonlinear changes occurring in ecosystems. Research findings published in 2008 on the accelerating rate of growth in the number of coastal "dead zones" vividly illustrate the nature of some of the changes in ecosystems during the recent past. That research reported that the "number of dead zones has approximately doubled each decade since the 1960s."[127] With only 49 dead zones recorded during the 1960s, the number of these oxygen-depleted zones exploded to 405 during the first decade of the century. The noted examples of nonlinear changes occurring in ecosystems by the *Millennium Ecosystem Assessment* report do not represent the only accelerating changes being demon-strated by ecosystems across the planet. Scientists are reporting such rates of change in the loss of ice sheets, species losses, and global climate alterations, as other examples of threatening ecological changes being brought on by continued demographic, economic, and urban growth. Growth in all of these forms of human expansion will have to quickly wind down if there is to be any hope of stopping the ongoing ecological degradation that threatens both the future viability of the human community and the broader community of life on the planet.

The current consumption of the capital base of renewable resources rather than living off their sustainable annual income streams clearly illustrates the human enterprise has already surpassed planetary limits to growth. Current unsustainable demands on the planet's ecosystems and their life-support ser-vices further illustrate the human enterprise has exceeded ecological limits to growth. An exponentially growing human enterprise is simply not an option on a finite planet. As the prior survey of existent ecological limits to growth showed, the exponential demographic, economic, and urban growth that has occurred to date has already exceeded the support capabilities of the planet's ecological life-support services. The ultimate challenge, therefore, is one of conceding the irrelevance of the growth imperative to current ecological realities. If there is to be an indeterminate future for the human enterprise on a finite planet, it will undoubtedly have to be predicated on a prior widespread acceptance of the inherently unsustainable nature of growth.

The inherently unsustainable nature of growth

The current widespread acceptance of the possibility of "sustainable growth" may in large part be attributed to the influence of the Brundtland Commission Report of 1987.[128] That United Nations Commission Report realized world-wide recognition of the concept of sustainable development, and "set the standard and became the point of reference for every debate on sustainable development."[129] The report ended up influencing the nature of a nascent sustainable-development movement in two key ways. First, it provided what would come to be the most widely cited meaning for the term sustainable development by defining it as development that meets the needs of the present generation without compromising the ability of future generations to meet their own needs. Second, it influenced the emerging sustainable-development movement by laying out the case for the legitimacy of further economic growth in the pursuit of sustainable development. These respective emphases on development directed at satisfying human needs and the legitimacy of economic growth to realize that development produced a pro-growth sustainable-development model. That model was based on needs being met through the material output of industrial development and economic growth being based on ongoing industrialization. This focus on addressing human needs via the material output of industrial development within the context of continuing economic growth represents the central theme in the Brundtland Report.

The Brundtland Commission's stance on population and urban growth reflects more of an acceptance of "inevitable" growth in these areas than a pro-growth stance toward further expansion in either of these terms. However, the assumed "inevitability" of further demographic and urban growth served to support the Commission's pro-growth position on continued economic expansion, since economic growth was perceived as essential to address problems stemming from future demographic and urban increases. For the Commission, economic growth translated into both an automatic fix for excessive population growth and the resources to manage rapid urban growth. Under this line of reasoning the Commission perceived a need for a new era of global economic growth to relieve poverty across the planet. In extending the definition of sustainable development beyond the notion of meeting basic needs to the realm of encompassing aspirations,[130] the Commission argued the case for an explosion of global industrial growth to meet both the needs and aspirations of humans over the long term.

The Brundtland Commission left no doubt as to its expectations of both needs and aspirations being met by material goods produced by manufacturing industries.[131] It called for a 5–10-fold increase in manufacturing output to raise developing world consumption of manufactured goods to industrial world levels by the time population growth rates level off.[132] To further that end, the Commission called for a sustained economic growth rate of 5 to 6 percent in developing countries, and an ongoing growth rate of 3 to 4 percent in industrial countries.[133] Such growth was portrayed as essential to avert economic, social, and environmental catastrophes.[134] Ultimately, this line of reasoning led the Commission to make the case for the possibility of "long-term sustainable growth."[135] The Commission made its case for the possibility of "sustainable industrial growth" and "sustainable economic growth" on the basis of a few key arguments: an achievable compatibility between economic growth and ecological sustainability; possible dematerialization and efficiency gains; prospects for resource substitution; technological optimism; and changes in production and consumption patterns. These arguments in support of the idea of "sustainable growth" have demonstrated tremendous staying power since the publication of the Brundtland Report. However, the arguments used by the Commission to support the possibility of "sustainable growth" have not gone unchallenged.

The possibility of achieving compatibility between economic growth and ecological sustainability, or stated differently, that it is possible to realize ongoing economic growth without jeopardizing ecological sustainability, has certainly come to be challenged. Brian Czech, as the founder and president of the Center for the Advancement of the Steady State Economy, played a key role in having a few key professional associations in the United States adopt position statements endorsing the idea of an inherent conflict between economic growth and environmental protection. He drafted the template for such a position and initially proposed its adoption before a meeting of the Wildlife Society (TWS) in 2003, followed by similar proposals before members of the United States Society for Ecological Economics (USSEE) and the North American Section of the Society for Conservation Biology (SCB/NAS). In 2003 the USSEE adopted a position statement endorsing the inherent conflict between economic growth and environmental protection, followed by similar adoptions of the conflict statement in 2004 by SCB/NAS and TWS. The SCB/NAS position statement asserted "a fundamental conflict between economic growth and biodiversity conservation based on the ecological principle of competitive exclusion," as well as "a fundamental conflict between economic growth and the ecological services underpinning the human economy."[136] Subsequent endorsements of the same position statement followed, with support coming from such organizations as the British Columbia Field Ornithologists. With mounting evidence of existent ecological limits to growth along the lines surveyed in the prior section of this work, it should come as no surprise that some would question the possibility of realizing a form of "sustainable growth" that would not endanger ecosystems.

Objections have also surfaced to the Brundtland Commission's claim that "sustainable growth" would be made possible by dematerialization and eco-efficiency gains permitting dramatic reductions in the material and energy inputs needed to support ongoing growth. Taken together, dematerialization and eco-efficiency are credited with prospects for reducing material throughput by certain factors, such as the popular notion of Factor 4, or the more optimistic Factor 10 that would reduce inputs to 10 percent of current numbers. Under this line of reasoning both dematerialization and eco-efficiency fall back on a high degree of technological optimism, with the role of technology being principally that of raising output from scarce resources while reducing pollution effects. This viewpoint is countered by dissenting voices that challenge the optimistic assumptions regarding the possibility of transforming ongoing economic expansion into some form of "sustainable growth."

They point to the fact that even Europe, with its dramatic efficiency gains in terms of both material and energy inputs over the course of the past few decades, has seen its total material and energy requirements increase with GDP growth. An analysis of Germany, Japan, and the United States in 2005 showed they reduced the material intensity of a unit of GDP by 20–30 percent over the course of the last two decades of the twentieth century, but that this was offset by aggregate growth in GDP that produced an increase of almost 28 percent in total use of materials.[137] This illustrates the pernicious ability of the growth effect in being able to outgrow any resource productivity gains. It does not require higher math to understand that a reduction of the total material and energy requirements of any economy by 50 percent would be negated by a doubling in size of that economy. Even more dramatic eco-efficiency gains would likewise be nullified by the ongoing doublings associated with exponential economic growth rates that have the ability to produce huge economies with deceptive speed.

The remaining Brundtland Commission arguments used to support the possibility of "sustainable growth" are also subject to criticism. The claim that prospects for resource substitution create avenues for "sustainable growth" does not recognize the flawed nature of the idea of perfect substitutability, which discounts any problems with shortages of natural resources assuming they can effectively be replaced by human-made capital. Some natural capital such as water supplies, and a multitude of natural processes vital to human existence like photosynthesis, are simply incapable of being replaced by human-made substitutes. With respect to technological optimism, critics are apt to emphasize the chemical and physical laws that specify absolute maximum potentials for controlling pollution under continued economic growth and conversion efficiencies for the reuse of materials or energy. Again, it does not require higher math to understand that the gains associated with cutting pollution flowing from any economy in half would be negated by the next doubling in size of the economy. Similarly, any gains associated with changes in production and consumption practices would be nullified by ongoing growth. In the end, the ultimate challenge is one of conceding the inherently unsustainable nature of material increases that economic growth represents. The sustainable-development movement has been unable to concede this point, because "in almost all respects, the main organizing principle of sustainable development is economic growth."[138]

If even participants in the sustainable-development movement have been unable to recognize that the term "sustainable growth" is a fatuous oxymoron that impedes recognition of the inherently unsustainable nature of growth, the challenges associated with gaining widespread acceptance of this reality become obvious. However, transitioning to a sustainable future will require prior acknowledgement of the inherently unsustainable nature of demographic, economic, and urban growth. In the end, the most direct support for the assertion that growth in any of these terms is intrinsically unsustainable derives from the nature of the definition for sustainability. With definitions for *sustainable* including "capable of being upheld; maintainable," definitions of *to sustain* encompassing "to keep in existence; to maintain or prolong," and synonyms for *to sustain* listing "to maintain, continue, and prolong" the lexical meaning of sustainability provides little room for debate. As has been noted, when it comes to defining sustainability "the distinguishing characteristic is the ability to be continued."[139] In order for anything to be considered sustainable in these terms, it would have to exhibit prospective continuity over time. Which is to say, this line of reasoning would yield a definition of sustainability as behavior capable of being sustained, maintained, or continued indefinitely. Material growth on a finite planet simply fails to meet this definitional requirement. The fallacy of assuming material increases might somehow represent sustainable behavior ignores the incontrovertible axiom that infinite growth is impossible in a finite system presented in the 1972 book *Limits to Growth*. Suggestions that material increases can somehow be transformed into sustainable growth also ignore what may be thought of as the "First Law of Sustainability," Herman Daly's truism that "[i]t is development that can have the attribute of sustainability, not growth."[140] Demographic, economic, and urban increases simply fail to meet the definitional requirement of sustainability, and any transition to a sustainable future will require the concession of this reality even though it challenges the growth imperative inherent in today's dominant social paradigm.

Additional evidence of the intrinsically unsustainable nature of material increases is provided by the magnitudes capable of being generated by ongoing exponential growth. Take, for example, the mathematical calculation revealing that if our species had started with just two people at the time of the earliest agricultural practices some 10,000 years ago, and increased by 1 percent per year, today humanity would be a solid ball of flesh many thousand light years in diameter, and expanding with a radial velocity that, neglecting relativity, would be many times faster than the speed of light.[141] Clearly, even the apparently innocuous annual growth rate of 1 percent is incapable of being continued indefinitely. Even the recent annual demographic growth rate of 1.2 percent succeeded in adding an additional billion people to the planet in a mere 12 years. Higher annual growth rates are capable of producing similarly absurd numbers in much shorter time periods. With respect to economic growth, it has been pointed out that the growth in the world economy during just the 12 months of the year 2000 exceeded that during the entire nineteenth century.[142] Similarly, another calculation has revealed that just the growth in the output of goods and services in 2007 exceeded the total output of the global economy in 1900.[143] With the global economy having added the equivalent of nearly two American economies in a mere 8 years between 2000 and the onset of the global recession in 2008, the unsustainable nature of exponential economic growth was being dramatically illustrated during the first decade of the twenty-first century. If the global economy were to come out of the global recession and expand at an annual rate of 3 percent, in a mere 50 years it would realize two doublings, expanding it from $66 trillion dollars in 2006 to $264 trillion, a 4-fold increase. Global urban growth rates over the course of the past century have yielded similarly incomprehensible numbers. With almost all of the 80 million annual population increase being added to the world's cities and suburbs each year, and the nearly 1 billion current slum dwellers set to keep growing under current trends, the unsustainable nature of current urban growth rates is also being clearly demonstrated. In the end, the demographic, economic, and urban quantities being generated by the beginning of the twenty-first century illustrate the inherently unsustainable nature of material increases in any of these terms.

Finally, the intrinsically unsustainable nature of population, economic, and urban growth has been revealed by reports documenting existent ecological limits to further growth. Given what ecologists are now telling us about the effects of even the current scale of the human enterprise on other species and ecosystems, and that these effects are incongruous with ecological sustainability, it seems we have no option but to accept the current reality of present limits to any further demographic, economic, and urban increases. The idea of "sustainable growth" must be recognized as being worse than an "oxymoron" and elevated to the status of a "moronic oxymoron." Growth in material terms needs to be rejected on the grounds that it does not satisfy the definitional requirement of behavior capable of being continued indefinitely. It also needs to be rejected on the grounds of the absurd numbers generated by exponential growth during the recent past. And finally, it needs to be rejected on the grounds of what ecologists are reporting on existent ecological limits to further growth. With past growth having already initiated a systematic dismantling of the planet's ecosystems and their essential life-support services, the time has come to abandon the vacuous oxymoron of "sustainable growth" and undertake consideration of a truly sustainable development path. The current challenge is now much greater than merely attempting to realize more *efficient* growth, which would merely serve to slow down the ongoing unsustainable conversion of the natural world to a human-dominated world. The quest for more efficient economic and urban growth only serves to distract attention from the true need to quickly transition to a no-growth future capable of being sustained indefinitely. With the prospect of an indeterminate future for humankind being dependent on realizing a no-growth state, the ultimate rationale for stopping global material growth centers on the essential need to replace the growth imperative with a no-growth imperative. If the primacy of ecological sustainability can be accepted, the necessity of rejecting the growth imperative will become increasingly self-evident as mounting evidence reveals the ecological destruction attributable to ongoing growth. In the end, it must be conceded that our species can persist without growth, but not without sustainable ecosystems. If people can accept this obvious truism, the requisite transition from the artificial growth imperative to an indispensable no-growth imperative can finally begin.

2   The American community as a growth machine

Throughout American history the most consistent theme in local governance has been the pursuit of growth: more people, more jobs, and more real-estate development. Local democracy has been dominated by 'growth coalitions,' composed of individuals and enterprises with a direct stake in real-estate development.

Alan Altshuler and José Gómez-Ibáñez[1]

[T]he political and economic essence of virtually any given locality, in the present America context, is *growth* ... The city is, for those who count, a growth machine.

Harvey Molotch[2]

Understanding the challenges associated with stopping growth in America's communities requires an appreciation of the historical role of local governments as "growth machines." It also requires recognition of the historical role of state and federal governments in supporting the growth-promotion function enacted by American communities. Additionally, local efforts to stop growth will have to recognize the urban planning profession's historical pro-growth stance and the part the profession has played in facilitating the growth of America's communities. In a related vein, local no-growth initiatives will also have to contend with the pro-growth orientation of the growth-management movement in the United States. Since all of these factors represent serious barriers to realizing a state of no-growth in any local governmental context, the following observations on urban growth machines, state and federal support of these machines, and the pro-growth biases of the planning profession and the growth-management movement are all intended to illustrate the magnitude of challenges inherent in devising and implementing a strategy for stopping growth within local political jurisdictions.

The historical pro-growth bias of American communities

The above-cited claim that pursuit of growth has been the most consistent theme in local governance throughout American history may be traced back to the earliest colonial settlements in North America, while "growth coalitions" with a direct stake in real-estate development represent a subsequent historical phenomenon. Beginning with Jamestown in 1607, American colonies were designed to serve the needs of a mercantilist British Empire.[3] Colonial settlements were sources of English wealth that were supposed to benefit the Empire by shipping products of extractive industries back to the British Crown. Representing assumed profit-making enterprises, colonial towns were points of control where the Crown sought to regulate trade and check illicit businesses. For the first few generations residing in these towns their activities were heavily regulated, with the specific end of expanding their basic economic activities. The Crown chartered the towns, and they were expected to demonstrate growth as the central indicator of their success. By the end of the seventeenth century most colonial towns had secured their respective economic bases under ongoing growth, and by 1700 many communities were developing rapidly, with some legitimately deserving the title of city.

The growth experienced by colonial towns and cities would end up producing significant unintended consequences. Originally, colonial settlements were mostly maritime phenomena developed along the shores of the Atlantic with a dominant focus on serving an empire that lay to the east. However, the colonies radiated outward from urban centers that also faced westward. Over time they produced a new breed of entrepreneurs "who began to think of themselves as imperialists in their own right, and of their communities as nascent metropolitan centers which might command hinterlands of their own."[4] These entrepreneurs began to capitalize upon resources westward of their communities for their own benefit rather than that of the Crown under a growing belief that they possessed the same rights as their counterparts in the mother country. By 1750 local elites had appeared in each of the colonial cities, groups of merchants and land owners with considerable wealth for the day, who engaged in widespread systematized smuggling to advance their personal prosperity over that of the Crown. As noted by urban historians: "The cities nurtured economic life so successfully as to feed economic ambition."[5] While local elites originally sought prosperity through circumventing Navigation Acts established by the Crown to regulate trade, over time they also began "to look beyond the confines of imperial policy for real estate profits."[6] This constituted a significant break from the past, because "[a]ll of the colonial cities and towns were planned communities in origin; the idea that their growth might be shaped by individuals' interests in real estate speculation was to emerge only slowly."[7] But the idea did emerge during the last decades of the 1700s as part of a "passionate land hunger which increasingly dispersed American settlements all over the landscape,"[8] when land speculators increasingly saw profits to be made from escalating land values driven ever higher by ongoing population increases. This reality would eventually produce a view of cities as "growth machines" run by local elites seeking to increase their land values through intensification of land use, and the associated claim that these growth machines are historical, dating from frontier America, being "nowhere more clearly documented than in the histories of eighteenth- and nineteenth-century American cities."[9]

Between the American Revolution (1775–83) and the Civil War (1861–65) increasing numbers of Americans pushed far west of established settlements.[10] As early as 1785 the federal government provided for the rectangular survey of national lands into "townships" (each 6 miles square and comprised of 36 sections) and "sections" (each a mile square, or 640 acres), and in the process furthered the view of land as a commodity. "The simplest, most orderly, and most quickly remunerative program was to sell these large tracts to easterners with strong financial backing."[11] While the federal government held to a policy of retaining title to all land not granted to private owners, parcels turned over to private entrepreneurs became part of an ongoing process of real-estate speculation. By the late 1820s the picture was further complicated by some two-thirds of settlers being squatters on property still technically belonging to the federal government, with their claims only addressed with the opening of federal land offices under the Preemption Act of 1841,[12] but granted lands provided plenty of opportunities for new western towns that at an early stage became speculative enterprises.[13] In the early 1800s western urbanization represented an important index of national growth,[14] and particular speculative town projects purportedly resulted in city council lists reading like local business directories after leading businessmen received legislative authorizations from the states in the form of charters.[15]

Early in the nineteenth century the federal government again intervened in ways that would facilitate expansion of speculative town projects across the new nation state.[16] In 1803 the area of the United States was doubled with the Louisiana Purchase, pushing the nation further into a largely unknown west. In 1806 the federal government authorized surveys for a National Road or Turnpike that would come to be known as the Cumberland Road, which was constructed directly by the federal government. Starting in Cumberland, Maryland, and crossing the mountain barrier to Wheeling on the Ohio River and beyond, the road opened new land to speculative town developments. In 1808 a federal report on roads and canals laid out a comprehensive scheme for a federally aided transportation system connecting eastern rivers with the Mississippi basin. Projects in that scheme would be accomplished over the subsequent 60 years by varying combinations of private, local, state, and federal resources. In 1825 the Erie Canal opened, connecting Albany on the Hudson River with Buffalo on Lake Erie. That project, organized and financed by the state of New York, opened a waterway eastward from Ohio, Indiana, Michigan, Wisconsin, and Illinois. In 1828 the state of Maryland followed with support for the Chesapeake and Ohio Canal, while the city of Baltimore provided support for the Baltimore and Ohio Railroad, with both projects competing for the opportunity to help the community of Baltimore grow. Before 1830 speculative town projects competed for such government aid, and during this era "the town promoter was the true 'frontiersman' in the development of new regions of the country."[17] These town promoters competed for "government-aided canals and railroads [that] were built ahead of the traffic."[18] What would come to represent a legacy of federal, state, county, and city support for such transportation infrastructure projects emerged during the opening decades of the nineteenth century.

Daniel J. Boorstin, writing on the American national experience, described the role of the "businessman" in what he called "upstart cities" in the American West between the Revolution and the Civil War.[19] The key idea behind these upstart cities from their beginning was growth, and around 1830 the term businessman came into use just when new western cities were growing most rapidly. Rather than being merchants engaged in mercantile transactions, these businessmen were community makers and community leaders, with a foundational belief in the interfusing of public and private prosperity. "In the period when he first appeared, his primary commodity was land, and his secondary commodity transportation."[20] These businessmen understood that the value of land rose with population. Measuring their success by the rate of growth of their communities, such businessmen depended on transportation to attract settlers and handle the growing industrial commerce of their communities. Their primary community service was to make it easier for more people to join their upstart settlements. Thriving on growth and expansion, and recognizing the increasing role of railroads in realizing the success of their new settlements, these businessmen became what would retrospectively come to be known as "boosters." Their "booster railroads" relied upon help from public agencies, and governments responded with aid for railroads that brought into being the population that used them. During the so-called "pioneer age of railroad building" in the decades before the Civil War, the American idea of progress became equated with the ability of upstart communities to attract immigrants, and businessmen sought to further that end by realizing the railroads that would draw those immigrants.

Whether referred to as town promoters, businessmen, boosters, or real-estate speculators, advocates of speculative town projects were not alone in recognizing the profits that could be made through real-estate transactions in upstart communities. "From early on in the railroad era, railroad officials were well aware of the possibilities of profit in urban growth in the West."[21] The platting of town sites and the sale of town lots accompanied the building of railroads into new regions, and creation of new towns by companies building the lines permitted a larger share of profits from increased land values to go directly to railroad owners. For longer routes rail companies relied on support of federal and state governments in the form of public land grants. Land grants for railroads extended beyond right-of-way allotments to include alternate sections (640 acres) within a specified number of miles on either side of the line. State and local governments supplemented those land grants to rail companies with direct financial grants that further enhanced prospects of the upstart communities that sprang up along the rail lines. Town promoters and rail companies alike laid out a grid of streets and "measured their success in the number and prices of the lots sold, and such gains often proved sufficient to create a boom-town atmosphere, which encouraged still wider and more speculative subdivisions."[22] During the first half of the nineteenth century potential profits in real-estate speculation were impressive, as illustrated by the Chicago businessman William B. Ogden, who in 1844 recalled that he "purchased for $8,000, what 8 years thereafter, sold for 3 millions of dollars, and these cases could be extended almost indefinitely."[23] "If the American experience in pre-Civil War land settlement taught anything, it was that town-lot promotion and city building offered grand prospects to ambitious men."[24]

By 1850 profits from real-estate speculation in upstart communities paved the way for creation of new wealth through other means. "The successful townsman of the mid-century had a speculation, not a business."[25] A rapid advance in real-estate values provided the foundation of credit in most upstart communities, and businessmen took advantage of that credit to initiate new moneymaking ventures, including industrial undertakings that increasingly created the factory towns that transformed America during the latter half of the nineteenth century into an industrial nation. The 1850s represented a period of widespread town promoting and urban ambition, and in the interior of the country regional rail systems engendered the rapid growth of new communities. What remained to be exploited was an 1,800-mile expanse from the Missouri River to the Pacific Ocean across lands largely unsettled by the new Americans. While the notion of a divinely intended expansion of European settlers was arguably as old as their settlement of the continent, John L. O'Sullivan gave popular expression to the idea when he coined the phrase "Manifest Destiny" in an 1845 newspaper column. That phrase was then widely employed to justify settlement of the remaining continental landscape. Before the end of the 1850s the federal government again provided large-scale aid to railroads in the form of land grants. In 1862 and 1866 the Pacific Railroad Act and its subsequent amendment set new records for federal land grants to finance the first intercontinental rail line across the country's vast prairies and over the Rocky Mountains and the Sierra Nevadas. Completed in 1869, the first intercontinental line was followed by ventures to launch three additional lines spanning the continent within another decade. "The new western railroads, built far ahead of population, hastened to promote land sales and, like the Illinois Central and other Midwestern roads before them, founded many towns en route."[26] Those lines, and subsequent development of regional rail systems, greatly expanded the number of new urban settlements and associated prospects for real-estate speculation across the national landscape.

National recognition of the potential evil of rampant real-estate speculation surfaced during the 1850s, and played a role in the passage of the Homestead Act in 1862. For more than three decades Congress had debated the question of how best to dispose of the public domain with the greatest benefit. There were many who believed that people had a God-given right to land, that it was indispensable to the right of life, liberty, and the pursuit of happiness, and that its possession was one of the bases of citizenship. In the words of a British observer writing a century later, "the public demand for free access to the land was overwhelming."[27] The Homestead Act reflected the view that "a more democratic distribution of land would ... do much to stop the scandalous speculation in land, whereby large areas were held out from settlement, only to be disposed of later at an enormous profit."[28] However, the Act did little to quell rampant real-estate speculation associated with the western movement of immigrants. In keeping with prior established procedure, towns and cities spawned by development of a national transportation system continued to exhibit scandalous speculation in land. Towns that came into existence in the 1860s and 1870s continued to be laid out by land speculators seeking to cash in on the future prosperity of a town as a real-estate venture. By the 1880s, a decade of rapid urbanization, frantic speculation in real estate produced an "orgy of town-lot promotion" in Californian cities as part of a "great land boom, the most extravagant in American frontier experience."[29] That boom was fueled by the generation of the post-Civil War years, people who believed the country belonged to them by right of conquest and inheritance, and who believed it was theirs to do with as they pleased. This generation pursued the objective of growth, and more specifically, "growth of an unheard-of-sort, geometric and without discernible limits."[30]

By 1890 the national urban network had been substantially completed, and by 1910 the "new social order of the city was already being imposed on the country, and in large measure defined the characteristic of a national culture."[31] Towns and cities were reasonably compact until 1850, but during the second half of the nineteenth century steam-powered factories run by inexhaustible supplies of coal enabled horizontal expansion of seemingly limitless industrial growth parallel to railroad tracks. In the late nineteenth and early twentieth centuries cities spread out residentially along electric trolley lines and inter-urban railroads, but the most significant development stimulating rapid suburbanization during the opening decades of the new century was the tremendous increase in use of the automobile. The new system of urban transportation permitted American cities to spread out as they expanded their populations, which significantly enlarged their land areas. The Federal Highway Act of 1916 greatly expanded road building, and as a result "a great jump in suburban population occurred in the 1920s [sic] when the automobile became the main device of urban transportation."[32] With the end of an era of being able to profit from building towns in the wilderness along new rail lines, the suburbanization of the 1920s made it possible for promoters to continue their activities by building highly profitable suburbs along trolley lines and highways. By the 1920s the automobile made possible "the complete emergence of modern residential suburbs" that often exhibited "spectacular percentage growth rates."[33] "The expanding economic opportunities created by the automobile stimulated an urban land boom that radically inflated property values in American cities"[34] as they experienced suburban sprawl.

The 1920s represented an era when it was widely assumed "that the proper end of government was to encourage and nurture the business world."[35] It has been described as "the golden age of free enterprise and speculation in land."[36]

Ironically, the decade also represented a period of widespread adoption of land-use controls in the form of zoning and subdivision ordinances, which the business community reluctantly endorsed for "the greater safety and security to investment secured by definite restrictions."[37] The 1920s reflected "the exuberant confidence of that decade in future growth and business prosperity," which translated into "vast overzoning" and similarly absurd overplatting or subdividing of land.[38] As noted, "with few exceptions the allocations of the land resources of cities under these enactments were preposterous, often reflecting population densities and uses beyond any reasonable prospect of growth."[39] The first zoning ordinance for the city of New York "led to a zoning scheme under which a population as great as that of the whole United States in 1900 could be lodged in New York City."[40] "During the 1920's [sic] lots sufficient for all the inhabitants of the five boroughs of New York were platted on Long Island."[41] As part of the Florida land boom in the 1920s, speculative fever produced "enough platted lots to house the population of the whole United States."[42] Similarly absurd zoning and subdivision ordinances proliferated across the country during the decade, typically zoning and platting more land for development by multiple factors beyond any reasonable growth projections. This "era of runaway growth" and "excessive real estate speculation"[43] yielded a legacy of vastly overzoned and overplatted tracts of land. A continuation of that legacy would come to characterize zoning and subdivision activities of American communities during the latter half of the twentieth century and the opening decade of the twenty-first century. This vast overzoning and overplatting of typical American political jurisdictions presents a unique and significant challenge to realizing a state of no growth in local community settings, and will therefore be revisited while addressing strategies to stop growth in American communities later in this work.

The next great suburbanization binge occurred during the prosperity of the post-Second World War era of the 1950s and 1960s. That suburban boom took place within the context of "basic trends [that] were toward 'concentration and decentralization'—concentration from the country[side] into metropolitan areas, and decentralization within these areas."[44] This suburban sprawl continued the prewar trend of more rapid growth in the suburbs than in the central cities, but the pace of suburbanization increased dramatically. A "phenomenal outward surge of development" so dominated "suburban communities and metropolitan areas that were undergoing explosive growth" that the urban historian Lewis Mumford referred to the phenomenon as "the suburban fallout from the metropolitan explosion."[45] Wartime and postwar "baby booms" coupled with a continued population shift from rural to metropolitan areas fueled the suburban boom. The federal government played a key role in making the suburban boom of the 1950s and 1960s possible. "Following the war, FHA- and VA-insured mortgages fueled a period of unparalleled suburban housing development and a rapid growth in homeownership, from less than 45 percent of occupied housing in 1940 to more than 60 percent by 1960."[46] In 1956 a new Federal-Aid Highway Act initiated the largest construction program in American history. An estimated $100 billion over a 13-year period created an unprecedented highway construction program that greatly expanded and accelerated the activities of state highway departments. In addition to authorizing some $27 billion for a 41,000-mile national freeway system, the Act approved additional billions in federal aid for primary, secondary, and lesser roads within the states over a 3-year period. Though it was an undertaking equivalent to building some 60 Panama Canals, the proposed system when finished would constitute but 1 percent of the highway and street mileage of the United States.[47] Nevertheless, "the new routes would further extend the suburban fringe," and "proponents of the highway program spoke of ... the rise in the values per acre of undeveloped land along the expressways."[48] Taken together, the expenditures of federal, state, and local governments on a national transportation system during this era facilitated the suburbanization process and an associated land boom with wild real-estate speculation. Federal and state governments during this period also subsidized sprawling land development through grants for public water and sewer line extensions that helped make suburban land development possible.

From 1955 through 1978 federal aid to states and localities rose nearly eight times in real terms ($12.7 billion to $109.7 billion) and states followed with similar dramatic increases in aid to local jurisdictions.[49] After 1978 federal aid began to contract, and during the Reagan-era cutbacks they declined sharply, with federal grants to localities falling by 49 percent between 1979 and 1989. State aid to localities rose in absolute terms during this period, but failed to keep pace with local own-source revenue growth. By the 1980s localities found themselves increasingly on their own in terms of subsidizing new suburban sprawl. They responded by increasingly pushing the cost of infrastructure improvements for new suburban developments onto developers as a way of maintaining the role of local governments as "growth machines," a term coined by Harvey Molotch in 1976. Molotch described a process whereby land-based elites manipulate governmental authority to profit from increasing intensification of land use under ongoing growth. During the 1950s and 1960s much of the suburban growth associated with local growth machines was accommodated by existing cities, which repeatedly annexed new land to maintain their ongoing growth processes. By the 1970s an increasing number of suburban communities pushed for incorporation in attempts to consolidate control over their own suburban growth machines. During the 1980s and 1990s continued decentralization began to spill over into rural counties outside existing metropolitan areas as part of an "exurbanization" process. As noted previously, America set a new record by adding 33 million to its population during the 1990s, and that demographic growth contributed to an increase in land consumption that jumped from 1.4 million acres annually in the 1980s to 2.2 million acres annually in the 1990s. This decentralization of development into rural counties often produced an interest in these counties in staking out their own positions as county growth machines. This history of local governments operating as growth machines has continued into the twenty-first century.

The legacy of local jurisdictions serving as growth machines portrayed in the prior historical review supports the cited claim at the beginning of the review that the pursuit of growth has been the most consistent theme in local governance throughout American history. American colonial settlements measured their success in terms of the growth of basic economic activities that would profit the British Crown. Promoters of American towns and cities in the post-Revolution era began to pursue profits from escalating land values driven by population increases, and in the process these communities began to take on the features of growth machines serving interests of land-based elites seeking to increase their land values through intensification of local land use. This view of local governments dominated by "growth coalitions" and operating as "growth machines" for more than two centuries in the United States, coupled with the continued role of such local growth coalitions and growth machines in the twenty-first century, warrant a more detailed inquiry into the nature of such coalitions and machines. If American communities are to experiment with local strategies for stopping growth, they must understand the growth coalitions and growth machines that are certain to challenge any attempts to shut down growth in local jurisdictions.

The role of local political jurisdictions as growth machines in America

The term "growth machine" was coined by Harvey Molotch in a 1976 article,[50] while John Mollenkopf introduced the term "pro-growth coalition" in a 1983 book.[51] Both authors describe a situation, characteristic of nearly all localities, where a coalition of supporters back the consensual objective of continued land development. The primary objective of these supporters is ongoing growth in their respective local political jurisdictions. For Molotch, the primary group within this "pro-growth coalition" is the land-based elite who own real estate and seek to enhance the value of those land holdings through continued intensification of land use within their communities. In his 1976 article "The City as a Growth Machine" Molotch argued that "the desire for growth provides the key operative motivation toward consensus for members of politically mobilized local elites" and that this "common interest in growth is the overriding commonality among important people in a given locale."[52] He felt that this interest in growth rose to the level of a "growth imperative" in virtually all local jurisdictions; so much so that he argued that "the very essence of a locality is its operation as a growth machine."[53] Although he acknowledged that success at growth was typically associated with a rising population, and accepted such population growth as an index of a broader meaning for the term "growth," Molotch identified an "entire syndrome of associated events" that actually comprise growth. In this regard he referenced an expansion of basic industries, an expanding labor force, a rising scale of retail commerce, increased levels of financial activity, and most importantly from his perspective, higher population density and increasingly intensive land development. For

Molotch, occurrence of these latter "events" represented "the degree to which the land's profit potential is enhanced" and the owners' "own wealth is increased."[54] Stated directly, he portrayed political jurisdictions as settings where local elites use their combined power to promote growth for personal profits from land transactions.

In his 1976 article Molotch portrayed local communities in terms of land interests, where any given parcel of land represents an interest and communities constitute an aggregate of those land-based interests. Under his portrayal, individual property owners strive, at the expense of others, to enhance the land-use potential of their parcels, while at the same time recognizing the value of their individual parcels derives from the value of the proximate aggregate of parcels. This recognition produces a situation where "otherwise competing land-interest groups collude to achieve a common land-enhancement scheme."[55] Molotch argued that these growth coalitions typically attempt to use government to gain resources that will enhance the growth potential of their respective land holdings. The most active participants in these growth coalitions are the ones who have the most to gain or lose in land-use decisions, including businesspeople who deal in land, investors in local financial institutions, and the lawyers and realtors who serve those with property interests. From his point of view such growth-machine coalitions mobilize, legitimize, and sustain a civic jingoism and growth enthusiasm in American communities that will gain and then maintain general acceptance of growth-oriented programs. They are portrayed as being supported by other institutions, specifically newspapers, universities, and utilities. Molotch held that newspapers were the most important example of a business committed to the aggregate growth of their respective local jurisdictions, writing editorials that support growth-inducing investments and endorsing planning that creates ever more potential future growth. Spokespersons for the public and quasi-public agencies of universities and utilities are portrayed as being similar growth advocates to further their respective expansion plans.

In his 1976 article Molotch depicted typical politicians as businesspeople who became involved in local government for reasons of land business and related processes of resource distribution. He asserted that this land business was the key determinant of any local political dynamic. However, he also pointed out that emerging trends were "tending to enervate the local growth machines."[56] He noted that many people were increasingly associating ongoing growth with such outcomes as increasing pollution, traffic congestion, and overtaxed natural amenities. He additionally described a growing sentiment that growth was in fact only benefiting a small proportion of local residents, and cited studies showing that growth often resulted in higher costs for existing residents, as reflected in higher property taxes and utility bills. Molotch even cited a study for Palo Alto, California, indicating it would be cheaper for the city to acquire its remaining foothill open space at full market value than to assume the maintenance of facility and service costs under development. Finally, he refuted the oft-cited claim that growth "makes jobs" and is necessary to avoid unemployment by referencing studies that show no significant relationship between growth rates and unemployment rates. In the end, he suggested that "under many circumstances growth is a liability financially and in quality of life for the majority of local residents."[57] In concluding his article, Molotch made note of an emerging antigrowth movement that was achieving at least toeholds of political power in some localities. He saw these antigrowth forces as representing a shift in outlook away from a view of local communities as exploitable resources to seeing them as settings for life and work, where the focus would change from increasing the number of residents to improving the life of existing citizens. He foresaw the possible death of the growth machine, associated this with a tendency for an increased progressiveness in local politics, and envisioned a new form of land-use policy that would establish holding capacities for local jurisdictions and then legislate to limit population to those levels. A generation after the publication of his article there is still no evidence of any meaningful shift of local jurisdictions away from their historical role as growth machines. The overwhelming majority of cities, suburbs, and rural counties continue to operate as classical representations of their historical roles as growth machines.

In 1987 Molotch co-authored a book with John Logan that provided additional characterizations of the growth machine operating in local American jurisdictions. In that work they argued that the "growth ethic pervades virtually all aspects of local life, including the political system, the agenda for economic development, and even cultural organizations."[58] They painted a picture of local jurisdictions as places where aggregate growth is portrayed as a public good that is beneficial to all residents in all places at all times, with no acknowledgement of the reality that advantages and disadvantages of growth are unevenly distributed or that long-term consequences of growth can be negative. In these settings they asserted that local elites generate and sustain civic pride directly connected to a growth goal, where these elites regularly tie presumed economic and social benefits of growth in general to growth being experienced in local settings. In an environment where little effort is devoted to questioning a link between growth and public betterment, local elites are said to use the growth consensus they have created to eliminate any alternative vision of the purpose of government. As a result, Logan and Molotch maintained that local growth activism dominates local policy agendas. At the time of the publication of their work they opined that "celebration of local growth continues to be a theme in the culture of localities" and tends "to be equated with progress."[59]

In the context of local jurisdictions that afforded such primacy to growth, Logan and Molotch described the workings of the growth machine, which they defined as an "apparatus of interlocking progrowth associations and governmental units ... devoted to the increase of aggregate rent levels through the intensification of land use."[60] They argued that pursuit of escalating exchange values for land so permeates the life of local jurisdictions that cities in effect become growth-machine enterprises. In their treatment of exchange values associated with place, they identified these values as "rent," using a broad definition for rent that included both outright purchase expenditures, and associated payments that homebuyers and tenants make to landlords, realtors, mortgage lenders, real-estate lawyers, title companies, and so forth. Logan and Molotch used the terms "place entrepreneurs," "growth elites," and "rentier elites" to describe local actors who "strive to increase their rent by revamping the spatial organization of the city."[61] These actors are said to be chasing the pot of gold represented by more intense land use and thus higher rent collections. In attempting to create conditions that will intensify future land use, they are portrayed as being involved in a complex and subtle business of manipulating place for enhanced exchange values. As Logan and Molotch put it, these "entrepreneurs tie their futures to the manipulation of exchange values."[62] This quest for great rewards through land speculation is described as being supported by local media, utilities, and such auxiliary players as universities and professional sports teams, whose institutional goals are often said to depend on support of rentiers and politicians who are at the heart of local growth machines. While Logan and Molotch emphasized the role of cities as growth machines working to increase aggregate rents and trap related wealth, they acknowledged the role of such machines in other local jurisdictional settings extending from neighborhood shopping districts to national regions. They particularly addressed the operation of growth machines in the suburbs. As they put it: "Even in the case of suburban local government ... the development process is dominated by the search for rent and profit with the very creation of suburbs guided by such goals."[63] At other points in their book they commented on the significant role rentiers have played in the incorporation of suburbs under the recognition that suburban growth provided investors with new opportunities to create additional growth machines.

As part of their treatment of local jurisdictions as growth machines, Logan and Molotch pointed out that any given piece of real estate has both an exchange value and a use value. A residential structure may, for example, represent a "home" for residents (use value) while also representing a potential commodity for buying, selling, or renting (exchange value). The simultaneous push for both goals is said to be "inherently contradictory and a continuing source of tension, conflict, and irrational settlements."[64] Logan and Molotch suggested that management of conflict between use values and exchange values plays a key role in determining the shape of local communities. Consensus among local elite groups on the issue of growth is said to separate them from those who see the city principally as a place to live and work, and hence prioritize use values over the exchange values emphasized by elites. Since use values can threaten to undermine growth, Logan and Molotch observed that growth machine activists "tend to oppose any intervention that might regulate development on behalf of use values."[65] Conversely, "[t]hose with only use values at stake in a locality are always structurally available to oppose development."[66] In many instances those who prioritize use values are said to join voluntary organizations when they perceive exchange-value threats to their neighborhoods. As Logan and Molotch put it, "these voluntary organizations typically exist to enhance use values, often in the face of exchange threats."[67] In this same vein, they characterized "[e]nviornmental movements [as] efforts to preserve use values at the expense, if need be, of rents and profits."[68] In describing six categories of use values, including advantages derived from informal support networks and agglomeration benefits in the form of identity and security, they suggested that voluntary neighborhood community organizations might mount a serious future challenge to the exchange values that have traditionally driven local growth machines. In concluding their book they opined, "people *can* capture control over the places in which they live."[69] Ongoing conflict between the push for growth and higher rents versus a drive to enhance use values has the potential of altering the historical outcome in favor of exchange values as mounting evidence of the ecologically unsustainable nature of growth increasingly confronts people.

If local citizens are to mount a serious challenge to the ongoing operation of localities as growth machines, they will need to understand the historical role of local politicians in supporting the rentier elites in their drive for enhanced exchange values. As noted previously, Logan and Molotch asserted that it is the rentiers and politicians who are at the heart of local growth machines. In their view, rentiers have long recognized that "public decisions crucially influence which parcels will have the highest rents as well as the aggregate rent levels" for an entire community.[70] As a result, they argued that the "growth machine will sustain only certain persons as politicians."[71] With virtually all politicians being dependent on private campaign financing, and a disproportionate amount of that financing coming from real-estate entrepreneurs, Logan and Molotch argued that politicians are chosen for their acceptability to the rentier groups. From their perspective "this puts them squarely into the hands of growth machine coalitions."[72] In citing research on urban elites, they referenced findings concluding that "political power ... has typically been concentrated in the hands of those people most willing and able to sustain growth and expansion."[73] Rentier elites have long been aware that "[i]n order to keep the property market rising, government must act on behalf of the market."[74] The most typical forms of governmental action on behalf of rentiers have been rezones allowing more intense land use and public subsidies for infrastructure necessary for ongoing growth. These actions by local politicians will have to be directly acknowledged and addressed if any local initiative to stop growth is to succeed.

In addition to addressing the role of local politicians in supporting growth machines in virtually all localities, Logan and Molotch also addressed the role of urban planners in perpetuating the ongoing operation of growth machines in local jurisdictions. Members of the planning profession working for local governments are key actors in helping local jurisdictions develop land-use plans and associated land-use regulations that delimit prospects for future growth. As Logan and Molotch acknowledged, "any land-use designation distributes use and exchange values."[75] As planners, under the direction of politicians, designate future uses of land in both community comprehensive plans and the land-use regulations that serve to implement those plans, they are said to be engaged in a planning process that is inherently political. Logan and Molotch argued this was most evident in zoning actions spelling out permitted uses and densities for privately held land, actions which they believed to represent a tool for safeguarding and increasing rents. They claimed that "virtually all significant urban areas in the United States are zoned for population and industrial increases double or triple their current levels and that, if history is any guide, those levels will in turn be raised if growth approaches those ceilings."[76] From their perspective amendments to comprehensive land-use plans and regulations like zoning ordinances are regularly provided as new entrepreneurial needs are anticipated. They asserted that in using the vague phrase of "highest and best use" to justify land-use designations planners were aligning their work with the needs of local growth machines. Their less than flattering portrayal of urban planners ended with the observation that "the most durable feature in U.S. urban planning is the manipulation of governmental resources to serve the exchange interests of local elites, sometimes at the expense of one another and often at the expense of local citizens."[77] If it can be argued that urban planners in America function as handmaidens to conservative politicians who serve private land interests,[78] then a more comprehensive understanding of the planning profession and its role in supporting local growth machines would appear to represent a necessary prerequisite to any local no-growth initiatives. The following historical overview of the planning profession in the United States is intended to illustrate the degree to which it has been wedded to a pro-growth bias over time, and thus to shed light on likely obstacles that traditional planning might be expected to put in the way of any prospective strategies to stop growth in American communities.

The planning profession's historical pro-growth stance

A review of the evolution of the planning profession in the United States clearly reveals a strong pro-growth bias from its inception to its current continued endorsement of growth.[79] While origins of community planning can be traced to planning for some of the earliest colonial settings, the planning agency and planning profession are inventions of the twentieth century. The country's first professional planning association, the American City Planning Institute, was formed in 1917. However, it is possible to link roots of the profession to urban conditions existent in the nineteenth century. Conditions of disorder, ugliness, and inefficiency in American cities by the middle of the nineteenth century stimulated the formation of distinct interest groups that represent the forebears of America's planning profession.[80] The first forebears of the contemporary planning profession consisted of members of civic reform movements that emerged shortly before the Civil War. These reformers sought to restore physical, social, and political order in urban settings. Believing that much of the urban disorder was attributable to unfettered growth, they pushed for new legislation to regulate city growth. Those efforts represented some of the first steps in regulating private property as a way of avoiding the ills of overcrowding and congestion produced by growth. While these reformers would leave their mark on the future planning profession in the form of an ongoing tradition of planning for reform, before the end of the nineteenth century their position on growth would be displaced by a very different growth orientation on the part of the other forebears of the profession.

By the 1890s architects had joined social reformers as additional forebears of the planning profession. These architects were key players in the "City Beautiful" movement that occurred around the turn of the century, and their focus was on the ugliness of the city rather than its disorder. They championed the aesthetic end of beauty, which they proposed to address via design schemes for grandiose civic centers, boulevards, monuments, and parks. This emphasis on aesthetics tended to negate the earlier interest of reformers in a broader social agenda, and wittingly or unwittingly aligned these architects with businesspeople willing and interested in supporting the downtown improvement schemes proposed by the architects. Those schemes "were supported by [businesspeople with] downtown business and property interests, who wanted to promote land values in these [downtown] areas and also advocated efficiency in government to keep taxes low."[81] These new economic interests ultimately diverted attention from aesthetics to new planning ends, but before displacing the architects' focus on aesthetics their partnership with business interests lent a decidedly pro-growth bias to the "City Beautiful" movement. Ultimately, the role of architects as forebears of the planning profession gave way to the role of businesspeople as the last of the forebears of the forthcoming planning profession.

By 1910 the influence of architects on the evolving planning movement in the United States had waned, and those seeking to advance economic ends assumed a leading role in shaping the subsequent nature of planning. The second national conference on city planning held in 1910 was dominated by representatives of municipal efficiency groups and their architect–planner collaborators.[82] However, the economic considerations that began to increasingly influence planning during this period were not limited to a concern with efficiency. Businesspeople advancing their interests played a key role in a movement that was advocating municipal reform, and in the process of championing the benefits of efficiency they took advantage of a new acceptance of liberalized governmental intervention to further their interests in protecting and promoting property values. The influence of these interests within the emerging planning profession produced a focus on governmental intervention directed at planning for general urban development. As it turned out, the newly formed planning profession began to define itself at a time when business interests dominated the American landscape. Those interests would also end up dominating the evolving planning movement in the United States. In his historical review of city planning in America, Mel Scott referred to planning activity of the 1920s as "City Planning in the Age of Business," which he described as a time when planners were seeking to gain professional legitimacy and security.[83] The perceived path to realizing that legitimacy and security was to serve the prevailing interests of the time. In an era of business optimism, that meant subduing their interests in social reform and aesthetics and turning their attention to matters of efficiency and development. In short, members of the new profession recognized the professional gains that could be attained by serving the prevailing growth philosophy of the period. Planners adopted pro-growth, business-oriented postures to establish the legitimacy of their profession, and in the process ended up serving a conservative ideology interested in economic development.[84]

The affiliation between planners and businesspeople during the 1920s was clearly exhibited by the enthusiasm for zoning that swept the country over the course of that decade. Those with property interests supported zoning as a way of protecting and promoting property values, and as a tool for furthering economic development. Planners saw zoning as a vehicle for advancing their profession by serving the dominant economic interests of the day. Scott acknowledged the role this early preoccupation with zoning played in associating urban planners with business interests when he noted that "[p]opular enthusiasm for zoning threatened to overshadow comprehensive planning and to ally the new profession with dominant business interests."[85] Members of the new planning profession played an active role in creating and implementing what Scott referred to as "unrealistic" and "preposterous" zoning ordinances during the 1920s and 1930s. This willingness to support pro-growth, business-oriented interests via liberal zoning enactments intended to facilitate new development leaves little doubt as to the planning profession's growth orientation during its formative decades. While this early preoccupation with zoning detracted from the attention afforded community plans during this era, planners nevertheless also pursued their interest in community plans intended to guide zoning and other land-use regulations. These plans also tended to reflect the business optimism of the era, with plans typically designed to permit optimistic levels of future growth. As Scott observed in his historical review of planning in America, the rapidity of growth during the 1920s required "practical" plans that allowed for "reasonable progress" if planners were to realize their goal of achieving professional security. His review revealed that planners were just as willing to use community land-use plans as zoning ordinances to facilitate growth during the first decades after the planning profession's emergence. This use of the principal tools of their trade to further development clearly illustrated the profession's early stance on growth. The following review of the profession's posture on growth in subsequent decades is intended to reveal the strong pro-growth bias of planners over the entire history of the planning profession in the United States.

Members of the planning profession have engaged in an ongoing dialogue over what the profession's concerns actually are, or ought to be, since the profession's inception. The resulting varied views of planning have found expression in terms of different types of planning.[86] Two dominant types of planning have characterized the profession over the course of its history: Planning as a plan-making endeavor and planning as a rational decision-making process. The comprehensive plan-making approach has represented the principal type of planning practiced by members of the profession over time. However, by the 1950s the rational decision-making process began to compete with plan making as an alternative type of planning, and subsequently came to represent a second dominant type of planning in America. Over time, members of the profession were also asked to consider the merit of a number of other types of planning, including middle-range, social, advocacy, allocative, and radical planning. The nature of these alternative types of planning and their individual growth orientations are the central points of interest in the context of a review intended to shed light on how future no-growth initiatives might be expected to encounter challenges from members of the planning profession.

In terms of different types of planning, none have played as dominant a role in defining the planning profession over time as comprehensive plan making. Creating and revising what have alternatively been called general, master, or comprehensive land-use plans, which depict a community's arrangement of land uses some 20 or 30 years in the future, has represented the principal type of planning from the earliest days of the profession to the present. Reformers, architects, and businesspeople who represented forebears of the profession saw their respective ends of order, beauty, and efficiency being realized largely through alterations in the uses of land, which produced an interest in the physical planning addressed in local comprehensive plans. This interest in physical land-use planning was codified in the profession's constitution in 1938 with a statement prescribing the professional sphere of activity specifically as "the planning of the unified development of urban communities and their environs ... as expressed through determination of the comprehensive arrangement of land uses and land occupancy and the regulation thereof." While the profession agreed on the primacy of this type of planning throughout this period, an ongoing debate on the desirable nature of such plans regularly occupied the profession until mid-century.[87] There were professionals interested in ideal or utopian ends who believed that comprehensive plans should portray "desirable unitary end states" for communities in the form of "static long-range master plans." A far larger number believed that plans ought to be "practical" and allow for "reasonable progress" via endless growth accommodation. From the 1920s to the 1950s changes in these plans reflected critiques that faulted their emphasis on physical planning, portrayal of a static end-state, long-range, goal-attainment orientation, and their claimed representation of an apolitically derived route for furthering the public welfare. In order to maintain loyalty to this type of planning under such criticisms, the profession responded by redefining the nature of comprehensive plans. That redefinition centered on a shift away from a product-oriented approach intended to produce static, utopian, end-state plans to a focus on plan making as a continuing process of revising the comprehensive plan in response to changing circumstances. The process-oriented view of plan making continued to evolve in the decades following the 1920s, and by the 1950s the profession had largely succeeded in reformulating comprehensive plan making into a sort of "continuing process." The central feature of that reformulation exercise was the idea that it was both acceptable and necessary to continually amend the comprehensive plan. Being receptive to these continuous amendments obviously conveys a different prospect for further growth than that conveyed by a view of plans as end-state documents intended to prevent disturbing overgrowth. The process view of plan making won out within the profession, and with it came a receptiveness to change and a flexibility to help communities adapt to ongoing growth within the context of a business-dominated economy that characterized the 1950s.

Post-1950s planning literature continued to reflect a view of the superiority of the process-oriented approach to plan making. Observers suggested this was the direction that the profession was moving toward, both in terms of theory and practice. By the 1970s a planning academic claimed that "American planning theory is generally moving away from approaches based on a fixed 'end-state' plan to a more flexible, dynamic concept of land-use 'guidance' systems."[88] This plan-making process characterized by continuous amendments to comprehensive plans intended to "guide" development was firmly anchored in projections of existing circumstances, which represented facilitating the continuation of the assumed progress traditionally associated with ongoing growth. This view of plan making extended into the 1990s, as revealed by the 1995 edition of the profession's principle methods text for the creation of comprehensive plans, which identified the management of land-use change as the fundamental rationale for the practice of land-use planning. That text also referred to the planner as "a manager of urban change and growth."[89] In the end, this process-oriented approach represents a plan-making methodology based on determining a future demand for land and associated public facilities that comprehensive plans are then designed to accept.

Even a cursory reading of the profession's principle methods text on preparing comprehensive plans reveals how that text has maintained an accommodative orientation toward ongoing growth as it has gone through periodic updates. The original 1957 version of the text laid out a plan-making methodology that would subsequently come to be referred to as a "demand-based," "demand-activated," or "accommodative" method.[90] This method focused on determining demand for land and facilities by studies of the urban economy, employment, and population, and then accommodating that demand. The plan-making method may be portrayed in terms of three procedural steps: (1) Determination of demand for land and facilities by the study of population and business trends, (2) calculation of land and facilities required to meet that demand, and (3) accommodation of the demand via plans that provide for future growth, rezonings that permit more intense uses of land, and capital improvement programming expenditures that build public facilities required to service new development. A 1979 update of the same methods text reflected a new sensitivity to environmental considerations by including a section on environmental suitability analysis intended to provide information on the relative suitability of different sites for various types of development, but it maintained an ongoing allegiance to a demand-based, accommodative method of plan making. Similarly, the 1995 update expanded the realm of environmental considerations, including treatments of such concepts as carrying capacity and sustainable development, but the book maintained a demand-based approach to the creation of comprehensive plans. In doing so, it continued to reinforce the idea that ongoing growth is desirable if its ill effects are mitigated, and suggested that a balance can be achieved between continued growth and environmental protection. As stated by the authors of that 1995 text update: "The goal is economic growth that is socially and environmentally sustainable, balancing economy and ecology."[91] Rather than suggesting that plan making ought to shift to planning directed at stopping growth in response to growing evidence of ecological limits to growth, the text held out the prospect of realizing the oxymoronic idea of sustainable growth.

The history of plan-making activity by planning professionals in America has maintained a consistent pro-growth bias over time. The profession has shown no willingness to consider an alternative "supply-based," "supply-activated," or "allocative/carrying capacity" method for the creation and subsequent revision of local comprehensive plans. Such an alternative approach would be characterized by the following procedural steps: (1) Determination of the supply of available natural and institutional resources, (2) establishment of "acceptable" levels of demand that might be put on available resources, and (3) allocation of permissible levels of use to the sources of demand. This approach would acknowledge limits to growth in local settings and put the exercise of plan making on a very different path than its historical fealty to demand-based plans directed at endless growth accommodation. Since demand-based, accommodative plan-making activity has represented the principal type of planning practiced in America over time, one might con-clude the planning profession has exhibited a history of a pro-growth bias. However, the profession has engaged in other types of planning, so to draw conclusions about the profession's stance on growth requires an understanding of the growth orientation of these alternative types of planning.

By the 1950s a group of urban theorists suggested an alternative view of planning as a rational decision-making process.[92] This view of planning as something other than the creation and revision of land-use plans posited that planning was in fact independent of the object to which it was applied, and rather than focusing solely on land-use planning it ought to focus on helping local communities realize the benefits of engaging in a rational decision-making process. This type of planning focuses on the deliberate choice of ends and an analytic determination of the most effective means to achieve those ends, and in the process shifts the practice of planning to what it does and how it does it instead of simply concentrating on land use. It sees planning as a methodology consisting of five interrelated steps that have come to be labeled the rational decision-making process: Identifying problems or goals; designing alternative solutions or courses of action; comparing and evaluating alternatives and choosing or helping decision makers choose the "best" alternative; developing implementation measures; and adjusting steps one through four based on feedback and review. This alternative type of planning appealed to many planners because it opened the door to forms of planning other than land use. It also attracted practitioners by suggesting that planners reject the traditional view of planning as a technical, professional activity removed from politics in favor of a new role advising elected officials, which would put planners directly into the decision-making process shaping the future of communities. The appeal of these rationales would eventually elevate rational decision making to the status of a second dominant type of planning in the United States, putting it in the position of competing with plan making as the other primary expression of planning in America. Putting planners directly into the decision-making process as advisors to politicians, this type of planning suggested clear implications for its likely growth orientation.

The growth orientation of the rational decision-making process as a type of planning is revealed by its association with a pragmatic planning approach. To be pragmatic or practical in everyday affairs under this type of planning meant that planners had to accept the argument that planning was a process within a political decision-making environment. Rather than assuming that planners ought to select the ends toward which society should be steered based on planning ideology or a prior determination of the public interest, as in the traditional plan-making approach, the rational decision-making process model avowed that political or market processes ought to determine those ends. Having ends determined by political and market processes, when these processes have traditionally been wedded to the idea that growth represents societal progress, clearly reveals the pro-growth orientation of this type of planning. Planners attracted to this formulation of planning quickly recognized that their ability to affect desired change in community settings depended on developing practical plans, and that in a societal context that traditionally valued growth this meant they had to accept pro-growth planning postures. So rather than providing an alternative to the growth accommodation associated with the plan-making approach to planning, the rational decision-making process approach linked professional planning activity even more directly to the practice of growth accommodation.

Accepting the view of planning as a rational decision-making process opened the door to considering other types of planning activity as legitimate planning endeavors.[93] Most of these alternative subtypes of planning suggested refinements or extensions of the two dominant types of planning. In the mid-1950s, the first of these alternatives surfaced in the form of a call for middle-range planning functions to bridge the gap between traditional short- and long-range functions carried out by planning offices. It was suggested that these functions would improve decision making in the realm between decisions on projects and decisions on long-range plans, thereby improving prospects for rational decisions. A call for a "market analysis function" clearly revealed the growth orientation of this subtype of planning by noting this was intended "to aid the operations of the market," and by suggesting that planning agencies should act "to facilitate market operations" through market analyses that "lubricate the process of urban development."[94] By the 1960s these ideas had increasingly found their way into planning agencies, which often ceased to be thought of as merely planning organizations and typically began to be titled departments of planning *and* development. To the extent that middle-range planning as a new subtype of planning influenced the profession, it clearly maintained its pro-growth bias.

In the 1960s another subtype of planning emerged in the form of increased professional acceptance of the idea of social planning. This form of planning extended professional activity beyond physical land-use planning to such diverse areas as employment opportunities, social services, and elimination of racial discrimination. Like the nineteenth century social reformers who preceded them, these social planners sought to address the needs of disadvantaged groups in society. Their focus on these groups stimulated a natural interest and endorsement of continued economic growth, because social justice advocates have demonstrated a long-standing commitment to the idea that growth affords a means to remedy a host of social ills. In a similar vein, the 1960s also introduced the concept of advocacy planning as another subtype of planning activity. The principal focus of this form of planning was on gaining representation for formerly unrepresented groups in the planning process, such as the poor, the black, and the underprivileged. With an emphasis on improving the status of the disadvantaged, and a belief in growth as a means of accomplishing that improvement, advocacy planners typically offered a spirited defense of continued physical mobility and economic growth. In this regard they tended to strongly oppose any growth controls that would limit access to the suburbs that represented centers of economic expansion. As with social planning, advocacy planning provided further support for a pro-growth orientation amongst professional planners. Interest in yet another subtype of planning emerged in the 1960s in the form of allocative planning. This view of planning focused on distributing scarce governmental resources among a large number of different public needs. The growth orientation of allocative planning is suggested by its close ties to economic reasoning and the traditional growth fixation of such reasoning. With a strong belief in economic growth being absolutely necessary to meet the needs of a growing population, and a related belief that difficult allocation decisions would never occur within a nongrowing economy, a pro-growth bias for this subtype of planning was strongly demonstrated in writings on allocative planning.

Of all the subtypes of planning to emerge before the planning profession's active involvement in the growth-management movement by the 1970s, only formulations of so-called radical planning during the early 1970s offered planners an option to continued support of growth. Rather than representing

mere refinements or extensions of the two dominant types of planning represented by plan making or a rational decision-making process, these radical
planning formulations called for system transformation and societal change.
Proponents of radical planning accused the profession of perpetuating elitist,
centralized, and change-resistant tendencies. In its place they called for a
decentralized communal society that would facilitate human development in
the context of an ecological ethic by evolutionary social experimentation.
Advocates for radical planning especially condemned technological thinking
and the preoccupation with material affluence, arguing that unending economic
growth actually served to impede further development of the individual.
These viewpoints failed to gain traction within the planning profession,
which doggedly maintained its historical pro-growth stance. As the growth-
management era gained momentum during the early 1970s, the planning
profession seemed unable to consider an alternative perspective on growth. So
as the profession embarked on decades of participation in an emerging
growth-management movement, it continued to exhibit a decidedly pro-growth
posture.

The emergence of a growth-management movement in the United States
during the late 1960s and early 1970s appeared to challenge the traditional
pro-growth paradigm that has dominated America throughout its history.
A growing number of voices in that period began to question the merit of
continued growth, suggesting it needed at a minimum to be managed, if not
controlled. During the heated debate of the 1970s on the topic of possible
limits to growth, some even called for an end to growth. But the growth-
management movement endorsed the management option as the appropriate
response to growth-induced problems, and the planning profession would
assume a key role in that management effort in a way that allowed it to
remain loyal to its historical pro-growth stance. For those seeking to pursue
no-growth initiatives within local political jurisdictions, it is imperative to
understand the pro-growth orientation of the growth-management movement
in the United States and the potential obstacles that existing growth-
management programs present to any effort to stop growth in America's
communities.

The pro-growth orientation of the growth-management movement

The growth-management movement that emerged in the United States during
the late 1960s and early 1970s reflected an ideological shift in Americans'
attitudes toward growth. That shift challenged the traditional view of growth
that only cited its assumed benefits in terms of stronger local economies,
higher personal incomes, lower taxes, greater upward economic mobility for the
poor, and a wider range of lifestyle choices for urban consumers. A growing
number of critics were citing its potential ills in terms of overcrowded
schools, tax increases, rising crime rates, physical blight, traffic congestion,

loss of open space, the destruction of a "way of life," and increasing air and water pollution. The ideological shift also reflected new perspectives toward land development, increasingly associating it with the costly and destructive development pattern of urban sprawl, the loss of prime agricultural lands, an inefficient provision of public facilities and services, escalating housing prices, and pervasive environmental degradation beyond the initial focus on air and water pollution. These feelings increasingly found expression in what would come to be referred to as the growth-management movement. Most participants in that movement had come to think of growth as something to be managed, regulated, or controlled, rather than simply promoted as in the past. By the 1970s the "ethic of growth" was purportedly said to be giving way to an "ethos of managed growth."[95]

Cited growth-management objectives represented attempts to address the problems of growth in general and land development in particular. Growth-management advocates suggested avenues for avoiding loss of open space, prime agricultural tracts, and valuable resource lands. They offered containment strategies for reigning in costly and destructive sprawl. They provided techniques for realizing the efficient provision of public facilities and services. They proposed approaches for ensuring housing choices that would further affordability. They advanced measures for protecting environmentally sensitive lands, and held out the promise that properly managed growth would make it possible to avoid further environmental deterioration. Advocates also held out the hope that properly managed growth would not have to represent a destruction of community character and current ways of life. With such a wide range of possible benefits associated with the management of growth, both the term and the concept of growth management came to be popularized during the 1970s. By the mid-1970s it was possible to argue that "we are entering a new phase of urban development in this country—a phase dominated by the concept of growth management."[96]

It is possible to attribute the origins of the growth-management movement in the United States to the development and legalization of land-use regulations in America during the opening decades of the twentieth century.[97] The management of growth through traditional regulatory mechanisms like zoning and subdivision ordinances clearly grounded early management efforts in the exercise of the police power by local communities. As the inherent power of government to regulate private property based on health, safety, and general welfare rationales, the police power provides legal justification for public imposition of land-use regulations. Early zoning ordinances provided mechanisms for controlling the use of land, its density or intensity, and its character by way of bulk regulations governing setbacks and height.

Early subdivision ordinances imposed requirements for public infrastructure as preconditions for subdividing and developing private properties. These police-power mechanisms therefore permitted communities to manage growth for decades before the emergence of the growth-management movement. However, prior to the 1960s there was limited willingness to utilize zoning and subdivision ordinances to effectively manage growth. Public acceptance of these regulations tended to be based on their respective roles in protecting private property interests and assuring public improvements that would enhance development options. For the most part, these traditional land-use regulations were employed to *facilitate* development rather than to *manage* the growth that development represented. The traditional use of police-power regulations to manage growth reflected a positive view of growth, which in turn produced regulations that were inclined to *promote* and *facilitate* growth during the course of managing it. With the emergence of the growth-management movement the new sentiment toward growth tended to produce regulations deliberately intended to *regulate* and *control* growth during the course of the management process. In this respect, the management movement represented a significant change in how growth was to be considered and treated in the American context.

The prior consideration of the role of land-use regulations in growth management suggests the beginnings of the management movement may be traced to efforts of local governments to modify and expand land-use regulations so as to realize new abilities to manage growth. In fact, much of the controversy associated with the growth-management movement since its inception may be attributed to the acknowledgement that "[t]he essence of the term managed growth is regulatory."[98] Local regulation of land in an expanding number of ways has come to represent the primary expression of growth-management activity in the United States. New regulatory initiatives during the opening decades of the management movement included linking development permission to the availability of infrastructure improvements and requiring property owners to share the cost of providing the needed improvements. These regulations allowed communities to influence the *quality* of new development through requirements for public facilities and services as a necessary precondition for approval. Other initiatives imposed new land-use regulations designed to contain growth within designated growth boundaries. These regulations permitted control over the *location* of new development. In other instances communities instituted controls over the timing of new development by limiting the number of allowed permits in designated time periods. These initiatives afforded control over the *rate* of new development, which had previously been determined by individual property owners. Yet other initiatives restricted development options at specific sites based on desires to protect environmentally sensitive areas or conserve resource lands. These initiatives represented new attempts to regulate the *amount* of development in at least some locations within local communities. This expanded realm of land-use regulation implemented under the heading of growth management permitted local communities to manage all the principal attributes of growth: *quality*, *location*, *rate*, and *amount*.

The regulatory focus of local growth-management initiatives and the associated cost implications for property owners and developers produced a general condemnation of the new regulatory mechanisms that typified growth-management efforts. Many viewed the new regulations as disguised efforts to stop growth, and this produced a corresponding characterization of all growth-management programs as no-growth initiatives. Defenders of the growth imperative denounced growth-management efforts on multiple grounds,[99] also associating management programs with local efforts to limit or stop growth. Some focused on an asserted "inevitability" of further growth, and stressed the "irresponsible" nature of local efforts that divert growth to communities already accommodating their "fair share" of regional increases. Others stressed the aspect of socially unacceptable motives and undesirable consequences they associated with local management programs. These critics faulted growth management on the grounds of its assumed "tendencies toward exclusion and inequality."[100] During the early years of the movement a land-use attorney described management efforts in terms of "the wolf of exclusionary zoning under the environmental sheepskin worn by the stop-growth movement."[101] From this perspective local growth-management initiatives were viewed as little more than disguised efforts to keep out the "wrong kind" of people represented by certain income or minority groups. Yet others damned the initiatives as a form of "homeowner cartel" intended to increase property values of existing owners, or suggested they represented "hustles" designed to defend privilege. Critics additionally argued that local growth controls eliminated low-priced housing, increased land values, reduced incomes, and contributed to metropolitan sprawl. Even a quick survey of such writings can lead to the conclusion that "[m]any authors characterize municipal growth controls as the evil stepchild of land use planning."[102] The point of interest here is whether such critics were justified in characterizing all management initiatives as efforts to limit or stop growth.

In actual fact, growth-management initiatives over time have demonstrated variable postures toward growth. Those different postures and their respective growth orientations are evident in the various definitions that have been offered for growth management.[103] The traditional pro-growth perspective on growth is still alive and well for many in the growth-management movement, who see management as appropriately intended to *promote* or *stimulate* growth, or at least to *plan* for the growth that will "inevitably" occur. Others, who have come closer to accepting the reality of problems associated with ongoing growth, concede a need to *influence*, *guide*, *channel*, or *redistribute* growth in order to *minimize impacts*. Yet others, who have come to view growth even more critically, make the case for having to *regulate*, *control*, or *limit* growth. What one does not find among the various definitions of growth management is a definition of management activity directed at a deliberate attempt to *stop* growth. This omission reflects the fact that the management movement has simply refused to entertain the possibility of a no-growth focus for growth-management efforts. Instead, the emphasis has been on making ongoing growth possible. Spokespersons for the management movement have endorsed the concept of "balanced growth," which holds that it is possible to achieve a "balance" between the "equally legitimate needs of economic development and environmental protection."[104] Proponents of this position suggest that growth and environmental protection represent equally legitimate objectives, and that a balance can be achieved between these ends without compromising either. With an obvious ongoing allegiance to the growth imperative, spokespersons for the management movement have dismissed a no-growth option for growth-management programs, characterizing any attempts to stop growth as being *inefficient, unjust,* and *irresponsible.* The unquestionable pro-growth orientation of the movement is revealed by writings that clearly spell out its stance on growth.[105] Even management programs that have only sought to limit future growth, as an alternative to actually stopping it in the short term, have been labeled as the *worst, unenlightened, unrealistic, immature,* and *improperly defined* programs. In contrast, initiatives designed to accommodate ongoing growth have been characterized as the *best, enlightened, realistic, mature,* and *properly defined* programs. In terms of thousands of growth-management initiatives undertaken by local governments through the 1990s, the overwhelming majority represented continued growth accommodation programs that reflected the pro-growth bias evident in the characterizations of "proper" management efforts.

The historical pro-growth bias of local growth-management initiatives in America may be illustrated by way of observations on the distinction between *growth-management* measures and *growth-control* measures that appear in growth-management writings.[106] Under this distinction "management" measures are those that seek to *guide* or *redistribute* growth, while "control" measures extend to efforts to *slow* or *limit* growth. In terms of attempts to influence the principal attributes of growth, "management" measures focus on influencing the *quality* or *location* of growth, while "control" measures focus on affecting the *rate* or *quantity* of growth. Most local growth-management initiatives have been directed at efforts to affect the *quality* or *location* of growth, rather than its *rate* or *amount.* Research findings published in 1991 on the distinction between growth-management and growth-control measures in California reported that of 586 measures utilized by local jurisdictions only 17 percent fell into the growth-control category.[107] Fully 83 percent merely sought to influence the quality or location of development, rather than its rate or quantity. When local programs did address the rate of growth, those measures only served to slow growth by imposing annual limits on permits that would continue to allow new annual permit allotments each subsequent year. Similarly, management programs that addressed the amount of growth only restricted the amount in certain locations, as in attempts to limit growth in environmentally sensitive areas or outside designated urban growth boundaries, while keeping overall growth options open. These research findings typified local initiatives throughout the United States during this period, with the significant majority of local programs being directed at a "managing to grow" option, rather than real efforts to control or limit future growth.

Efforts to move beyond the management of ongoing growth to growth-control measures intended to slow or limit future growth during the early years of growth management in the United States were both controversial and limited in number.[108] Two highly publicized cases established the legality of rate controls during the late 1960s and early 1970s. In 1969, Ramapo, New York, amended its zoning ordinance to include a development-timing component designed to control the rate of growth within the community. That requirement conditioned new development upon availability of facilities and services, and postponed development in some outlying areas for up to 18 years when those areas were scheduled to receive facilities and services. In 1972, Petaluma, California, followed suit with a rate-control measure that limited the number of residential building permits to 500 per year, at a time when the development community had been building some 2,500 units annually. Although these efforts only served to slow growth, and not to actually stop it, even this form of interference with the growth imperative produced legal challenges that were in both cases appealed to the U.S. Supreme Court. Both of these programs survived their respective legal challenges, so by the mid-1970s rate controls that had the effect of slowing growth had been established as a permissible form of growth control. However, the controversy of rate controls serving as an impediment to market-driven growth rates restricted experimentation with this form of growth control to a small minority of overall growth-management programs throughout the United States. Most programs voluntarily limited themselves to attempts to influence the quality or location of new development.

Early efforts to actually limit future growth in local political jurisdictions by setting an ultimate cap on allowable growth were even more restricted in number, and they did not enjoy the success of growth-control measures merely imposing rate controls. In 1971 citizens of Boulder, Colorado, collected sufficient signatures under the state's initiative process to have a measure put on the ballot that, if passed by voters, would have imposed a "population cap" for the city of around 100,000, or some 30,000 above the approximately 70,000 that were already in the city. The city's elected officials responded by putting an alternative advisory measure on the same ballot with wording encouraging the city council to keep the city's growth rate "substantially below the rates experienced during the 1960s." With the city council assuming a role as key actors in the city's growth-machine coalition, they used the advantage of their political pulpits to convince citizens of the wisdom of voting for rate control measures over a cap to limit future growth. The voters responded by rejecting the cap measure and passing the advisory measure recommending adoption of a rate control ordinance. The nation's first attempt by a local jurisdiction to cap future growth failed. In 1972, the city of Boca Raton, Florida, also used the ballot in an attempt to limit the amount of future growth that would be permitted in the community. Voters passed a charter referendum placing a cap on total housing units that would have capped the city's population at approximately 105,000 residents, versus some 40,000 in the city at the time of the vote. In this instance the attempt to place an absolute limit on the amount of future growth was invalidated by a court ruling. Other similar efforts would fail, as in the case of Fort Collins, Colorado, where a growth-limitation initiative similar to Boulder's was soundly defeated by voters in the late 1970s after the city's growth-machine coalition finished propagandizing the potential dangers of any growth-limitation measure. It is a fact that few local governments have attempted to set absolute limits to future growth within their jurisdictions, and that far fewer have actually succeeded. One is hard pressed to identify any local jurisdictions that have implemented absolute caps on future growth. By the 1980s loss of federal aid to local governments under the "new federalism" diverted attention from such possible no-growth initiatives as communities scrambled to pursue economic growth to make up for the withdrawal of federal funds. Under these new fiscal realities attention shifted from the growth/no-growth debate to a sprawl versus compact development debate during the 1980s and 1990s. However, the 1970s did yield at least one classic example of a local jurisdiction that succeeded in setting a cap on the number of future dwelling units. Residents of Sanibel Island, Florida, rebelled against county officials in that instance, who had approved a plan and associated land-use regulations that would have allowed some 35,000 dwelling units on the island. The residents passed a ballot measure to incorporate as a city and thereby gain control over future development, and subsequently adopted a new land-use plan and regulations limiting future development to 6,000 dwelling units. The progressive nature of that planning effort included basing the growth cap in part on development tolerances of different ecozones on the island. Legal challenges to the innovative effort were largely averted by sound planning rationales supported by professional studies that were used to justify the dramatic curtailment of development options. Another successful attempt to cap future growth occurred in Florida during the same era. In 1983 the same district court of appeal that denied a cap in the Boca Raton case upheld a cap adopted by the city of Hollywood, Florida, noting the cap on growth was justifiably based on plans, studies, reports, and public meetings, and adequately linked to substantial advancement of the community's health, safety, and welfare. These examples illustrate that while there are significant challenges associated with placing limits on future growth, those challenges need not be considered insurmountable. While the overwhelming majority of local growth-management initiatives have demonstrated a growth-accommodation orientation, there are clearly defensible options for devising future growth-management programs specifically intended to stop growth at some specified level if those programs are wisely crafted to withstand political and legal challenges.

Further insight into the typical pro-growth bias of growth-management programs in America may be gained by understanding the nature of statewide growth-management laws passed to date.[109] Before the advent of the growth-management era, planning and regulation of land had been considered primarily a concern of local governments. States had, in effect, relinquished the regulatory means to control land use and thereby manage growth to local jurisdictions. Statewide growth-management laws served to reclaim a certain degree of state control over the use of land within states that passed such laws. Motivations for passage of these laws varied. In some instances the case was made that local controls were inadequate to deal with extralocal issues. In other instances the reason for intervening centered on the need for coordinating areawide funding and development of essential facilities and services. Loss of state resource lands, environmental damage, and inefficient infrastructure investments resulting from ongoing sprawl provided further motivation. With the new federalism reducing local revenues during the 1980s other states saw a need to add economic development requirements to local management programs as a way of facilitating local economic activity that would further state economic solvency. An interest in protecting private property rights prompted some states to impose consistency requirements on local governments, which meant that land-use regulations had to be consistent with previously adopted comprehensive plans as a perceived way of avoiding regulations that were arbitrary or capricious. A concern with social problems like affordable housing provided yet further motivation for increased state involvement in local growth-management efforts. These and other motivations prompted the passage of statewide growth-management laws in 11 states between 1961 and 1998.

The state of Hawaii (1961) passed the first of the statewide growth-management laws during the 1960s. Subsequent statewide management laws were passed during the 1970s in Vermont (1970), Florida (1972), and Oregon (1973). Following an absence of enactments over an entire decade, Florida supplemented its law in 1984 and 1985, and New Jersey (1986), Maine (1988), Rhode Island (1988), Vermont with supplemental legislation in 1988, and Georgia (1989), all passed statewide laws during the 1980s. The 1990s yielded statewide laws in Washington (1990 and 1991), Maryland (1992), and Tennessee (1998). The focus of these statewide laws changed over time. Laws passed through the 1970s reflected a strong, natural-systems orientation in response to the rising tide of public concern for the environment during that period. By the 1980s, statewide laws did not abandon environmental components, but they did move toward becoming more balanced in attempting to integrate economic development mandates with environmental protection requirements. When "balanced growth" became the catchphrase of the growth-management movement, statewide enactments of the 1990s reflected an even stronger commitment to the idea that growth-management initiatives could legitimately pursue both growth and environmental protection without compromising either. While statewide management laws passed in the noted 11 states through 1998 reflected different areas of emphasis, they uniformly demonstrated support for the growth imperative. Laws in all 11 states exhibited elements intended to further ongoing growth accommodation. All the laws contained provisions intended to promote ongoing growth, and in eight of the 11 states the laws actually mandated ongoing growth accommodation by local governments.[110] As a researcher noted during the 1990s, statewide growth-management laws passed up to that point merely suggested "different paths to accommodating growth."[111]

By the late 1990s, the growth-management movement that had emerged in the United States during the latter 1960s and early 1970s had evolved into a smart-growth movement. As the latest incarnation of growth management, smart-growth initiatives both encompassed and extended growth-management efforts of previous decades. This current manifestation of growth management has been portrayed via lists of principles describing the nature of smart growth envisioned by proponents of such an alternative management paradigm. The varied smart-growth principles in those lists may all be encompassed under a short list of five major tenets of smart growth: growth containment in compact settlements; protection of the environment, resource lands, and open space; multi-modal transportation systems; mixed-use development; and collaborative planning and decision making.[112] In terms of significant extensions to earlier growth-management efforts, smart-growth advocates expanded the prior focus on containing sprawl in compact settlements to a corresponding call for higher densities. With respect to protection of the environment, resource lands, and open space, smart-growth advocates introduced a need to address these considerations within urban growth areas as well as on outlying lands. The multi-modal transportation systems tenet as envisioned by smart-growth proponents extended the former emphasis on automobiles and public transit to encompass connections between and among different transportation modes embodied in the term intermodalism, as well as a related focus on non-motorized forms of transportation represented by walking and bicycling. With respect to the tenet of collaborative planning and decision making, smart-growth proponents have made the case for nongovernmental stake-holders becoming players as a way of advancing the disparate ends of smart growth, and for an implementation focus that favors incentives over controls. While the noted changes represent departures from earlier growth-management endeavors, urban design innovations embodied in the mixed-use development tenet represent the most significant shift in growth-management thinking introduced by smart-growth advocates. Concerns about the design of neigh-borhoods and cities gave rise to a "new-urbanism" movement during the 1990s, and many of the design elements advanced by members of this group ended up being embodied in smart-growth principles formulated during that decade. Both movements bought into the idea that specific physical designs were capable of yielding a high quality of community life. Those design features included diverse land uses, walkable districts, human-scale buildings, modi-fied street grid patterns, narrow streets lined with trees and sidewalks, shorter setbacks of residences from streets, front porches, alley-loaded garages, useable open spaces, among a broad range of specific design considerations. Smart-growth advocates argued that if smart growth was to succeed as a viable alternative to sprawl, it would require more than merely realizing compact development at higher densities. Compared to earlier growth-management concerns that paid little or no attention to matters of design, the smart-growth tenet of mixed-use development introduced a significant design component into current growth-management considerations.

As the prior portrayal of smart-growth thinking reveals, growth management in the United States was significantly altered by its evolution into a smart-growth movement during the 1990s. The smart-growth movement expanded the realm of growth-management concerns by advocating higher densities, new environmental sensitivities, a transportation reorientation away from the automobile, an implementation focus that calls for participation of new stakeholders and favors incentives over regulations, and for the introduction of new-urbanism design considerations into growth management. Aspects of these new concerns began to find their way into the first statewide smart-growth laws enacted during the latter 1990s and subsequent laws adopted after 2000.[113] In 1997 Maryland passed the first statewide management law carrying a smart-growth heading. Wisconsin followed with a smart-growth bill in 1999. Pennsylvania passed its smart-growth bills in 1999 and 2000. Delaware passed legislation in 2001 and 2003 advancing a smart-growth agenda in that state. What did not change under the new smart-growth orientation and legislation was the management movement's historical pro-growth bias. The smart-growth movement has maintained the prior growth-accommodation orientation of the management movement, and arguably even strengthened its pro-growth bias. In 2000 researchers investigating the nature of smart-growth initiatives in America concluded smart growth "is much more pro-growth and much less pro-conservation than earlier growth-management efforts."[114]

Advocates of a no-growth agenda in the context of local political jurisdictions need to recognize the pro-growth bias of growth management as it has been practiced in the United States. With widespread acceptance of a pro-growth position within the management movement, it has come to represent "a wholehearted endorsement of ongoing growth accommodation."[115] For those seeking to advance a no-growth agenda within local political jurisdictions, the "growth-management movement in America must come to be recognized for what it really is: an institutionalized form of support for the growth imperative"[116] that pervades all aspects of our national culture. The overwhelming majority of local growth-management programs implemented to date have clearly reflected continued growth accommodation. In the majority of states that have passed statewide growth-management laws, ongoing growth accommodation on the part of local governments is actually *mandated* under those legislative enactments. The recent evolution of the growth-management movement into a smart-growth movement has not changed this growth-accommodation bias. Smart-growth advocates clearly believe the problem is not growth per se, but rather the "dumb growth" represented by sprawling, low-density development. For them the challenge is merely one of realizing more efficient development patterns embodied in smart-growth principles and more effectively mitigating growth-induced problems. Defenders of the management movement's continuing growth-accommodation focus have even suggested the possibility of "sustainable growth."[117] In spite of mounting evidence of existent ecological limits to further growth, the growth-management movement remains committed to an increasingly obsolete growth imperative.

In communities with existing growth-management programs, the pro-growth orientation of those programs will obviously present significant challenges to formulating and implementing a no-growth agenda.

The prior portrayals of local jurisdictions as growth machines, the historical pro-growth stance of the planning profession, and the historical growth-accommodation bias of local growth-management initiatives in America all suggest that a transition to a no-growth future in local communities will not come easily. The "growth coalitions" that comprise local growth machines represent a formidable alliance of pro-growth interests. Land-based elites and politicians whose campaigns they have funded represent the central core of local growth machines that work for more intense land use and enhanced property values. They are supported by a broad array of other growth-coalition members, including local financial institutions, lawyers and realtors serving property interests, local media, construction industry representatives, labor unions, retailers, universities, utilities, and so on. These growth coalitions have imposed their will on local jurisdictions for so long that the growth ethic pervades virtually all aspects of local life. They have succeeded in implanting a common interest in growth and realizing consensus on the merit of continued land development. Building an alternative coalition based upon the consensual objective of enhancing "use values" rather than "exchange values" of land will be absolutely essential if local jurisdictions are ever to realize a sustainable state of no-growth. Similarly, advocates of such a no-growth agenda will have to recognize and contend with potential impediments stemming from the historical pro-growth stance of urban planners in America. Members of the planning profession gained and maintained professional legitimacy by serving the needs of local growth machines. The profession's theories, methods, and techniques evolved in a manner supportive of those machines. One of the most obvious manifestations of that support found expression in land-use plans and associated land-use regulations created by planners that have typically made allowances for preposterous levels of future growth. Changing this pro-growth bias of planners and directly engaging them in creation of plans and regulations intended to realize a state of no growth will therefore present another significant challenge. However, the work of professional planners employed by local political jurisdictions is invariably directed by local politicians, so if such guidance can be directed toward a no-growth end, planners can be enlisted to rework community plans and regulations to serve the new end of stopping growth just as effectively as they have historically served to facilitate growth. Finally, in communities with existing growth-management programs, no-growth advocates will have to contend with reversing the growth-accommodation orientation of those programs. In communities operating under statewide management laws mandating continued accommodation, that reversal will likely entail litigation contending that specific communities can no longer accommodate growth and meet their legal obligations to protect local health, safety, and general welfare. In the end, local management programs are just as capable of being designed to shut down future growth as they have been historically designed to facilitate ongoing growth. Changing local politics, planning, and growth-management programs to serve the new end of realizing a sustainable state of no growth, will obviously present significant challenges to no-growth advocates in virtually every local political setting. While those challenges may be substantial, they are not insurmountable. Strategies for addressing these challenges and advancing the end of stopping growth in America's communities are the subject of forthcoming sections of this work.

3 Rationales and strategies for stopping growth in America's communities

Growth can be restrained temporarily or permanently, as long as there are valid public welfare concerns being addressed by the process.

Eben Fodor[1]

If the federal government will not do it, and the state governments will not do it, then the ethical thing is to begin at the local level, insisting upon growth limits. If the impetus needs to come from the bottom up, so be it.

Daniel M. Warner[2]

With America's local governments having operated as "growth machines" for more than two centuries, redirecting the focus of these jurisdictions to a no-growth end will certainly present significant challenges. "Unfortunately, many local governments are thoroughly entwined with the narrow, special interests of the growth machine."[3] Throughout the county's history the nation has been a "growth-oriented culture," which is arguably better characterized by the operative motto "In Growth We Trust" than by the official motto "In God We Trust."[4] Within the context of such a growth-oriented culture it is possible to characterize local governments as "growth-addicted communities" that "have become a part of the growth machine whose primary function is to build roads and infrastructure and to provide development services for an ever-expanding mass of subdivisions, industrial parks, and shopping centers."[5] The former chapter's characterization of local governments as growth machines addressed the role of urban planners in helping local jurisdictions further their pursuit of growth. Under the direction of local politicians, planners have historically produced comprehensive land-use plans and associated land-use regulations designed to accommodate growth. This growth-facilitating role has been bluntly acknowledged by a member of the planning profession in the following terms: "The business of planning has become primarily the process of accommodating growth."[6] With the advent of the growth-management movement during the late 1960s and early 1970s, planners assumed key roles in helping local governments devise management strategies intended to support ongoing growth accommodation. As conceded by an identified expert on growth management: "With a few exceptions, communities generally formulate growth management programs to accommodate rather than limit expected growth."[7] This pro-growth orientation did not change when the growth-management movement transitioned into a smart-growth movement during the latter 1990s. Local smart-growth programs have demonstrated the same growth-accommodation orientation as earlier growth-management programs. In the words of the expert cited above, "[s]mart growth offers a 21st-century, pro-growth path to creating livable communities."[8] Taken together, the combined influences of local governments historically operating as growth machines, planners facilitating ongoing growth accommodation, and growth-management programs serving to assure further growth, have made it difficult to envision stopping growth within local political jurisdictions. These pro-growth influences have produced responses by those who have come to question the possibility or wisdom of additional growth. These responses have stopped short of suggesting strategies to actually *stop* growth, and have instead proposed more restricted agendas, such as strategies intended to *oppose* development or *slow* growth.

An example of a publication intended to guide citizen activists in local efforts to *oppose* specific development proposals was published in 2004 under the title of *Citizen's Primer for Conservation Activism: How to Fight Development in Your Community*.[9] That work by Judith Perlman identifies strategies for defeating what is alternatively referred to as "unwanted," "undesirable," "unplanned," or "destructive" development proposals in local settings. Identified strategies include issues identification, leadership development, hiring and working with legal counsel, building coalitions and partnerships, conducting a media campaign, raising money, and managing the process. The publication's position on growth is revealed in its portrayal of specific case studies. At one point Perlman recalls: "We talked about growth to make it clear that we were not 'antigrowth,' something the village officials and developers alleged."[10] At another point in the publication Perlman addresses the importance of an "extensive community vision" in defeating undesirable development, and in one of her case studies such a vision included "[r]ecommendations on how to grow and maintain the quality of life."[11] A noted mission statement for a group opposing development in a specific case study reflected a clear stance on growth in the following terms: "To encourage a long-range plan for growth ... which is in harmony with nature and consistent with the values of our community."[12] Elsewhere in the book Perlman notes that "around the country, 'smart growth' plans are becoming requirements ... and the existence of those plans [provides] a strong legal basis for challenging decisions inconsistent with the plans."[13] These views place Perlman's opposition to undesirable development firmly within the smart-growth movement. Throughout the publication expressed opposition is not directed at growth per se, but rather at the "dumb growth" of sprawl that threatens conservation efforts in outlying areas. This position supports the belief within the smart-growth movement that continued growth without compromising environmental or ecological values is possible if dumb growth is eschewed in favor of smart growth.

Potential shortcomings associated with the strategy of limiting opposition to growth only to those forms that represent "undesirable" development are indirectly acknowledged in Perlman's guidebook. Perlman concedes the difficulty of defeating even undesirable forms of dumb growth in many communities, due to the fact that "[s]ome local board and plan commission members are deeply prejudiced in favor of development."[14] At another point in her work, she admits to being "so often amazed at the partnership of local officials and developers."[15] She also acknowledges that in some "situations, the [local unit of government] is prejudiced in favor of development and is clearly adversarial to citizens proposing alternatives to development."[16] Perlman recognizes the reoccurring problem of defeating an undesirable development proposal only to have to fight the battle all over again with a subsequent proposal. As she put it, "[i]n defeating one petition for annexation, we were not assured of continued success as petition after petition was filed seeking to annex and develop for profit this highly desirable parcel."[17] Even the most committed citizen activists are apt to be worn down over time under such a relentless stream of unending development proposals. Ongoing development will likely triumph even over efforts that are limited to merely opposing certain kinds of development. However, the most serious shortcoming with strategies restricted to opposing only dumb growth and supporting smart growth is not addressed in Perlman's work. She fails to acknowledge the inherently unsustainable nature of any kind of material growth. As Daniel Warner has noted: "Smart Growth leads to a dead end."[18] Warner refers to smart growth as cutting-edge, land-use planning theory for attractive places that produces solid urbanization, an outcome he considers undesirable, unsustainable, and impossible. His conclusion supports the argument advanced here that merely *opposing* certain types of growth, while endorsing other types, represents an insufficient response to mounting evidence that past growth has already surpassed existent ecological limits to growth.

A classic example of a publication intended to guide citizen activists in local efforts to *slow* growth was published in 1999 under the title *Better Not Bigger: How to Take Control of Urban Growth and Improve Your Community*.[19] Eben Fodor's book focuses on "those approaches to growth management that have the potential to moderate or restrain growth (slow it down) rather than accommodate it."[20] He writes that "[t]here are ... many effective strategies in use today that will moderate or restrict growth in desirable ways" and that his "emphasis [would be] on those policies that will actually slow growth in your community."[21] Fodor attributes a range of negative impacts to rapid urban growth, including lost open space and environmental quality, overcrowded schools, traffic congestion, noise, rising crime rates, higher cost of living, unaffordable housing, a lost sense of community, and so on.[22] He criticizes the growth-management strategy of smart growth on the grounds that it limits options to what he considers to be two unpleasant choices: Growing out (low density sprawl) and growing up (high density infill). Fodor believes communities facing what he calls "tough growth pressures" ought to have a third option: Slowing or limiting growth.[23] In the end, he chose to focus on strategies and techniques intended to *slow* growth, rather than those that might significantly *limit* or even *stop* growth. Electing to emphasize control of the *rate* rather than the *amount* of growth allowed Fodor to stake out a position within the broader growth-management movement, because the movement had reluctantly accepted a possible role for *growth controls* in the form of *timing* controls after court decisions had sanctioned control of the pace of development. On the other hand, controlling the amount of growth via an eventual future *limit* on growth, or taking the even more radical action of implementing strategies to *stop* growth in the short term, have been condemned by spokespersons for the growth-management movement. If Fodor had suggested an emphasis on actions to limit or stop growth it would have put him outside the pale of "acceptable" growth-management practices. As a practicing planning consultant one might surmise that political expediency played a part in his decision to emphasize rate controls rather than controls intended to limit or stop growth, because a call for growth-management services beyond those focusing on the quality, location, and rate of growth do not yet exist. However, there is ample evidence in his book to indicate he recognizes a need to go beyond actions that merely *slow* growth.

Fodor faults the smart-growth approach to growth management for focusing only on *how* growth ought to occur, and suggests a need for an alternative approach to growth management that "focuses on *whether* growth should occur, and, if so, how much and how fast."[24] He refers to the latter approach as *finite world planning*, because it "recognizes limits to growth and makes the reasonable assumption that our communities cannot grow forever."[25] He believes this approach could yield an optimum or maximum size for each community beyond which its livability and quality will decline. In contrast to the smart-growth view that communities can keep on growing indefinitely if development occurs as smart growth, he posits that some communities are growing too fast and need to slow their rate of growth, while others may have already exceeded their optimum size and need to limit additional growth. Fodor credits smart growth with only slowing the rate of inevitable environmental deterioration, noting that "no matter how you dress it up, growth is still growth"[26] that will ultimately get you to exactly the same place as dumb growth. He suggests communities have a choice between endless growth that is forced to stop by intolerable conditions, or establishing an ideal or optimal size and engaging in management strategies to realize and maintain that size. This view assumes at least a willingness to entertain management strategies specifically intended to stop growth in some local settings. A general receptivity to stopping growth appears in other forms in Fodor's book. He cites numerous examples to make the point that growth results in steady erosion in the integrity of the natural environment. He refers to ecological footprint analyses clearly indicating the planet is incapable of supporting even its present residents under American lifestyles, let alone a continually growing human enterprise. He notes there is no possibility of a net growth in the planet's biota, and that our expansion can only occur at the expense of other species. He asserts that we must learn to integrate ecological principles of sustainability into public policies for managing growth. He identifies a list of positive opportunities and possibilities associated with stable, sustainable communities. However, these rationales for endorsing management initiatives to *stop* growth did not translate into that emphasis in Fodor's book; instead he chose to focus on strategies and techniques to *slow* growth. As he optimistically declared, "[t]here are dozens of effective ways to manage and slow growth."[27] The good news for those seeking to go beyond efforts to merely slow growth, and actually engage in deliberate attempts to stop growth, is that many of the strategies and techniques identified by Fodor to slow growth are capable of being modified to achieve the end of stopping growth. Those strategies and techniques will be credited in the forthcoming treatment of strategies for stopping growth in America's communities.

The subsequent elaboration of strategies for stopping growth in local jurisdictions is predicated on the belief that current ecological realities require more than merely opposing certain types of development or slowing the rate of ongoing growth. Success in defeating certain kinds of development or reducing annual growth pressures would only serve to retard the pace of continued growth. Realizing that end would not stop further growth in the scale of the human enterprise, and as a result would only slow the rate at which human expansion continued to dismantle and destroy the planet's ecosystems and the essential life-support services they provide. With mounting evidence that past growth has already surpassed global ecological limits, merely growing more efficiently would only delay an inevitable ecological catastrophe. Having already encountered existent ecological limits to global growth, the actual challenge will be one of "downsizing and redesigning the human enterprise to a level and form that is ecologically sustainable."[28] In many American communities, historic violations of local carrying capacities will actually require a period of negative growth until their populations and associated economies reach a level that can be maintained indefinitely (sustained) without impairing the functional integrity and productivity of local ecosystems.[29] Realizing such a period of negative growth will undoubtedly represent an even more daunting task than stopping growth, but the alternative option of attempting to maintain growth is simply not an ecological option. Implementing local strategies to stop growth represents an essential first step in moving American communities toward a state of sustainable behavior. Growth of the human enterprise does not represent sustainable behavior. No amount of wishful thinking, verbal gymnastics, or elaborate management practices will make it sustainable. In the end, "smart growth" is just as unsustainable as dumb growth. Under current ecological realities "smart growth" represents a false pursuit in the quest to realize and then maintain livable and sustainable communities.

If a growing number of progressive communities were to implement strategies to stop growth in their local jurisdictions, it would inevitably force a response by federal and state governments. A supportive response would represent the necessary rejection of growth as a viable policy option or survival strategy at all governmental levels. The subsequent treatment of political, economic, and planning and regulatory strategies to stop growth in America's communities is intended to provide local jurisdictions with tactics to shut down growth and begin the process of transitioning to stable, sustainable communities. With the understanding that implementation of many of these tactics might result in court challenges, the treatment of no-growth strategies is followed by a review of legal considerations in stopping growth in local communities. While that review is intended to convey that there are significant legal challenges associated with local efforts to stop growth, these challenges "need not be considered an insurmountable obstacle to stopping growth."[30]

Political strategies for stopping growth

The previous chapter's portrayal of local governments operating as growth machines described powerful local growth coalitions that represent a formidable alliance of pro-growth interests. Individuals and enterprises that make up these coalitions all end up supporting the consensual objective of continued growth manifested through ongoing land development. Assuming primary status within the coalitions are land-based elites who seek to enhance the value of their land holdings through continued intensification of land use in local political jurisdictions. The noted coalitions of supporters backing the land-based elites were said to include: mortgage lenders, realtors, real-estate lawyers, title companies, real-estate speculators, construction industry representatives, labor unions, retailers, newspapers, universities, utilities, professional sports organizations, planners, growth-management proponents, and individual property owners. Eben Fodor's treatment of local growth machines added additional growth coalition members due to his particular focus expressed in the following terms: "The engine of the growth machine is powered by the fortunes resulting from land speculation and real estate development."[31] That focus had Fodor identify the primary business interests within the coalition as landowners, real-estate developers, mortgage bankers, realtors, construction companies and contractors, cement and sand and gravel companies, and building suppliers. He noted that many of these parties have organized into groups like Associations of Realtors and Home Builder Associations to advance their interests. He also expanded coalition membership by identifying professionals in addition to planners that often support the growth machine: Architects, landscapers, engineers, surveyors, interior decorators, home inspectors, appraisers, and even wetland consultants. Such an expanded list of growth coalition members certainly represents a formidable alliance of pro-growth interests even before adding the role of politicians as powerful members of local growth coalitions.

In many communities typical politicians end up being businesspeople who have gained political office for reasons of land development and related processes of resource distribution that serve land interests. All too often lists of elected officials read like local business directories. In other communities a disproportionate amount of local campaign financing comes from real-estate entrepreneurs and others with a vested interest in continued growth. This financial support makes elected politicians who are not businesspeople beholden to the central interest of growth-machine coalitions in ensuring continued growth. If these politicians fail to support growth-promotion initiatives they risk losing campaign funding in subsequent elections. As a result, local governments become co-opted to such a degree that any alternative vision of the purpose of government beyond growth facilitation ends up being ignored, suppressed, or eliminated. In these local environments land-based elites are able to manipulate government authority in ways that allow them to profit from intensification of land use under continued growth. Under such a system land-based elites and the politicians they seek to control represent the heart of local growth machines. These elites use the combined influence of local growth coalitions to lobby for governmental actions that will enhance the growth potential of their land holdings. This puts elected officials in positions of being key actors in local growth-machine coalitions, because land-based elites recognize the profit potential of their land depends on a range of public actions.

Eben Fodor identified four types of governmental action capable of improving the profitability of local land development: Increasing the intensity of permitted land uses through changes in land-use regulations; diverting public resources to infrastructure expenditures in support of land development; reducing the cost of development through reduced regulations, fees, and delays; and stimulating demand for new development via economic development programs, tax incentives, and other subsidies.[32] Local politicians are empowered to approve the upzonings and subdivision plats that enable more intense and hence profitable uses of land. They possess the authority to approve public expenditures on new roads, sewers, and other facilities without which land development would often be unprofitable. They also have the power to reduce regulations, development fees, and delays that impede the development process. Additionally, they command fiscal resources to stimulate economic development with a range of expenditures, plus authority to approve incentives and subsidies intended to promote growth. Taken together these actions by local elected officials position them as powerful players in growth coalitions that comprise local growth machines. Local politicians have historically utilized all of the noted actions to promote the growth traditionally equated with progress in the United States.

All too often local politicians assume the position of spokespersons for growth machines in their jurisdictions. Even without support of local politicians, growth coalitions have done a masterful job of promoting growth. "The major growth machine players tend to be wealthy, well organized, and politically influential in their communities."[33] When they are joined and supported by elected representatives of local government they become a formidable alliance of pro-growth interests committed to reinforcing and maintaining the historically popular wisdom that "growth is good." Such popular wisdom is part of a cultural story that demonstrates tremendous staying power even when its claims are clearly more mythical than factual. In Daniel Quinn's novel, *Ishmael*, he conveys the idea of a culture being a people enacting a story, and addresses the difficulty of abandoning a story without an accepted replacement story to enact.[34] The "growth is good" myth represents a key component of the American cultural story that persists in spite of the declining quality of life inherent in further adherence to the growth path propounded by local growth machines.

> To act in a more discerning manner we must be aware of the story; we
> must think about it and decide what is myth that enriches only a few,
> and what in the story is a truth that applies to all of us.[35]

Over the past few decades a growing number of Americans have been increasingly willing to question the merit of further growth in their communities. Surveys undertaken in rapidly growing areas during the last two decades of the twentieth century showed that a majority of residents were already supportive of public actions to slow or stop growth.[36] As these residents experienced such growth-induced effects as traffic congestion, higher taxes, environmental degradation, and a general decline in the quality of life in spite of growth-management programs, they appeared increasingly willing to reject the "growth is good" myth. Some would undoubtedly have been sympathetic to the view that growth in their areas resulted in a minority of winners and a majority of losers, as expressed by the Oregon environmental leader Andy Kerr who has referred to urban growth as "a pyramid scheme in which a relatively few make a killing, some others make a living, but most [of us] pay for it."[37] If the public at large is to accept such an alternative view of growth, other myths that have traditionally been used to support ongoing growth will also have to be discredited.

A rich source of information and associated references for debunking traditional growth myths may be found in the third chapter of Fodor's 1999 book *Better Not Bigger*.[38] Fodor rejects the "growth is inevitable" myth and the associated claim that growth forces are such that growth-management programs are incapable of impeding continued growth. He asserts communities have a wide range of responsible policies and regulations capable of influencing whether or not individuals and businesses choose to locate in their jurisdictions. He states communities can set limits to their rate of growth and even cap their ultimate size. He derides the idea of unlimited growth on grounds of it being analogous to cancer, and argues communities can limit growth to achieve such legitimate objectives as protecting their local quality of life and honoring physical limitations of their natural environments. In declaring that quantitative growth of any kind is unsustainable toward the end of his book, it was surprising Fodor neglected to directly fault the "growth is inevitable" myth on the basis that it implies we have no choice about our collective behavior other than to continue to behave unsustainably.

Fodor also dismisses the economically derived idea that we have to "grow or die" as another historical growth myth. He points out that under traditional economic terminology a non-growing economy is pejoratively referred to as "stagnant" or even "recessionary," rather than by the more accurate and neutral term, "stable." He notes the choice of terms is significant, because the former imply rot, decay, and decline, while the latter implies balance and equilibrium. Fodor cites research indicating that when social and ecological costs are incorporated into measures of economic welfare, Americans have experienced a declining level of prosperity since the mid-1970s. He acknowledges that crafting a sustainable, stable economy will be challenging, but asserts there is no option to devising an economy that is non-growing in terms of material consumption and pollution emission if we are to realize a state of ecological sustainability. In the closing chapter of his book he describes features of a stable, sustainable economy for local communities and outlines steps to move local economies toward that end. He and others clearly envision prospects for an alternative to growing communities other than their inevitable decline and death if they cease to grow.

Another economic myth debunked by Fodor is the often-cited claim that growth is necessary to provide jobs and reduce unemployment. In Molotch's 1976 classic article on cities as growth machines he argued the total number of societal jobs is dependent upon such factors as federal monetary policy and rates of return on investment, and has very little to do with local decision making. As a result, he pointed out that local growth only tends to *distribute* jobs rather than *make* jobs. Fodor draws on another of Molotch's findings, noting that there is no statistical correlation between growth rates and unemployment rates across America's fastest and slowest cities. In fact, Molotch identified research indicating a tendency for rapid growth to be associated with higher rates of unemployment, and concluded that data indicate local population growth is no solution to the problem of local unemployment. As Fodor explains, faster growing cities can create jobs that attract new residents who don't succeed in finding employment, which results in a larger city with a similar unemployment rate to that prior to its growth spurt and a larger number of unemployed. Economic security for local residents is clearly more complex and difficult to achieve than just realizing continued growth.

Fodor also discredits the common economic myth that growth provides needed tax revenues that make it possible to avoid increasing individual tax burdens. As Fodor points out, growth does result in a larger overall tax base, but usually generates more costs than revenues, largely due to the fact that it creates a need for costly new infrastructure. He references research indicating that per capita taxes tend to increase with city size, and experience the greatest increases in communities with the most rapid growth rates. Fodor concludes: "The bottom line on urban growth is that it rarely pays its own way."[39] While many are willing to concede that residential development does not generate the taxes to pay for its costs, there is still widespread support for commercial and industrial development under the reasoning that they do pay their own way. However, the argument that these forms of development are necessary to generate taxes that help pay for services residents demand may be criticized on the grounds of the circular nature of the process: Commercial and industrial developments demand new workers; new workers and their families demand low-cost services.[40] As a general rule, growth results in higher taxes. Growth typically generates a need for a higher level of costly facilities or services, and generally drives up assessed values; both result in people paying more in taxes even if actual tax *rates* are held steady. In the introduction to Perlman's book on opposing development, she declares that the book is being written in part for those who "are sick of seeing [their] taxes increase to pay for all the services needed by so much 'progress.'"[41]

Fodor additionally challenges the frequently asserted myth that any attempts to limit growth will negatively affect housing affordability. He notes that the development industry regularly argues against growth controls on the grounds that they will drive up housing prices. Fodor cites a study from California indicating housing prices did not rise any faster or to higher levels in cities with growth controls than in pro-growth cities. He cites another California survey that showed communities with growth controls had enacted more affordable-housing incentives than communities without controls. With respect to the claim that land prices rise faster in communities with growth boundaries than in those without boundaries, he references data showing that lot prices rose faster over a 5-year period in Oklahoma City, Charlotte, Chattanooga, Salt Lake City, and Houston in the absence of growth boundaries than in Portland after the adoption of its boundary. In the end, he concedes growth limits may affect housing prices, but he suggests the rate of growth, the types of new jobs being created, and the kinds of housing policies enacted are likely to be more important influences.

Perhaps the most intriguing myth contested by Fodor is the claim that leaving land vacant or undeveloped is wasteful and unproductive. The fact that he clearly disagrees with this claim is evident in his list of productive land values that are often permanently destroyed by growth: Food production potential; outdoor recreation opportunities; open space; fresh air; quiet and serenity; beautiful views; watershed quality (water purification, groundwater recharging, and flood control); wildlife habitats; species diversity; and ecosystem functions. In terms of financial implications of undeveloped land, Fodor cites studies from Maryland and New Hampshire showing that open space generates more in tax revenues than it requires in service costs. This favorable outcome stems from the fact that undeveloped land requires few, if any, public services, which means there are minimal or no public costs required to maintain it. Most surprisingly, Fodor references studies from New Jersey, California, Maine, New Hampshire, and New York showing instances where it would be cheaper for communities to purchase undeveloped land or its development rights than to allow it to be developed and then have to assume the increased costs of providing and maintaining infrastructure and services.

Fodor's critique of growth debunks other myths, including the claims we have to stimulate and subsidize business growth to have good jobs and community prosperity, environmental protection hurts the economy, and most people really don't support growth management or environmental protection. When considered in conjunction with the formerly discounted myths, a compelling case against further growth emerges. As noted earlier, a growing number of Americans are becoming disenchanted with growth in their communities. They are increasingly associating it with traffic congestion, higher taxes, a higher cost of living, overcrowded schools, rising crime rates, unaffordable housing, environmental degradation, noise, lost open space, a lost sense of community, and a general decline in the quality of life. While defenders of the historic growth paradigm acknowledged these growth-induced problems, they have tended to argue they can effectively be mitigated under responsible growth-management programs, and that the costs of growth must be considered in light of tradeoffs associated with growth benefits. In enumerating those benefits they have deployed the historic myths debunked above, claiming growth would result in job creation, community prosperity, reduced unemployment, needed tax revenues, more affordable housing, and more economically productive use of land. However, if all of these touted benefits represent more in the way of myth than fact, communities are really being asked to sacrifice their livability and overall quality of life for little or nothing in terms of tangible gains.

The true nature of ongoing growth in local jurisdictions presents potential rationales for stopping growth in America's communities. If local growth tends to merely distribute rather than create jobs, the job creation myth provides little or no justification for supporting growth and its associated problems. If local growth tends to enrich the few at the expense of the majority, the community prosperity myth fails to compensate for growth-induced problems. If community growth tends to maintain the unemployment rate while increasing the actual number of unemployed, the reduced unemployment myth provides nothing in the way of a gain to balance diminished livability. If local growth increases tax revenues while also increasing individual tax burdens, the revenue myth actually represents a double loss for citizens as they pay more for a declining quality of life. If community growth actually drives up the cost of housing rather than maintaining reasonable prices, the affordability myth constitutes another lose/lose situation as local livability is sacrificed for higher housing costs. Finally, if local growth requires sacrificing a range of productive values associated with undeveloped land, while simultaneously requiring increased costs for public services, citizens are again forced to accept another lose/lose situation. In the end, each of the debunked growth myths provides an individual rationale for stopping growth in local communities. These rationales may serve to support the broader rationales for stopping growth, such as the inherently unsustainable nature of community growth expressed through demographic, economic, and urban increases, or the current ecological reality of existent ecological limits to growth.

By the opening decade of the twenty-first century polls increasingly revealed that in a growing number of areas "the 'system's' insistence on promoting growth collides with the majority's wish for low or no growth."[42] In a 2006 journal article on "post-growthism" Daniel Warner cited a number of surveys indicating that a majority of citizens no longer equate growth with progress. He cites a survey in 2000 revealing that 54 percent of residents in Virginia and 69 percent in Maryland thought growth was eroding their quality of life. He also cites results from California polls in 2000 and 2002, with the former indicating that 58 percent of citizens favored slowing development even if it resulted in less economic growth, and the latter revealing that a majority (52 percent) felt population growth should be discouraged in their communities. Referring to poll results from 2002 out of Washington State, Warner notes a survey indicating that over 60 percent of suburban voters favor strong limits on development to protect quality of life. Drawing on these results, he concludes: "It is not public opinion that drives growth, then; it is 'the growth machine.'"[43] Noting that what he calls "pro-growthers" have lobbied local governments assiduously, and acknowledging their role in "controlling elections" to obtain politicians supportive of growth, he concedes "pro-growthers" have traditionally won political battles over growth. Warner describes what he sees as a necessary response in the following terms: "Their lobbying and representations must be countered by equally powerful lobbying and representations from the other side, in order for the popular will to express itself."[44] The development of no-growth coalitions to counter the influence of growth-machine coalitions operating in local jurisdictions represents a key component of any political strategies that might be devised to stop growth in America's communities.

The politics of stopping growth in local jurisdictions may be thought of as a political battle between traditional growth-machine coalitions and newly emerging no-growth coalitions. For nascent no-growth coalitions to prevail in these battles, they will have to become more politically influential in conveying the actual "public will" on the politically charged issue of growth. Realizing the requisite degree of political influence to get local politicians to take the actions necessary to stop growth will ultimately depend on whether no-growth coalitions succeed in overcoming the historical dominance of growth coalitions. To succeed in displacing that dominance, no-growth coalitions will have to effectively counter the pro-growth mythology propounded by local growth machines. They will also have to convince local politicians that the majority of citizens are more interested in what Molotch called the "use" values of community land than in its "exchange" values, i.e., they place a higher value on maintaining the quality of their communities as places to live and work than on realizing potential profits from the sale of land holdings. To realize these ends, no-growth coalitions will have to mimic the efforts of growth coalitions in two key ways: Being well-organized and well-funded. Pursuit of either of these objectives presumes the prior establishment of a coalition specifically intended to move local communities toward stable, sustainable entities by stopping growth. Therefore, *a key political strategy for stopping growth in local jurisdictions is the establishment of a no-growth coalition focused on shutting down growth*. Such a coalition would be predicated on conveying the essential message that stopping growth represents an indispensable prerequisite for realizing stable, sustainable communities.

A rich source of information pertinent to building a coalition appeared in 2004 with the publication of Judith Perlman's book on fighting development in local communities.[45] Perlman addresses the initial need to find a group of like-minded individuals, and to identify one or two key actors capable of launching the initiative and creating momentum. She suggests that a good way to start building a coalition is by networking, with an initial undertaking of making a list of every individual and organization potentially sympathetic to the cause. She discusses the importance of forming partnerships with other organizations capable of being enlisted as supporters, partners, or members of the coalition. Perlman notes organizational support builds credibility, makes it easier to muster additional organizational support, and serves as an efficient way of getting additional individual support through the members of other organizations who might be rallied to the cause of a no-growth coalition. In terms of linking with organizations potentially sympathetic to a different growth orientation, she mentions connecting with a range of conservation and environmental groups, including river and watershed organizations, local chapters of national organizations such as Audubon, local fish and game chapters of organizations such as Trout Unlimited or Ducks Unlimited, and directors of any local environmental centers. Support for a no-growth agenda amongst these groups might be assessed and promoted by determining their respective sympathies to the position statement made in 2004 by the North American Section of the Society for Conservation Biology asserting a fundamental conflict between economic growth and biodiversity conservation. She also suggests partnering with land trusts in using tools like conservation easements to reduce development options in communities and preserve land permanently. Perlman even advocates speaking before organizations unlikely to support an anti-growth stance, like the Rotary Club, the Lions, and the Kiwanis, since individual members of these groups might become supporters. She addresses gathering possible support from individuals in a variety of governmental units and agencies, who might lend their support outside their official professional responsibilities. She additionally acknowledges the critical role of academics in building credibility, garnering media attention, and building momentum for a coalition's cause. Perlman devotes an entire chapter of her book to conducting a media campaign, which she credits with lending credibility to a coalition. She also commits a chapter to hiring legal counsel for the coalition to advise on intricate state-specific requirements related to things like state legislative directives on growth management and the use of initiatives and referenda in instituting growth limits. She even addresses the importance of selecting a proper name and logo for a coalition in terms of their potential contributions to a group's credibility. As part of her extensive treatment on establishing local coalitions to fight development, Perlman acknowledges the purpose is "to build a coalition for its electoral power."[46] In the context of a local campaign to stop growth, this would translate into enlisting a sufficient number of voters to convince elected officials to abandon their traditional support of growth in favor of a new public consensus that rejects the merit of further growth. A key component of attempting to convince local politicians of actual public sentiment in favor of stopping growth would be a local survey eliciting public opinion on different possible public responses to ongoing growth pressures. If a no-growth coalition is unable to change the traditional voting behavior of elected officials in support of a local growth machine even under evidence of public backing for a no-growth policy, the coalition would be left with having to turn to a more direct political strategy to realize its end of stopping growth.

In communities where it becomes evident that there is little prospect of changing the hearts and minds of individual local elected officials with respect to their roles as key members of community growth machines, citizens would be faced with "the eventuality of voting out of office certain intransigent government officials."[47] Replacing elected officials who are unsympathetic to a new public will regarding growth may be thought of as part of the natural progression of implementing any new public policy, which is to change the people serving in office if you can't change their minds.[48] In some of America's more conservative communities elected officials wedded to the growth machine may dominate, making an electoral shift to a no-growth position extremely difficult. However, in many communities an alternative stance on growth is already represented among elected officials, and in some instances all that would be required would be a swing vote in favor of implementing a new public will regarding growth. The important point to recognize is that local resistance to growth "can lead to expulsion of public officials sympathetic to the pro-growth side."[49] Local campaigns seeking to elect officials with an alternative growth orientation would have to push to "[e]lect public officials whose campaign funding is not dominated by Growth Machine money" and who are "not bound by philosophy or money to the Growth Machine."[50] *The ultimate quest and central political strategy for stopping growth in local jurisdictions would be to "{e}liminate the growth-promotion focus of local government by election or initiative."*[51] Eliminating supporters of the growth machine from local government would be essential to any effort to stop growth in local jurisdictions, because, as noted previously, under typical state laws local politicians have the final say over public actions capable of promoting or retarding growth. They are singularly empowered to institute the land-use plans and regulations, public expenditures on infrastructure and economic development, and incentives and subsidies that determine prospects for growth in any local setting.

Clearly, the best way to eliminate the growth-promotion focus of local governments that has dominated American history for more than two centuries would be to elect local officials willing to support a no-growth agenda. Where the strength of the local growth machine makes this unlikely or impossible, an alternative approach would be to force such an agenda on reluctant or unwilling local officials with a public initiative. The prospective use of an initiative as an alternative approach for stopping growth in local jurisdictions represents another political avenue for achieving a no-growth end. Electing sympathetic politicians and instituting a new growth policy by initiative both present unique challenges, but neither represents impossible paths to redefining a community's growth orientation. Both avenues involve the use of the ballot to commence the process of stopping growth in America's communities. In the case of local initiatives (establishing new policies or laws by ballot) and referenda (overturning existing policies or laws by ballot), these tools typically end up being constrained by state laws governing the use of these electoral mechanisms. In most states, both are governed by the requirements that they may only be used to decide legislative matters (those affecting many, rather than one or a few) and may not conflict with state laws (those specifically specifying decision-making processes). For example, with the exception of California, where the state's supreme court has liberally allowed rezoning actions to be decided by ballot, other states effectively block such rezones of individual properties by classifying them as non-legislative decisions and/or by pointing to state laws specifically restricting rezoning authority to elected officials. However, even in California the power to rezone by ballot is constrained by another state law requiring all rezones to be consistent with a previously adopted comprehensive plan approved by elected officials. While the power to implement a no-growth policy by downzoning permitted intensities of use via the ballot may therefore be severely restricted or effectively prohibited, other ballot measures may effectively serve to stop growth in local jurisdictions.

A local initiative could, for example, require elected officials to fund research to determine natural limits to growth within an area's political jurisdiction and then cap growth at a level that respects those limits.[52] Once that initiative identified limits based upon considerations like sustainable water yield from an aquifer or the ability to maintain biodiversity in local habitats, programs to cap growth within those established ecological limits could be devised and implemented. Local initiatives could also require establishment of growth threshold standards.[53] These standards would be intended to preserve or improve an existing quality of life in a local setting. By way of illustration, these standards could prohibit any deterioration, or even require improvements, in things like environmental quality (e.g., air or water quality), community services (e.g., police or fire protection, library capacity), or travel times on a community's road network (e.g., congestion levels). An example of such standards appeared early in the growth-management era when Livermore, California, adopted an adequate public facilities (APF) ordinance by initiative in 1972, which imposed the requirement that approval for new development would be dependent upon complying with specific standards for local educational, sewage disposal, and water supply facilities.[54] A recognized growth-management expert has acknowledged that APF ordinances "appear to operate in many communities as devices to limit growth" and that the effect is "particularly significant in communities that set severe standards of adequacy that immediately restrict development."[55] In many local settings the cost of overcoming constraints established by rigorous standards would effectively serve to shut down further growth.

If local no-growth coalitions succeeded in convincing elected officials of the wisdom of a no-growth position, prevailed in electing new no-growth politicians, or realized a no-growth agenda by initiative, they would still be faced with implementation of that agenda via a number of other strategies. Local communities would, for example, have to implement a few key economic strategies in order to stop growth. These strategies would have to be adopted by sympathetic politicians, or again imposed upon intransigent government officials by initiative, in order to stop local growth. These required economic strategies, coupled with other regulatory and planning strategies, impose challenges beyond the initial political obstacle of electing sympathetic politicians or forcing their hands by initiative. While challenges associated with overcoming the inertia of local growth machines are undoubtedly significant, they are not insurmountable. As one participant in local development battles has noted: "To an ordinary citizen trying to stop the steamroller of development, the force of big money allied with government may seem unstoppable. But ... individuals and small groups of citizens are challenging these forces and winning."[56]

Economic strategies for stopping growth

Ending public subsidies for infrastructure improvements that support ongoing development would represent an essential economic strategy for stopping growth in local jurisdictions. Public investments in capital facilities make ongoing growth possible, and to the extent that these investments are subsidized, the subsidies provided to development corporations may be thought of as a form of "corporate welfare."[57] The extent of such public subsidies is illustrated by two studies carried out by Eben Fodor on growth-induced infrastructure costs in the Pacific Northwest. In 1996 Fodor showed that the price for seven categories of off-site infrastructure improvements in Oregon amounted to $24,500 for a typical new single-family house.[58] In that initial investigation Fodor limited the inquiry to the off-site infrastructure costs for school, sanitary sewerage, transportation, water system, parks and recreation, stormwater drainage, and fire protection and police facilities. His subsequent 2000 study of an expanded list of off-site infrastructure costs for a typical residential structure in Washington state concluded each new residence required approximately $83,000 in facilities expenditures.[59] That study expanded the prior seven categories of infrastructure costs to include consideration of expenditures for libraries and electric power generation and distribution facilities.

Fodor's studies clearly illustrated the significant infrastructure costs associated with new development. Historically, local communities have viewed ongoing development so favorably they gladly subsidized continuing growth by funding associated infrastructure improvements out of general revenues. "The near universal norm in the U.S. is that the costs of infrastructure to support new development are shared among all taxpayers."[60] To the extent that communities moved toward imposition of impact fees on new development during the growth-management era to help pay for new infrastructure requirements, they tended to impose fees that represented only a small fraction of the actual costs of required facilities. In most local settings the majority of such costs are still subsidized by residents who live in those jurisdictions, which often translates into the general public subsidizing the new development that degrades the livability and quality of life in local communities.

An alternative approach would be to stop all such subsidies and to "[m]ake new development pay its way."[61] In states that have legislatively authorized impact fees, communities could use those fees "to recover the full costs for all types of public infrastructure required to serve new development."[62] Within states that have not enabled impact fees, and in which the attempted use of such fees under general home-rule authority may be invalidated as an unauthorized tax, communities might still be able to require developers to fund needed infrastructure via local improvement districts. Whatever the approach, the end of infrastructure subsidies would typically require developers to absorb additional costs to the tune of tens of thousands of dollars for each additional residence they constructed. The presumed short-term effect in many localities would likely be the diversion of most development to surrounding communities that had not instituted full-cost impact fees, while advancing the end of stopping growth in communities that ended subsidies and adopted such fees. As a growing number of communities joined the ranks of local jurisdictions unwilling to subsidize the growth jeopardizing their futures, their collective interest in stable, sustainable communities would eventually force state and federal governments to acknowledge a new national sentiment on growth. In this respect, ending infrastructure subsidies could not only serve to advance the goal of stopping growth in America's communities, it might also serve to trigger a new national stance on growth at all political levels.

Acquiring private land and holding it in public trust to reduce development prospects would represent another possible economic strategy for stopping growth in local jurisdictions. In many communities purchasing some private properties rather than subsidizing the infrastructure and subsequent maintenance costs associated with the development of those parcels would make economic sense. As noted previously, studies from five states revealed it would be cheaper for communities to purchase some undeveloped land or its development rights than allow it to be developed and have to assume the increased costs of providing and maintaining infrastructure and services. These land acquisitions would have to extend beyond the purchase of land designated for residential uses if communities hoped to achieve the end of stopping growth in their local settings, because realizing that end would also require stopping the redistribution of jobs that fuels further growth at the expense of neighboring communities. In 1997 Boulder, Colorado recognized that its residential controls had slowed population growth, but had done little to curb commercial or industrial development; so the city acted to reduce the number of new jobs the city could accommodate by purchasing some of the commercially and industrially zoned properties within its jurisdiction.[63] Since purchasing all properties zoned for commercial and industrial uses would have been financially prohibitive, the city supplemented the purchase of selective properties with rezonings to residential uses and downzonings to reduce the size and density of possible developments on remaining commercial and industrial lands. Such regulatory changes would in fact represent the backbone of any local effort to stop growth, because inflated real-estate prices in many communities would make it impractical, if not impossible, to stop growth by purchasing all remaining undeveloped land. The critically important role of revamped land-use regulations in stopping local growth is acknowledged and addressed in the subsequent section of this chapter. However, selective purchases, especially of vacant parcels zoned for commercial and industrial uses, could play an important role in stopping local growth by shutting down the employment gains historically realized through public actions intended to entice the relocation of employers from other locales.

In addition to infrastructure subsidies for new development, local communities have demonstrated established track records in providing a range of other subsidies and incentives intended to further growth. *Eliminating an array of subsidies and incentives traditionally employed to encourage growth would represent another important economic strategy for stopping growth in local jurisdictions.* In many intermediate- and large-size communities, local jurisdictions fund governmental agencies specifically charged with promoting local growth through their oversight of a range of such growth subsidies and incentives. As has been acknowledged, "[t]he growth machine function of local governments is carried out most conspicuously by the Economic Development agencies."[64] In smaller communities without resources to fund such agencies, these jurisdictions typically provide annual monetary contributions to Chambers of Commerce to recruit new businesses or encourage their expansion. Economic development agencies and Chambers of Commerce end up overseeing local efforts to entice businesses to locate or expand within their jurisdictions via a host of local economic development techniques.[65] Those techniques typically include formulation of an economic development strategy that targets businesses and employment opportunities compatible with community resources. Another technique widely utilized is the creation of a marketing program that emphasizes community assets, e.g., labor availability, transportation facilities, tax structure, accessibility to resources and related business, and attractive sites. In many communities financial tools are also usually arranged to aid development, including tax abatements and waivers, the establishment of community development corporations to serve as conduits for public grants and low-cost loans to pursued firms, and targeted financial mechanisms like special taxing districts. A popular form of these special taxing districts consists of tax increment financing districts, where a portion of tax revenues stemming from increases in assessed values over time are put back into such districts rather than being allocated based upon established formulas to support schools, police, etc. Another common local economic development technique consists of assembling and improving potential sites for development, including obtaining appropriate zoning, mitigating environmental site problems, and providing basic infrastructure. In some jurisdictions public land is made available, or favorable public lease commitments are provided, while in other instances communities offer supportive facilities, such as parking, child-care centers, or services like job-training programs. Additionally, many local jurisdictions expedite the development approval process; subsidize the cost of processing permits, reviewing plans, and performing inspections; and reduce the complexity of existing zoning and building codes, all to facilitate development. In the same way that general subsidies for infrastructure improvements often benefit the few at the expense of the larger community, the above subsidies and incentives used to attract new businesses typically also benefit a small number of local residents while degrading the quality of life for the majority. Under recognition of this reality:

> It is difficult to reconcile the practice of spending tax dollars to attract new businesses at the same time we are spending tax dollars to mitigate the congestion and [other problems] caused by the addition of new businesses to the area.[66]

Ending the growth subsidies and incentives noted above would represent another important component in an overall effort to stop growth in local jurisdictions, but when added to the prior political and economic strategies needed to realize such an end, the objective could still not be met without planning and regulatory strategies specifically intended to shut down future growth.

Planning and regulatory strategies for stopping growth

Comprehensive plans and associated land-use regulations adopted by local jurisdictions spell out prospects for future growth in America's communities. As noted in the prior review of the historical growth-orientation of urban planners in the United States, the plans and regulations they helped create generally tended to make allowances for preposterous levels of future growth. Under the direction of local politicians, planners have historically utilized a demand-based planning approach to determine the amount of land and facilities needed to accommodate projections of ongoing growth. Under wildly optimistic growth projections endorsed by politicians, local comprehensive plans have typically made allowances for dramatic increases over the 20- to 30-year time horizons of such plans. In helping communities craft land-use regulations to implement those plans, planners have usually served the interests of local growth machines and their political allies by developing permissive regulations intended to facilitate, rather than restrain, growth. As noted, zoning ordinances governing permitted uses and intensities of development have tended to allow for "unrealistic" or "preposterous" levels of possible growth, often beyond any reasonable prospects. A cited claim by Logan and Molotch in their description of urban growth machines asserted that virtually all significant urban areas in the United States are zoned for population and industrial increases double or triple their current levels. Actually, that estimate might understate the true nature of the "vast overzoning" that characterizes most American communities.

In 1999 a report in Florida revealed that community plans and associated zoning ordinances would permit the state to grow from its then 15 million to over 100 million under development based on the highest density permitted by those documents.[67] Most American communities are also "vastly overplatted," with approved subdivisions of land far beyond realistic prospects for development in the foreseeable future. The fact that most communities are vastly overzoned and overplatted obviously presents a major obstacle to stopping growth. Existing zoning districts and previously approved subdivisions of land represent enormous unrealized capacity for future land development. That situation is compounded by the fact that local communities are continuously being bombarded by requests for additional rezones for more intense uses and further subdivisions of land, many of which end up being granted under intense political pressure to meet the interests of private property owners. The resulting absurdity of the growth potential embodied in existing community plans and land-use regulations will have to be addressed if communities hope to stop growth within their jurisdictions.

Any attempt to modify comprehensive land-use plans and land-use regulations in a manner that closes out options for further growth would certainly elicit responses from members of local growth coalitions. A likely initial response would consist of attempts to "vest" development rights under existing lax community plans and regulations before communities have the opportunity to amend those public documents in ways that eliminate future growth options. The concept of "vested rights" with respect to private property consists of realizing a position where owners are no longer subject to governmental interference in attempts to develop their land. In most states property owners must obtain a building permit and spend a substantial sum based on that permit (e.g., land grading costs) in order to vest, or lock in, their development rights, while in a minority of states they only have to obtain a valid building permit in order to vest their rights. In other states, legislation has granted additional forms of vested rights to property owners, as illustrated by the "complete application" rule in Washington State. Under that rule, owners vest their rights to have development applications considered under regulations in place at the time of their applications once they submit complete applications, which consist of whatever local communities require in terms of submitted materials. If owners anticipated new community plans and regulations specifically intended to close out future development options, they would clearly be motivated to vest their rights to develop under existing plans and regulations that usually embody tremendous potential for further growth. In order to avoid a flood of permit applications intended to vest development rights before new rules go into effect, communities would have to halt all further processing and issuing of building permits with moratoria during the time period needed to amend their plans and regulations.

The adoption of moratoria to block the establishment of vested rights to considerable additional growth would represent an indispensable strategy for stopping growth in local jurisdictions. In the absence of a moratorium, developers would be able to impose significant additional growth on communities before they had the opportunity to adopt amended plans and regulations intended to shut down growth in their jurisdictions. "The legality of moratoriums has been well established in the courts."[68] They are generally considered within the rights of local governments if they represent a response to a public emergency in the form of defined problems that would be created or worsened by development, and only extend for a reasonable time period required for resolution of the problems that triggered the moratoria.[69] As traditionally applied, moratoria "must demonstrate a health, safety, or welfare basis for halting development and then move to determine a solution that will permit development to resume."[70] The stated intent here is very different, in that the suggested outcome of the moratoria would extend beyond merely halting development in order to overcome a development-induced problem to realizing a permanent end to the growth that inevitably results in problems that diminish the livability and quality of life in America's communities.

> Courts have allowed moratoria to block development during the time required to amend plans or regulations, when ongoing development would defeat the stated intent of revising these public documents in response to an emergency consisting of threats to a community's health, safety, and general welfare.[71]

The legal issue therefore is not one of the legality of moratoria to buy time to change plans and regulations in ways that respond to problems threatening communities, it is rather one of whether the courts will accept the health, safety, and general welfare rationales for stopping growth via the new plans and regulations created under those moratoria. That legal issue and related legal considerations are treated in the subsequent section on legal matters raised by pursuing an overall no-growth strategy.

Once communities have instituted moratoria to buy time to respond to the threats of ongoing growth, *any attempt to stop growth in local jurisdictions would have to implement the critical strategy of modifying community land-use plans and regulations in ways that close out options for further growth.* Traditional land-use plans and regulations have historically reflected a pro-growth bias and embodied absurd prospects for further growth. Any attempt to realize a no-growth state in local jurisdictions would have to revamp these public documents to serve the new public end of realizing stable, sustainable communities. In a growing number of states, communities would have to change their comprehensive plans to reflect a no-growth stance before undertaking revisions of their land-use regulations, due to a trend in favor of a so-called "consistency" requirement. This requirement, imposed either by state legislation or court rulings, prohibits any regulatory decisions affecting private property that are not consistent with a previously adopted local plan. In states that are subject to such a consistency requirement, comprehensive plans would have to be changed to reflect studies justifying a cap on growth before regulatory actions, like downzonings and plat vacations that eliminate existing subdivisions of land, could be legally undertaken to curb land development. Once communities have changed their comprehensive plans to reflect a no-growth end, they could legally proceed with changing the zoning and subdivision ordinances that currently ensure ongoing growth.

As has been emphasized previously, America's local jurisdictions tend to be vastly overzoned and overplatted. "Their existing zoning districts and previously approved subdivisions of land represent enormous unrealized capacity for future land development."[72] The absurdity of the growth potential embodied in existing community plans and associated regulations was illustrated by statewide calculations carried out in Florida in 1999, indicating local plans and zoning ordinances in the state embodied the potential to expand its population 7-fold to over 100 million. An equivalent calculation for any local jurisdiction would be apt to yield similarly ludicrous growth prospects, which no-growth coalitions might effectively utilize to gain public support for their campaigns to realize stable, sustainable communities. Such a calculation would merely entail accessing public records on vacant residentially zoned land, applying the allowable densities under existing zoning to determine the prospective number of residential units on each vacant parcel, and converting the number of residential units into population figures based on past census figures for the likely number of individuals in different types of residential units within the community. In order to stop the ongoing growth that would inevitably move communities toward the ridiculous population levels suggested by such calculations, local jurisdictions would have to downzone land and vacate previously approved subdivisions. The legacy of vastly overzoned and overplatted local landscapes guarantee ongoing land development, and represent the past successes of local growth machines that would have to be reversed if further growth is to be curtailed.

The growth potential of any local jurisdiction could be reduced tremendously by downzoning properties and vacating existing subdivisions that only exist as so-called "paper plats" (i.e., approved subdivisions that have not been built or had facility improvements installed). While reductions in permitted intensities of use on undeveloped land, and the associated reductions in land value accompanying downzoning and plat vacation actions, would undoubtedly be controversial, both actions are clearly legal if they can be justified on health, safety, and general welfare rationales embodied in a community's comprehensive plan.[73] Take, for instance, the following hypothetical examples. If a community still possessed resource lands within its boundaries that permitted 5-acre hobby farms, it could legally downzone those land holdings to large agricultural parcels if the land were capable of being viably farmed. Similarly, downzoning land from 1-acre residential lots to 40-acre parcels would be legal if the action were required to protect a community's aquifer or other environmentally sensitive lands. In terms of lands already zoned for higher densities, communities could dramatically downzone those properties under public welfare rationales indicating the community could not accommodate those densities without violating local public facility and service standards established to protect livability and quality of life. Such downzonings could be supplemented by the selective purchase of development rights to reduce growth prospects even further. With respect to possible prospects for vacating existing subdivisions of land that exist only as paper plats or prospective developments, communities could similarly reduce or drastically curtail possible development outcomes based upon important public interest rationales. For instance, an existing registered subdivision that permitted 20 single-acre lots on a 20-acre parcel, with associated zoning that allowed densities ranging from 1 to 20 housing units per 20 acres, could be vacated to allow only a single house on the 20-acre land holding, if the action was based on a justifiable public-interest rationale. It is important to understand that existing zoning designations and publicly recorded plats do not typically confer any sort of inalienable development rights; those rights are usually not established until property owners vest their rights by applying for and acting on development permits. Until development rights are vested, communities have the authority to alter development outcomes by actions like downzonings and plat vacations, as long as they can provide legitimate public-interest justifications for reducing development options and associated land values. The vast overzoning and overplatting of America's communities does not, therefore, represent an insurmountable obstacle to changing land rights in ways that would enable the creation of stable, sustainable communities.

If a community succeeded in shutting down development options within its political boundaries via downzonings and plat vacations, it would still have to contend with prospective development influences immediately outside its borders that could potentially affect its desired planning outcomes. While downzonings to lower densities are capable of blocking *upward* expansion within a community, local jurisdictions would still have to contend with eliminating prospects for growing *outward* in order to effectively shut down further growth. *A permanent urban growth boundary would, therefore, represent yet another key strategy for stopping growth in local jurisdictions.* In order to gain control over development options on land outside that boundary, a community could annex surrounding vacant land. The intent of such an annexation would not be the traditional aim of providing urban services for further development, but rather one of establishing a greenbelt of protected land around the community. That greenbelt could be created by regulatory techniques like exclusive agricultural zones, large-parcel zoning with associated clustering of any limited development, and land-use regulations used in conjunction with techniques such as conservation easements and development rights purchases.

A number of the aforementioned strategies for stopping growth in America's communities raise potential legal issues. For example, the call for a permanent urban growth boundary as a necessary strategy for shutting down growth would clearly raise questions about the potential legality of such an action in states where statewide growth-management laws mandate ongoing adjustments of those boundaries in response to continued growth. Regulatory strategies that significantly curtail property rights and values would also raise a number of legal issues specifically related to their constitutionality. In many instances, these arguments might be expected to lead to claims that the suggested strategies are illegal under constitutional, statutory, or case law considerations. In order to counter likely claims of illegality, and to make a case for the defensibility of specific suggested strategies, legal considerations in pursuing a no-growth strategy need to be explicated.

Legal considerations in pursuing a no-growth strategy

The growth-management era that emerged in the United States during the latter 1960s and early 1970s represented a new degree of interference with private property rights. By extending earlier forms of regulation in order to manage and control the location, quality, rate, and amount of growth, local jurisdictions imposed an unprecedented level of restrictions on individual land holdings. With respect to *location* controls, some local management programs severely restricted permissible levels of development outside designated urban growth areas. In other communities management programs addressed attempts to influence the *quality* of development by requiring adequate public facilities ordinances that effectively served to constrain development options in many locations. Elsewhere, some locales instituted *rate* controls to slow down or postpone development prospects, as in the landmark Ramapo case out of New York state upholding such timing controls,[74] which in that particular case survived a legal challenge in spite of eliminating development options on some parcels for up to 18 years. In other local settings management programs severely restricted the *amount* of development in some areas due to the presence of environmentally sensitive lands, even though these communities typically refused to consider an ultimate cap on growth for their entire jurisdictions. While all of these new regulatory initiatives represented further intrusions into the realm of private property rights, often imposing new levels of restriction on allowable use, "most police-power regulations that have been commonly employed while attempting to manage growth have survived legal challenges."[75] However, the overwhelming majority of growth-management programs implemented to date have allowed growth to continue in spite of their new restrictions on private property. The main point to be considered here is whether management programs intended to realize a state of no growth, with presumed additional limitations on property rights and associated values, might also be able to survive inevitable legal challenges.

The management of growth via land-use regulations grounds such management efforts in the exercise of the police power by local communities. Public use of these regulations "is based on the police power—the right and obligation granted to the states by the Tenth Amendment to the Constitution—to protect the health, safety, and general welfare of citizens."[76] This right and obligation to protect the public welfare implies local communities can use their state-delegated, police-power authority to impose even extreme forms of land-use regulation if public interests require such regulation. As an acknowledged growth-management expert has observed: "Under the police power, governments may severely limit private property owners' rights to use of their property ... so long as they [have] established a legitimate public interest for the action and [have] followed due process in adopting and administering it."[77] These use limitations have been upheld by the courts even when they have severely reduced the value of private property. In 1915 the U.S. Supreme Court established the right of local governments to regulate development even when that regulation dramatically reduced use and value. In that *Hadacheck* v. *Sebastian* ruling, the Court upheld a prohibition on manufacturing within designated areas on nuisance grounds as a proper exercise of the police power even though the imposed use limitations resulted in an 8-fold diminution in the value of privately held land.[78] In its landmark 1926 ruling in *Euclid* v. *Ambler Realty* the Court upheld the constitutionality of zoning as a valid form of regulation under the police power in spite of use limitations that produced a 4-fold diminution of value.[79] As an expert in land-use law has noted, the U.S. Supreme Court has "repeatedly upheld regulations that destroyed or adversely affected real property interests, provided that the state's interest in the regulation was ... strong enough."[80] However, the ability of local jurisdictions to utilize land-use regulations for the public good has not been unlimited. Over time an elaborate set of *constitutional*, *statutory*, and *case-law* standards have emerged to limit the permissible degree of public interference with the property rights of individuals. These standards have been established by legislatures and court rulings spelling out the extent to which private property rights (use rights) and associated interests (economic interests) would be protected when regulations were litigated. New growth-management regulations intended to stop growth in local jurisdictions could be expected to push the boundaries of permissible reductions in the use and value of private land holdings to new levels. The point of interest is whether the more significant limitations on property rights likely to be associated with local no-growth programs might be expected to survive legal challenges under the standards courts have established to protect property rights.

Historically, most land-use litigation in the United States has occurred in the form of substantive due process challenges. In 1894 the U.S. Supreme Court set out standards for judging the legality of land-use regulations under the due process clause of the Fourteenth Amendment in its *Lawton* v. *Steele* ruling.[81] Those standards consisted of three requirements under what would come to be referred to as the "reasonableness test": The regulation had to advance a legitimate public purpose, it had to employ means reasonably necessary for accomplishment of that purpose, and it could not be unduly oppressive on the individual property owner.[82] With respect to the first requirement of having to advance a legitimate purpose (i.e., one that protected, furthered, or promoted the public health, safety, or general welfare), courts have traditionally applied a "presumption of constitutionality" or "presumption of validity" in reviewing the legitimacy of stated purposes, meaning purposes have been accepted if they were reasonably debatable. During the growth-management era courts accepted the legitimacy of such new regulatory purposes as environmental protection and growth management itself, so if emerging problems require new public responses in the future, one might expect the courts to sanction the legitimacy of new purposes even if they served to severely restrict private property rights. The second component of the due process inquiry requires that there be a reasonable relationship between the regulation's legitimate purpose and the means or regulations selected to accomplish that purpose or objective. Out of recognition of the separation of powers principle, and an assumed expertise on the part of legislative bodies in deciding local policy matters, "the courts are extremely reluctant to strike down legislative determinations of means for accomplishing a given end."[83] So the courts have afforded local jurisdictions considerable latitude in adopting both "legitimate purposes" and "reasonable means," leaving fairly debatable questions as to wisdom and propriety on these matters to local legislative bodies. These components of the due process inquiry have not, therefore, presented serious obstacles to adoption of new land-use regulations to protect the general welfare, even when the regulations represented significant new intrusions into property rights. In fact, most litigation under due process challenges has been decided under the third component of the reasonableness test, the determination of whether or not the regulation has been "unduly oppressive" upon a property owner.

The third prong of the reasonableness test under substantive due process challenges focuses on the impact of specific land-use regulations on individual properties. In requiring that regulations not be "unduly oppressive," this component of the test has come to be interpreted as a prohibition against regulations that are judged to be "confiscatory." Under this standard, a regulation would be unreasonable if it rendered property unsuitable for any use to which it was adapted, and thus destroyed all, or virtually all, of its value. As this wording implies, "it would take a substantial amount of injury before the court would invalidate a regulation on this ground,"[84] because it is assumed that some injury accompanies any legitimate regulation, and courts are reluctant to usurp the legislative role in making determinations of the need for particular regulations. Even severe land-use regulations have typically been able to withstand legal challenges under this standard, since these regulations have typically stopped short of legislating away all, or virtually all, use and value. As long as local regulations have permitted some remaining use and resultant value, the courts have been reluctant to invalidate them on "confiscatory" grounds. When courts have judged regulations to be confiscatory, property rights advocates have been dissatisfied with the judicial remedy, because the due process clause of the Fourteenth Amendment provides for no compensation for such a regulatory "taking" of property. The clause merely affords the remedy of invalidation of the excessive regulation. As a result, aggrieved property owners have sought other litigation routes to obtain relief from what they considered to be unreasonable regulations.

By the 1990s law textbooks and court rulings referred to lawsuits against proclaimed confiscatory regulations as a "substantive due process taking claim."[85] In essence, property owners were arguing that excessive land-use controls were effectively serving to "take" private property. In their view, regulations were capable of going so far, and destroying the value of property to such an extent, that they had the same effect as a taking by eminent domain. Since the due process litigation route only afforded invalidation as a possible remedy for such excessive regulations, an obvious interest in other possible litigation routes had existed for decades. Before the Supreme Court's landmark 1987 *First English* ruling that the compensation provision of the Fifth Amendment's takings clause did apply to the regulation of private property,[86] property owners were limited to seeking possible compensation for excessive regulations via the doctrine of inverse condemnation.[87] That doctrine embodied the idea that government actions could serve to take private property without formal condemnation procedures. The phrase "inverse condemnation" suggests an action that is the inverse or reverse of a condemnation proceeding, in that the taking precedes the usual affirmative actions required of formal eminent domain acquisitions. While the doctrine encompasses possible physical, title, and economic takings, the vast majority of suits filed under the doctrine have claimed takings in the form of imposed economic losses on property owners. These claims of economic takings under the doctrine of inverse condemnation often ended up falling short of meeting property owners' expectations. First, standards used by the courts to judge takings claims under the doctrine provided less than definitive guidelines for assessing whether a particular regulation constituted a taking. The "harm/benefit" standard provided for possible compensation if a regulation went beyond preventing a public harm to realizing a public benefit, but many regulations are capable of being characterized both in harm-prevention and benefit-attainment terms. The "diminution of value" standard implied denial of reasonable use, usually meaning no economically profitable use, represented a taking, but the standard offered no set diminution of value that had been identified as the point at which regulations became unreasonable. The "balancing test" as a third standard suggested a taking when the degree of intrusion into property rights was judged to be out of proportion to any needed furtherance of a specific public end, but again the standard provided little in the way of a definitive guideline for judging when a regulation would rise to the level of a taking. In terms of a second short-coming associated with litigating under the doctrine, even in those instances when courts found a taking there was no guarantee of a compensation award, because the courts have awarded other forms of relief for violations under the doctrine beyond compensation. These shortcomings prompted interest in yet another possible litigation route for excessive land-use regulations, and the Supreme Court's 1987 *First English* ruling provided such a new litigation path for contesting extreme forms of regulation.

In *First English* the Court ruled that the just compensation clause of the Fifth Amendment requires compensation for a taking of property effected by regulatory action. That so-called "compensation ruling" opened the door to directly litigating excessive land-use regulations as violations of the Fifth Amendment's takings clause, and eliminated any question as to whether compensation was required for such regulatory takings. In that opinion, and in a number of other regulatory taking rulings during the growth-management era, the Court provided a refined and expanded set of standards for judging regulatory taking claims. Although the Court did not abandon the "balancing test" for making regulatory taking determinations, it appeared to evidence a "growing preference for categorical answers over balancing tests."[88] Such *categorical* or *per se* takings represent regulatory actions the Court automatically considered to represent takings irrespective of whether they achieved important public purposes or had only a minimal economic impact on property owners. The first of these categorical or per se takings rules was announced in the *Loretto* decision, where the Court stated "a permanent physical occupation is a governmental action of such a unique character that it is a taking without regard to other factors that a court might consider."[89] The second categorical or per se takings rule identified limits to the degree of permissible economic impact associated with applications of land-use regulations. In the *First English* ruling the Supreme Court stated that a denial of "all use" constituted a categorical taking requiring compensation in addition to invalidation. Variations on this second categorical rule describing so-called "total takings" were provided by the Court in its *Agins* ruling and its *Lucas* decision. In the *Agins* case the Court declared a denial of "economically viable use" to be a taking regardless of the government's intent.[90] In its *Lucas* ruling the Court referred to a denial of "all economically beneficial or productive use of land" as "compensable without case-specific inquiry into the public interest advanced in support of the restraint."[91] Whatever the wording, the opinions clearly declared that regulatory destruction of all of a property's use and associated economic value would always constitute a "total taking" requiring compensation. If local governments' regulations either imposed permanent physical occupations on property owners or realized "total takings" via the denial of all economically viable use and associated economic value, the Court clearly established that both actions would always constitute takings requiring governmental com-pensation. However, as with "substantive due process taking claims" asserting "confiscation," these categorical or per se takings rules do not present serious obstacles to even extreme forms of land-use regulation since most regulations have typically stopped well short of legislating away all, or virtually all, use and value.

In addressing regulatory takings claims as violations of Fifth Amendment protections afforded private property, the Supreme Court acknowledged that specific land-use actions could rise to the level of requiring compensation even if they did not represent "total takings." According to rules laid down by the Court, these "partial takings" claims would be decided under the so-called "multi-factor balancing test."[92] Emphasizing the importance of weighing several factors in resolving takings claims under that test, the Court identified the relevant factors as: The *character of the governmental action*; the *economic impact* of the regulation; and the extent to which the regulation has interfered with *distinct investment-backed expectations*.[93] Because of uncertainties associated with applying the character of governmental actions and interference with distinct investment-backed expectations considerations, courts have tended to resolve partial takings claims based on economic impacts, or what may be thought of as a "diminution of value" test.[94] With respect to that test, the Court has said its prior opinions "uniformly reject the proposition that diminution in property value, standing alone, can establish a 'taking'" when regulations are reasonably related to promotion of the general welfare, and that "the 'taking' issue in these contexts is resolved by focusing on the uses the regulations permit."[95] With a bias in favor of applying the "mere diminution rule," litigation under that rule "has given rise to a common notion that a regulation must restrict all reasonable economic use before it can be recognized as a taking."[96] Even regulations that have significantly interfered with property rights have not tended to push regulation to the point of restricting all reasonable economic use. As a result, taking claims decided on the basis of the multi-factor balancing test have typically concluded that no taking had occurred.[97] Again, litigation under this test would appear to represent little in the way of obstacles to significant restrictions on private property as long as those regulations did not restrict all reasonable economic uses.

Finally, any attempt to assess whether courts might be expected to sanction serious use restrictions on private land holdings would have to acknowledge the possible role of the so-called "whole-parcel rule" in making those determinations. In making determinations of permissible degrees of interference with economic interests in land, the Supreme Court has determined that a landowner's entire parcel of property was to be considered as the unit of land against which interference was to be assessed.[98] Under that rule, courts do not divide a single parcel into discrete segments to determine if rights in a particular segment have been taken. Instead, they assess the impact of a regulation against the entire land holding. Under this standard, land-use regulations may legally deny *all* use on a portion of a single landholding, as long as some reasonable use remains for the entire property. For example, regulations might prohibit all development on environmentally sensitive lands, even if those lands constituted the majority of an owner's landholding, as long as some reasonable economic use remained on the remaining portion of the property. As an example, this rule might allow a community to deny all use on some 90 percent of a landholding under legitimate public purpose rationales, if the owner were permitted to make economically viable use of the remaining 10 percent of the landholding and thus retain some reasonable use for the entire property. This rule serves to further reduce the threat of possible taking challenges to land-use regulations that seriously restrict use rights if communities are able to base such restrictions on legitimate health, safety, and general welfare rationales.

The prior review of legal standards that courts might apply in adjudicating the legality of significant restrictions on private property directly bears on the question of whether courts might uphold the serious limitations on property rights that would be required to stop growth in local jurisdictions. Members of local growth machines might be expected to assert that such serious limitations would represent *unconstitutional* restrictions on private property. However, as the review of substantive due process challenges to arguably excessive land-use regulations revealed, courts would only invalidate regulations using a "confiscatory" standard under the due process review if they rendered property unsuitable for any use to which it was adapted, and thus destroyed all, or virtually all, of its value. Similarly, litigation under the doctrine of inverse condemnation was shown to require denial of reasonable use, usually meaning no economically profitable use, before courts would be apt to declare a taking and provide some form of judicial relief. Under litigation asserting violations of protections provided by the Fifth Amendment's takings clause, the review revealed that categorical takings only occur in instances where regulations impose permanent physical occupations on property owners or realize "total takings" via denial of "all use," "economically viable use," or "all economically beneficial or productive use." Under Fifth Amendment "partial takings" claims decided via the multi-factor balancing test, a bias in favor of using the diminution in value standard under that test showed that a regulation would have to restrict all reasonable economic use before it constituted a taking. Reference to the "whole-parcel rule" showed that land-use restrictions could legally deny *all* use on a portion of a single landholding, as long as some reasonable economic use remained for the entire property. These legal standards used in substantive due process challenges and regulatory takings challenges all suggest the courts will tolerate significant limitations on property rights, if regulations imposing those limitations are based upon legitimate public purpose rationales and do not extinguish all use and value. Regulations devised to stop growth in local jurisdictions will clearly have to leave affected parties with some reasonable remaining economic use and associated value under the reviewed standards. *However, while communities may be legally bound to permit economically viable uses of private land, they are under no legal obligation to allow the most profitable use of any particular parcel.*

Local jurisdictions seeking to stop growth will be faced with the challenge of identifying economically viable uses other than commercial and industrial uses which generate growth through expanding employment opportunities or residential uses that serve to house a growing population. Constitutional protections afforded property owners clearly rule out some regulatory options. For example, communities would be unable to take regulatory actions that resulted in permanent physical occupations of private property, such as zoning parcels for public open space or for storage of public vehicles, because such actions would both deny economically viable use of private landholdings and violate owners' rights to exclude people from their properties. Communities would also be unable to implement land-use regulations that extinguished all, or virtually all, reasonable economic use and associated value. Under constitutional interpretations, communities are obliged to permit some reasonable remaining use of regulated land, usually interpreted to mean that regulations may not extinguish all economically profitable use; however, as noted, communities are under no constitutional obligation to maximize the profit potential of private properties. Under legitimate public welfare rationales communities could legally reduce development options to the point of leaving only marginally profitable uses on regulated landholdings. The "whole-parcel rule" would, in turn, legally permit dramatic reductions of use potential on individual properties, so long as owners were still permitted some economically viable use of their entire landholding. On other properties communities could legally close out some future development options via conservation easements and development rights purchases. Communities could also use land-use regulations to limit development options on some properties to a number of income-producing agricultural and recreational uses capable of representing economically viable uses without associated growth-inducing effects. Identifying economically viable uses that minimize or stop further growth would represent a central challenge in devising local land-use controls intended to stop growth. Where the desired restrictions on individual properties could not be achieved by land-use restrictions without denying economically viable use, communities would have to abandon the regulatory approach and purchase those properties to stop growth. *Creative use of all of these approaches under a unified growth-management program would permit local jurisdictions to advance the end of shutting down growth without violating constitutional protections afforded private property rights in America.* If done imaginatively, and with due diligence to legal considerations, such management programs could certainly counter the claim that no-growth programs would impose unconstitutional restrictions on private property.

Members of growth coalitions that comprise local growth machines could also be expected to claim that no-growth programs would impose *unconstitutional* restrictions on Americans' fundamental right to travel and settle in communities of their choice. They could claim court decisions have affirmed that the "constitutional right to travel encompasses transient passage from state to state as well as interstate migration and settlement."[99] They could also assert that federal courts have held that the right to travel includes intrastate travel as well,[100] and go on to argue that this infers a corresponding right to settlement in any community of one's choice. They might additionally point out that this fundamental personal liberty is protected from infringement under the "compelling state interest test" used in equal protection challenges,[101] and that land-use regulations that serve to block travel and settlement have little hope of surviving such challenges because they would be unable to provide the compelling state interest arguments needed to justify regulatory interference with the right to travel.

No-growth proponents could effectively counter each of the prior claims used to argue that no-growth programs would be unconstitutional based upon their interference with the fundamental right to travel that has been established by the courts. They could point out that the Supreme Court has ruled that the right to travel is not absolute, but rather subject to reasonable limitations.[102] They could also make note of the fact that federal courts have rejected the idea that the interstate right to travel includes the right to settle in any community during the course of litigation addressing low-income housing and single-family zoning.[103] Finally, they could argue that possible litigation addressing the fundamental right to travel under the compelling state interest test could not be expected to present serious challenges to instituting local no-growth programs on two grounds. First, the requirement regarding "standing to sue" makes such litigation unlikely, because landowners or developers cannot assert the rights of others in order to obtain relief for themselves. Second, even if the standing requirement were to be overcome, there would still be the fact that courts have been reluctant to apply the rigorous compelling state interest test in cases alleging interference with the right to travel.[104] For example, in reviewing a contested growth-management program in the city of Livermore, the California state Supreme Court decreed that land-use ordinances that substantially limit immigration into a community need not be sustained under the compelling state interest test, and are constitutional if they are reasonably related to the welfare of the region affected by the ordinance.[105] Even if the courts were to assess a claim of illegal interference with the fundamental right to travel under the compelling state interest test, one might assume that some current environmental rationales might suffice to qualify as the compelling public interest needed to justify interference with the right to travel and settle. If communities could, for example, show that they lacked sufficient sustainable groundwater supplies for even their current population base, let alone an expanding one, one might assume the courts would accept this as a sufficiently compelling basis for blocking further in-migration and settlement. Based on these arguments, *it would appear as though the fundamental right to travel need not be considered an insurmountable barrier to growth controls directed at stopping growth.*

In terms of a possible *statutory* law rationale for asserting the illegality of local efforts to stop growth, members of local growth coalitions could be expected to assert that no-growth programs would violate statewide growth-management statutes in states that have adopted these laws. As noted previously, the majority of statewide management statutes passed to date actually mandate ongoing growth accommodation on the part of local governments. Defenders of the growth imperative in these states might be expected to argue that management efforts directed at stopping growth would be illegal, because under state law communities are required to comply with accommodation directives spelled out in statewide growth-management enactments. The actual legal issue ends up being considerably more complicated due to the existence of other state laws. These other state statutes may, in fact, impose legal requirements that are quite different from, and potentially in conflict with, continued growth accommodation. For example, all of the states that have passed these statewide growth-management laws to date also have environmental statutes that direct local governments to protect the environment. If ongoing growth accommodation were to threaten the ability of a local government to fulfill other state-legislated requirements, the courts would have to resolve the conflict between state laws. In these instances the courts try to "harmonize" the conflicting laws, but when they are unable to achieve that end they eventually decide in favor of one of the statutes based upon an interpretation of legislative intent. Under mounting environmental and ecological problems one might expect some courts to exempt specific local settings from further growth if they face pressing natural limitations, even if statewide laws mandate continued development. On a more general level, it has been noted that local governments have a legal obligation to protect the health, safety, and general welfare of their citizens. In local settings where communities are able to make the case that it has become impossible for them to fulfill that obligation while at the same time complying with a state mandate to continue accommodating growth, courts might be expected to exempt them from the growth mandate. "There may, therefore, be a legal out even from a state statutory requirement forcing continued growth on local communities."[106] Local jurisdictions may have to litigate to be exempted from state-imposed, growth-accommodation mandates, but a potential legal avenue does exist to pursue a no-growth program even in states with statewide growth-management laws. A more daunting undertaking would be formation of a coalition of local governments pushing to amend the growth-accommodation provisions in such statewide laws. That possibility was acknowledged by one critic of these laws in the following terms: "The most serious legal impediment to growth constraints is Smart Growth legislation that mandates upzoning to accommodate future populations. That legislation is amendable."[107] There can be little doubt that statewide growth mandates imposed by statutes represent very real obstacles to shutting down further growth, and attempts to pass such laws in other states ought to be vigorously opposed by those who have come to accept existent ecological limits to growth. However, obstacles presented by these statewide growth-accommodation laws are impediments that might nevertheless be overcome.

Members of local growth coalitions might also be expected to use *case-law* rulings to support their position on the assumed illegality of local efforts to stop growth. An example of such possible court-imposed restraints on limiting growth has been decreed by state courts that have established a regional welfare standard for judging the legality of land-use regulations. In a few of those states (Pennsylvania, New Jersey, Michigan, Massachusetts, and New York) the regional welfare standard has translated into court mandates to accommodate growth in furtherance of the general welfare. In these states the courts have considered housing opportunities for all income groups as essential to promotion of the general welfare, and assumed that ongoing growth accommodation furthers increased housing opportunities. In some of these rulings the courts have said that land-use regulations may not be used to avoid "natural" or "normal" growth, and in effect imposed a legal requirement to address growth with "open doors."[108] Proponents of ongoing growth in these states might be expected to argue that the regional-welfare standard established by court rulings effectively prohibits local attempts to stop growth. No-growth proponents could counter that argument by referencing court decisions indicating the growth-accommodation requirement associated with the regional-welfare standard may be waived in certain circumstances. In the *Albano* decision out of New Jersey a court allowed for reasonable interference with ongoing growth based on environmental considerations, reaffirming the general rule that regulations "cannot be used to thwart growth," but conditioning that rule by permitting regulatory interference with growth when "reasonably necessary for public protection of a vital interest."[109] Similarly, the *Sturges* ruling by a Massachusetts court conceded that, at least in some circumstances, "the public interest in preserving the environment ... may outweigh whatever undesirable economic and social consequences inhere in partly 'closing the door.'"[110] So while the regional-welfare standard may seriously impede attempts to stop growth in states that have adopted such a case-law standard, it need not be considered an insuperable roadblock to growth controls directed at stopping growth if imposed limits are based upon compelling and vital public interests.

The prior review of legal considerations in pursing a no-growth strategy within local jurisdictions concedes that there are potential constitutional, statutory, and case-law barriers to implementing no-growth programs. Yet the review also suggests that none of these possible legal constraints need be viewed as presenting insurmountable obstacles to stopping growth in America's communities. Local growth-management programs are capable of being fashioned in a manner that addresses constitutional, statutory, and case-law considerations. Properly crafted programs that address legal issues raised by these different judicial concerns ought to be able to overcome many of the legal challenges associated with implementing no-growth programs when courts are asked to resolve the matter of whether local jurisdictions have the legal authority to realize stable, sustainable communities. Unfortunately, there are few court opinions available to shed light on the matter of whether the American judicial system will sanction the ultimate form of growth control under growth management represented by local efforts to stop growth. In a highly publicized 1979 *Boca Raton* case, a Florida district court of appeal upheld a lower court's invalidation of a cap on the maximum number of dwelling units that would be allowed within the city.[111] The trial judge's opinion held that the city had the power to establish a "cap" on growth, but that it had failed to show that its cap, established by public vote, bore a rational relationship to a permissible municipal purpose, i.e., one that promoted the public health, safety, or welfare of the community. In 1983 the same Florida district court of appeal was willing to uphold a cap in a decision involving the city of Hollywood, noting the city *"presented a more than adequate case for the proposition that the proposed cap would contribute substantially to the public health, morals, safety and welfare of its citizens."*[112] The court noted the public record was replete with plans, reports, and studies justifying the cap. If that court ruling reveals a willingness to accept an absolute cap on future growth based on justifiable public welfare grounds, one might surmise that another court might sanction the more radical step of stopping growth in the short term, rather than at some future point when a community reaches a designated cap, if a community were able to present compelling public welfare rationales for its no-growth program.

In terms of courts being willing to tolerate dramatic reductions in the growth potential embodied in existing community plans and land-use regulations, no-growth proponents have the intriguing example of another community in Florida that radically reduced its growth prospects without having its actions contested in the courts.[113] As an unincorporated area in Florida subject to a county plan and land-use regulations, Sanibel Island residents rebelled at the notion of their island being zoned for up to 35,000 dwelling units by elected county officials. The residents voted to incorporate, elect their own city officials, and hire their own planners to create a new community plan and associated land-use regulations. Their new zoning ordinance reduced the number of permitted residences from 35,000 to 6,000 under the ultimate "buildout" of the city. According to lawyers writing a case-study description of the city's experience, the professional nature of the community's plan and land-use controls, which included such progressive features as basing the number of permitted residences at least in part on development tolerances of different ecozones on the island, provided few opportunities to litigate the dramatic reduction in allowable uses of land on the island. The Sanibel Island case study suggests local jurisdictions might be able to overcome legal challenges associated with dramatically reducing the absurd growth potential typically embodied in existing community plans and land-use regulations.

The prior treatment of stopping growth in America's communities identified rationales for pursuing a no-growth end, which are summarized in Table 3.1. Those rationales embody responses to the flawed reasoning that has continued to be deployed in defense of growth in geographical settings ranging from global to local. At the global level, even academics speak of "sustainable growth" as an actual option, even though the phrase represents a moronic oxymoron that ignores existing ecological realities. At local levels, proclaimed benefits of continued growth tend to represent myths that are increasingly capable of being debunked. The identified rationales collectively represent a

Table 3.1 Rationales for stopping growth in America's communities

1) Demographic, economic, and urban growth are inherently unsustainable.
2) Global ecological limits to growth have already been surpassed.
3) Growth has produced a declining level of prosperity for Americans since the mid-1970s due to rising social and ecological costs associated with ongoing growth.
4) Rather than providing jobs and reducing unemployment, local growth only tends to redistribute jobs among communities, and in the process typically maintains the unemployment rate while increasing the total number of unemployed in individual communities.
5) Growth usually generates more infrastructure costs than tax revenues, typically resulting in higher per capita taxes.
6) Instead of increasing prospects for affordable housing, growth tends to drive up housing prices.
7) Public acquisition of undeveloped land or its development rights may prove less expensive than allowing land to be developed and having to assume the increased costs of providing and maintaining public infrastructure and services.
8) Over time ongoing growth inevitably degrades the livability and quality of life of local jurisdictions due to the deterioration of ecosystems and their life-support services.

basis for justifying local no-growth programs, and a unified foundation upon which to build coalitions needed to push a no-growth agenda in America's communities. The former treatment of stopping growth in local jurisdictions also identified strategies for realizing a no-growth end, which are summarized in Table 3.2.

Those political, economic, and planning and regulatory strategies suggest multiple approaches to shutting down the local growth machines that have historically dominated American communities. A subsequent review of potential constitutional, statutory, and case-law barriers to implementing no-growth programs conceded possible legal constraints, yet suggested they did not constitute insurmountable obstacles to stopping growth in America's communities.

Table 3.2 Strategies for stopping growth in America's communities

Political strategies
1) Establish a local no-growth coalition focused on shutting down growth.
2) Eliminate the growth-promotion focus of local government by election or initiative.

Economic strategies
3) Stop the public subsidies for infrastructure that support ongoing development.
4) Acquire select private lands and hold them in public trust to reduce development prospects.
5) Terminate the array of growth subsidies and incentives traditionally employed to encourage growth.

Planning and regulatory strategies
6) Adopt a moratorium to block establishment of vested rights to considerable additional growth under existing lax plans and regulations that usually embody tremendous potential for further growth.
7) Modify communities' comprehensive plans and associated land-use regulations in ways that close out options for further growth.
8) Institute a permanent urban growth boundary to avoid outward community expansion.

With compelling rationales and legally defensible strategies, perhaps the greatest challenge in implementing local no-growth programs will consist of mustering the social and political courage to undertake such a radical and unprecedented course of action. The hope of realizing such courage will rest in part on the ability of local no-growth proponents to understand the ongoing dogged support for the growth imperative at all jurisdictional levels outside of local communities. The following chapter explores the extent to which continued support for the growth imperative outside of local jurisdictions can be expected to impede local efforts to stop growth, but also surveys the principles and tenets of the bioregionalism movement to illustrate the guidance this regional framework might provide in initiating a societal rejection of the growth imperative and the associated adoption of a no-growth imperative.

4   The no-growth path to sustainability

What an astounding thing it is to watch a civilization destroy itself because it is unable to re-examine the validity, under totally new circumstances, of an economic ideology.

James Goldsmith[1]

It is development that can have the attribute of sustainability, not growth.

Herman E. Daly[2]

An "ideology of growth"[3] lies at the very core of today's worldwide cultural network driven by a universally accepted growth imperative.[4] Centuries of positive perceptions of demographic, economic, and urban increases have stood in the way of reassessing the merits of continued growth in human populations, economies, and cities. While some have been willing to question the wisdom of further demographic and urban growth, the most difficult conceptual leap has been that of attempting to visualize economies characterized by stability rather than growth. A "world fixated on growth"[5] has been unable to let go of the idea of economic growth as progress. In 1973 the steady-state economist Herman E. Daly described what he called the malady of growthmania, which he referred to as "the paradigm or mind-set that always puts growth in first place—the attitude that there is no such thing as enough," even though "[w]e may already have passed the point where the marginal cost of growth exceeds the marginal benefit."[6] Daly specifically labeled GNP accounting that neglected to count the costs of growth as "growthmania," and the associated counting of those costs as benefits in GNP calculations as "hyper-growthmania."[7] As Daly noted, "Growthmania is the paradigm upon which stand the models and policies of our current political economy."[8] Local jurisdictions seeking to stop growth will have to recognize the ongoing dogged support for the growth imperative outside local settings, especially the unwavering continued endorsement of economic growth, and the challenges that such a pro-growth bias present to moving local communities toward a state of no growth. Communities wanting to shut down growth and transition to stable, sustainable futures will have to contend with growth myths that still extol the virtues of demographic and urban growth, but the greatest challenge will undoubtedly come from having to counter the pro-growth mythology associated with economic growth. Current international and national stances on economic growth clearly evidence a virulent form of growthmania, in that both demonstrate an excessive enthusiasm or obsession with continued economic expansion. The respective stances of states and existing regional jurisdictions towards growth, and economic growth in particular, are almost as obsessive. The first three sections of this chapter are intended to portray the nature of these persistent pro-growth attitudes in international, national, state, and regional contexts, in order to convey the extent to which local jurisdictions will have to go it alone in attempting to stop local growth and move their communities toward stable, sustainable entities. The third of these sections acknowledges the pro-growth orientations of most regional entities in America, but suggests that a past willingness to consider strong growth controls in a few of those entities holds out the hope of bioregionalism becoming a new organizational framework for realizing no-growth communities. The final section of the chapter addresses the critical role of urban places in realizing sustainability, and argues that cities will only be able to further the transition to a sustainable future if they first realize stable, sustainable states of no growth.

The challenge of international and national growthmania

The current obsession with economic growth evidenced by ongoing globalization and national development initiatives may be traced back to theoretical formulations advanced by early economists. Adam Smith, the founder of the classical school of economics, set out to explain how the wealth of a nation could be increased in his 1776 publication *Wealth of Nations*. That early focus on increasing national wealth would continue to dominate economic thinking in subsequent centuries. "Economics thus became a science geared toward justifying and facilitating the pursuit of wealth by individuals and nations."[9] A few key aspects of Adam Smith's reasoning have continued to captivate economic theorists. His emphasis on "individual self-seeking as the mainspring of social benefit, the beneficent 'invisible hand'"[10] produced an ongoing fealty to the "idea that individuals, pursuing their own individual interests in a market society, make one another richer."[11] The idea that "the 'invisible hand' leads self-interested individual actions to positive collective outcomes"[12] has been idealized by a former chair of the president's Council of Economic Advisors in the following terms: "Harnessing the 'base' motive of material self-interest to promote the common good is perhaps the most important social invention mankind has achieved."[13] Economists have also remained loyal to Smith's view that increased wealth depended on the skill and efficiency with which labor was applied to the production of material goods from natural resources. For Smith, the basic means of increasing production were through a high degree of specialization in the division of labor and the introduction of machinery.[14] Smith lived at the beginning of the Industrial Revolution, and the "new regime of private enterprise in manufacture by power-driven machinery needed a system of ideas to justify it ... so

Adam Smith and his followers played the role of advocates for the rising industrialists."[15] Smith argued "prosperity was dependent on specialization" that "made workers more productive" through the realization of greater efficiencies in production processes.[16] The "idea that increasing efficiency, usually by increasing scale, is the key to increasing wealth" has demonstrated tremendous staying power, with an ongoing quest "to keep us becoming ever more efficient, achieving ever greater economies of scale."[17] An eventual "efficiency revolution" would encompass far more than factory work, but under an initial focus on industrial processes "efficiency became the ultimate tool for exploiting the earth's resources in order to advance material wealth and human progress."[18] Equating human progress with material wealth has persisted over the centuries since Adam Smith's contributions to economic thinking, and has resulted in a "dogged pursuit of maximum economic production"[19] from his day to the present. Over time, a sort of "evangelism for efficiency and growth" produced a "growth-centered, efficiency-obsessed economy."[20] Preoccupation with productivity and growth has resulted in an idolatry of growth, where even ecological disasters looming on the immediate horizon have yet to "shake the conviction so deeply rooted in the discipline [of economics] that growth is both the supreme end and the supreme means for achieving that end."[21]

Other aspects of classical economic dogma have continued to influence current positive perspectives on economic expansion. Adam Smith reasoned that "the chance to apply a high degree of specialization depends on wide extension of the market, since large numbers of a given product cannot be sold in a small or local community."[22] It naturally followed that widening markets, through improvements in transportation, would be seen as making possible the growth of commerce and industry, resulting, in turn, in gains in national wealth. This line of reasoning sounds like something one might expect from proponents of global markets in today's headlong rush into economic globalization. Smith also argued the case for the necessity of competition as a condition of his system of "natural liberty" playing out under free markets and free trade. He was an ardent disciple of laissez-faire principles, believing individuals ought to be free to act in their own self-interest without governmental interference, and that under competition everyone would gain from a free market and free trade. One of the noted gains would be the prospect of individuals obtaining what they want at the lowest possible price, which again sounds like a contemporary rationale for global markets. If specialization, competition, free markets and freedom of trade were desirable within a nation, Smith reasoned that they must be equally desirable among nations. It naturally followed that "[n]o nation can gain by making something which it could buy more cheaply elsewhere."[23] David Ricardo, another celebrated classical economist and principal theoretician of free trade, formulated the principle of comparative advantage to address this point. Believing in specialization like Smith, Ricardo argued each nation should specialize in those activities in which it excels, so that it can have the greatest advantage relative to other countries. By narrowing its focus of industrial activity to those in which it has the largest comparative advantage, international trade would grow through the export of surpluses produced under higher efficiency and productivity, and prosperity would be enhanced. Again, this reads like a rationale for global markets and free trade in the current era.

Defenders of private enterprise and free-market capitalism have continued to espouse the virtues of doctrines formulated by classical economists to the present day. They accept the principle premise of human progress being represented by material wealth, and therefore endorse the ongoing pursuit of maximum economic production. In quest of that end, they accept the need for specialization of labor to increase productivity, as well as the claim that increased efficiency is associated with increased scale. These orientations yield a natural preoccupation with productivity and growth, and an associated support for other doctrines espoused by classical economists. Advocates of free-market capitalism believe laissez-faire principles afford the best route to increased national wealth, with the greatest gains stemming from individuals responding to market price signals in a competitive free market unimpeded by government regulations. The resulting efficiencies in labor productivity and use of scarce resources are assumed to ensure the greatest production of material wealth. Proponents of free-market capitalism suggest that the extension of operations of the "invisible hand," where individuals are free to pursue their self-interests unimpeded by governments, to a global market under free trade represents the best route to universal material affluence.

With the advent of the Industrial Revolution, free-market capitalists were presented with an economic development paradigm that seemed to support their affinity for maximizing the production of material wealth. Industrial "production in line requires a large scale of total output before it becomes feasible" and "international trade provided a market of sufficient scale."[24] "Although industrialism grew up historically under capitalist institutions, it ... prov[ed] to be compatible with socialist institutions as well."[25] Marxist socialism ended up being as committed to the desirability and possibility of industrialism as capitalism. Conflict between the two economic systems ended up centering on which afforded the best route to maximizing the growth of material goods and equitably spreading the benefits of the industrial mode of production. "Whatever their ideological differences both systems [ended up being] fully committed to large-scale, factory-style energy and capital-intensive, specialized production units that are hierarchically managed."[26] Capitalists believed the best route to universal material affluence consisted of private ownership of the means of production, with allocation and distribution provided by the market. Socialists believed the best route to be government ownership of the means of production, with allocation and distribution realized by central planning. Under Marxist materialism the "emergence of the new socialist man in the classless society ... require[d] the material precondition of overwhelming abundance, which in turn require[d] rapid growth."[27] In the end, both free-market capitalism and Marxist socialism represented "growth economies"[28] intended to advance the quest for universal material affluence. When the economies of Eastern Europe and the former Soviet Union collapsed during the last decades of the twentieth century, and their governments embraced free markets, it appeared as though free-market capitalism stood alone as the vehicle for helping nation states pursue their respective quests for material affluence through unending growth. The doctrines of free-market capitalism seemed to endorse both the possibility and desirability of such unending growth.

It should be acknowledged that classical economists did not envision a prospective path of unending growth. "The classical economists saw a temporary phase of growth that must culminate in a new steady state economy."[29] Adam Smith and his close friend David Hume had both looked into the distant future and seen "an end to the accumulation process."[30] Thomas Malthus contributed the idea of the "law" of diminishing returns in relation to the use of land, noting there comes a point beyond which it does not pay to apply additional fertilizer and labor because the additional increments of expense do not correspondingly increase yield. He also had "declared the mathematical certainty of populations outstripping their food supply, and David Ricardo had incorporated a similar assumption in his model of the economy."[31] In 1848 John Stuart Mill provided a reformulation of the classical doctrine in his *Principles of Political Economy*, where he wrote "in sweeping terms about the limits to economic expansion."[32]

> He fore[saw] an ultimate 'stationary' state of society, in which population growth would be voluntarily limited, there [would] be ample means to maintain all in reasonable comfort, and attention [would] be directed to a better distribution of the product rather than merely to increasing it without limit.[33]

As Mill wrote: "It must always have been seen, more or less distinctly, by political economists, that the increase in wealth is not boundless: that at the end of what they term the progressive state lies the stationary state."[34] Mill expressed his positive view of such a stationary state in unequivocal terms: "I cannot ... regard the stationary state of capital and wealth with the unaffected aversion so generally manifested towards it ... I am inclined to believe it would be, on the whole, a very considerable improvement on our present condition."[35] These acknowledgements of a future stationary or steady-state economy on the part of classical economists would eventually yield to the arguments of twentieth-century "neoclassical growth economists"[36] suggesting that economic growth could continue in perpetuity.

The idea of unlimited economic growth potential is championed by neoclassical growth economists, whose views represent the dominant economic paradigm of the current era. "Substitutability, efficiency, and human capital have been the bulwarks of the neoclassical theory that economic growth may continue in perpetuity."[37] Neoclassical growth economists developed these three theoretical concepts to support their faith in perpetual economic growth.

With respect to *substitutability*, they argued resource limitations would not serve to constrain future growth because resource scarcities could be effectively addressed by substituting other available resources. In its broadest application, the concept of substitutability suggested the factors of production (land, labor, and capital) could be substituted among themselves. Land, which in these formulations includes natural resources, need not limit growth, because "[i]f human-made and natural capital were good substitutes for one another, then natural capital could be totally replaced."[38] Under this line of reasoning, "neoclassical economic theory has taught that humanly created capital is a near-perfect substitute for natural resources, and consequently for the stock of natural capital that yields the flow of these natural resources."[39] For neoclassical growth economists, "[n]ature may be finite, but it is seen as just one sector of the economy, for which other sectors can substitute without limiting overall growth."[40] The economy's growth is therefore unconstrained by natural resource considerations in the view of growth economists. These economists also employ the concept of *efficiency* to tout the infinitude of economic growth. The focus of economic growth theory is on productive efficiency or productivity. Productivity is the output per unit of input employed, and increases in efficiency are seen to depend on the increased efficiency in the use of labor or capital. For growth economists increasing efficiency provides the route to continued growth via the production of more goods with less labor, capital, or natural resources. In this regard they draw on the reasoning of classical economists that efficiency is generally obtained through specialization of the production process, division of labor, and technological progress. In the end, such efficiency improvements are assumed to afford unlimited prospects for further growth. Finally, growth economists also employed the concept of *human capital* to back their claims of the possibility of perpetual economic growth. With human capital being "jargon for intelligence, education, and knowledge" this concept may simply be thought of as "a fancy representation of the older concepts of substitutability and efficiency."[41] In other words, human ingenuity is seen to provide unlimited prospects for realizing new substitutions and efficiencies that will permit unending growth. These concepts in support of perpetual economic growth reveal the extent of the commitment to continued economic growth by neoclassical economists who represent today's dominant economic paradigm. "Neoclassical economics is too firmly invested in the perpetuity of economic growth for its practitioners to acknowledge growth limits."[42] The concepts in support of the infinitude of economic growth have also provided a theoretical foundation for the argument that it is possible to extend free-market capitalism to every corner of the planet as part of an economic globalization effort that will yield a material paradise.

According to one interpretation, the ideological principles underlying the global economy include:

> [T]he primacy of economic growth; the need for free trade to stimulate the growth; the unrestricted 'free market'; the absence of governmental

regulation; and voracious consumerism combined with an aggressive advocacy of a uniform worldwide development model that faithfully reflects
the Western corporate vision and serves corporate interests.[43]

The free-market capitalism underlying such a global economy has, in turn,
been portrayed via its basic tenets in the following manner: Sustained
economic growth as measured by Gross National Product represents the
foundation of human progress and is essential to alleviate poverty and protect
the environment; free markets, unencumbered by governmental interference or
regulation, result in the most efficient and socially optimal allocation of
resources; economic globalization, under which goods and capital flow freely
across national borders in a single integrated world market, spurs competition, increases economic efficiency and growth, and is generally beneficial to
everyone; and localities achieve economic success by abandoning goals of self-
sufficiency and aspiring to become internationally competitive in providing
conditions that attract outside investors.[44] Finally, a set of fundamental
assumptions on which the doctrine of free-market capitalism rests has been
suggested in the following terms: Humans are motivated by self-interest,
expressed principally through a quest for financial gain; the action that yields
the greatest financial return for the individual or firm is the one that is most
beneficial to society; competitive behavior is more rational for the individual
and the firm and more beneficial to society than cooperative behavior;
and human progress is best measured by increases in the value of what the
members of society consume, and those who consume the most contribute
the most to that progress.[45] Taken together, these principles, tenets, and
assumptions are presumed to represent a roadmap to realizing an unending
state of societal progress through global economic expansion. That progress is
seen as being dependent upon "an ever-continuing expansion of economic
output—*economic growth*—and the integration of national economies into a
seamless global economy."[46] This orientation suggests that economic growth,
and more specifically exponential economic growth, represents the principle
measure to gauge the success of nations. For nation states it affirms that
"progress and national well-being should be judged according to only one
standard: the volume of production and consumption."[47] Hence the pervasive
use of Gross Domestic Product as a measure of "progress." Under early
formulations of economic globalization it was widely assumed that "the
full forces of the market could now be unleashed to focus human attention exclusively on the production and consumption of endless material
wealth."[48] The creation of a global consumer culture coupled with boom-
ing global commerce has been sold as a path to unprecedented material
abundance. As one critic has summed it up, economic globalization "is
believed to provide a means of creating a material and technological paradise
on Earth."[49]

"The modern worldview is that the more material goods you have, the better
your life will be."[50] With this worldview it is possible to conclude that global

free trade is based on the assumption that "the highest good is to shop."[51] In order to help their citizens realize a state of material paradise, it is believed nation states merely need to implement some of the previously noted principles and tenets of free-market capitalism. An emphasis on commodity accumulation as part of a commodity-intensive lifestyle produces a natural interest in consumers being able to access affordable goods. The tenets of free trade drawn from the reasoning of classical economists are said to ensure these affordable prices: Competition spurs innovation, raises productivity, and lowers prices; the division of labor allows specialization, which raises productivity and lowers prices; the larger the production unit, the greater the division of labor and specialization, and thus the greater the benefits in terms of lower prices.[52] Reasoning has it that if governments allow free markets unencumbered by governmental interference or regulation then consumers will be able to benefit from such lower prices. Conventional wisdom also has it that nation-states need to emphasize production of export goods for which they have a "comparative advantage" and import everything else as another strategy for ensuring affordable prices. To realize these prices they are additionally told they need to allow free trade unimpeded by tariffs or other requirements (i.e., minimum wage laws, environmental protection dictates, national health insurance mandates, etc.) that would impede international competition in a global market. And finally, nation states are told they need to accept a uniform worldwide industrial development model that faithfully reflects the Western corporate vision and serves corporate interests if they hope to realize material affluence for their citizens via lower prices. This last requirement acknowledges that corporations have "an inexorable, unabatable, voracious need to grow and expand" due to the fact that the "profit imperative and the growth imperative are the most fundamental corporate drives."[53] Ongoing pursuits of profits and growth in an industrial system yield large-scale, centralized production processes feeding standardized markets. This "infatuation with large-scale systems leads logically to [a] postulate of free trade: the need for global markets."[54] Reasoning has it that "[a]nything that sets up barriers to ever-wider markets reduces the possibility of specialization and thus raises costs, making [a nation] less competitive."[55] When corporations, and increasingly transnational corporations, are accepted as essential players in realizing national material wealth, it naturally follows that corporations' "profit objective [ends up being] reformulated as a question of broad national economic policy—how to stimulate the economic growth from which the multitudes will presumably benefit."[56] If nation states realize all the former requirements of economic globalization, it is believed they will benefit in ways that extend far beyond just lower prices for goods. "The philosophy allegedly behind the globalization agenda is that maximizing global economic liberalization will result in broadly based economic and social benefits."[57] Defenders of the globalization of market capitalism suggest that it will solve a broad array of social problems. In addition to advancing the social goal of expanding material wealth globally.

[today's] prevailing wisdom continues to maintain that economic growth offers the answer to poverty, environmental security, and a strong social fabric, and that economic globalization—erasing economic borders to allow the free flow of goods and money—is the key to such growth.[58]

However, the claimed benefits of economic globalization have not gone uncontested.

Critics of economic globalization find fault with many of the touted benefits presumed to flow from the ongoing spread of free-market capitalism. With respect to the claim that economic globalization will reduce poverty worldwide, they point to statistics indicating that it has actually increased unemployment and thereby exacerbated poverty across the globe.[59] In a competitive global marketplace, transnational corporations are driven to realize greater production efficiencies, including reductions in labor inputs per unit of output. Critics point out that "[s]pecialization inevitably leads to chronic unemployment and to lower wages."[60] In order to compete effectively, corporations engage in "downsizing, streamlining, and automating their operations, using the most advanced technologies to eliminate hundreds of thousands of jobs."[61] The result ends up being "jobless economic growth."[62] Globally, "transnational companies build state-of-the-art, high-tech production facilities, and shed millions of low-wage laborers who can no longer compete with the cost efficiency, quality control, and speed of delivery achieved by automated manufacturing."[63] Jobs are being lost in "all three key employment sectors—agriculture, manufacturing, and services—[because] machines are quickly replacing human labor."[64] In terms of another economic shortcoming associated with globalization, critics point to growing income and wealth disparities nationally and globally associated with the spread of free-market capitalism. To illustrate the point, the income gap between the bottom 20 percent and the top 20 percent of the world's population has more than doubled since 1950, growing from 30 times in 1950 to more than 60 times as large today.[65]

In terms of other economic drawbacks for nation states, critics point to threats associated with the homogenization of global culture.[66] They point out that the push for standardization of markets within the Western conceptual framework serves to diminish the viability of traditional local cultures and tastes. Threats to local cultures and the traditional communities from which they spring are of concern, since any losses of cultural diversity are believed to impoverish the earth. This viewpoint draws on the idea propounded by environmentalists that biological diversity is a precious global resource worthy of protection because it ensures ecosystem resilience beneficial to humans and all of life. In a similar vein, loss of cultural diversity is seen as a degradation of world culture, which also increases vulnerability and endangers humanity. Critics also argue that economic globalization serves to undermine national economic, health, safety, and environmental standards. All such standards come to be seen as trade barriers that harm a county's competitive standing in a free-trade world. "Wage raises, environmental protection, national health insurance, and liability lawsuits—anything that raises the cost of production and makes a corporation less competitive—threatens [a country's] economy."[67] As summed up by one critic, "free international trade encourages industries to shift their production activities to the countries that have the lowest standards of cost internalization."[68] "In effect, unrestricted trade imposes lower standards."[69] In what is seen as a "race to the bottom," transnational corporations "are free to scour the globe and establish themselves wherever labor is the cheapest, environmental laws are the laxest, fiscal regimes are the least onerous, and subsidies are the most generous."[70]

Critics of economic globalization also fault its ongoing destruction of local communities and their economies. They consider globalization to be a zero-sum game, where "the global economy ... can only expand at the expense of the local economy, whose environment it degrades, whose communities it destroys, and whose resources (land, forests, water, and labor) it systematically appropriates for its own use."[71] They point to "the marginalization of local banks, local financial services, and professional services"[72] that undermine the ability to carry out local commerce and sustain local economies. Critics lament the globalization pressures that force a shift from "an inward-looking import-substitution industrialization model of development" to "an export-oriented economic model,"[73] believing this effectively destroys activities capable of supporting local economies. They condemn the spread of corporate agribusiness under globalization, noting that under its growing dominance "family-farm agriculture and the rural communities that depend on it are destroyed."[74] Naysayers criticize the huge public subsidies for large-scale industrial infrastructure associated with globalization, claiming it "allows goods produced on a large scale and transported long distances to be sold at artificially low prices—in many cases at lower prices than goods produced locally."[75] They argue that if the true "costs of increased transport were properly internalized, much of world trade would be revealed as uneconomic."[76] The combined effects of these influences devastate local economies and their communities. As one observer notes, the "rapid replacement of secure jobs by short-term contracts, part-time or lower-paid work, or unemployment sharply reduces overall effective purchasing power and is introducing a spreading culture of insecurity."[77] Critics of globalization point to the social or psychological dimensions of that insecurity: "[T]he stress, the loneliness, the fear of growing old."[78] In response to these threats, critics suggest an alternative system for the preservation of local communities, economies, and livelihoods, which they envision as "a return to the security provided by local self-sufficiency that emphasizes local economic control and local production for local consumption."[79]

Some of the most damning criticism of economic globalization has come from those who address its environmental and ecological consequences. Critics point out that the principle consequence of globalization will be to "intensify competition for already overstressed environmental space" and that "this intensified competition accelerates destruction of the regenerative capacities of the ecosystem on which we and future generations depend."[80] They believe "our environment is becoming ever less capable of sustaining the growing impact of our economic activities."[81] Ecological economist Herman E. Daly has expressed his belief that we have already surpassed the ecological capacity of the planet to sustain further growth in the following terms: "The regenerative and assimilative capacities of the biosphere cannot support even the current levels of resource consumption, much less the manifold increase required to generalize the higher standards worldwide."[82] Daly clearly dismisses prospects for multiplying the scale of the human economy by a factor of 5 to 10 as called for by the Brundtland Commission in its 1989 report on a global transition to sustainable development. He points to research findings by Vitousek and others from the mid-1980s showing the human economy had already preempted 40 percent of the global net primary product (NPP) of photosynthesis.[83] He recognizes that even a single doubling of the human economy would move it toward appropriating all of global NPP, and that this could only occur at the expense of other species. As he sees it, "it is ridiculous to urge the preservation of biodiversity without being willing to halt the economic growth that requires human takeover of all places in the sun now occupied by other species."[84] Daly is not alone in believing the human enterprise has already exceeded the planet's ecological carrying capacity. A growing number of voices argue that "the services [nature] offers as source and sink for economic growth have become depleted or saturated"[85] and that "we have reached the limits of the ecosystem's regenerative and assimilative capacities."[86] It turns out the first limits to have been exceeded "are not the limits to nonrenewable resource exploitation, as many once anticipated, but rather the limits to renewable resources and to the environment's *sink functions*— its ability to absorb our wastes."[87] The most pressing of those limits has turned out to be the planet's ability to absorb CO_2 emissions. As Robert Goodland has observed, "[c]limate change is a compelling indication that limits have been exceeded because it is globally pervasive rather than limited to the atmosphere of the region where the CO_2 is generated."[88] These critics believe the current global economic paradigm has "led us to the near breakdown of the natural world,"[89] and that "the world is on the verge of an ecological holocaust."[90] They therefore reject a global economic system based on growth, and argue "we have no real option other than to adapt our economic institutions to the reality of a 'full world'."[91]

Previously noted criticisms of economic globalization have produced resounding condemnations of current efforts to extend free-market capitalism to every nation state on the planet. Critics point out that world GNP increased by five times, and world trade by 12 times, during the latter half of the twentieth century. Rather than alleviating problems of poverty, unemployment, malnutrition, homelessness, disease, and environmental disruption, critics point to data indicating that these problems have become more serious and more widespread.[92] They therefore express sarcastic skepticism about prospective outcomes associated with further globalization along the following lines:

> We are now being asked to believe that the development processes that have further impoverished people and devastated the planet will lead to diametrically different and highly beneficial outcomes, if only they can be accelerated and applied everywhere, freely, without restriction; that is, when they are *globalized*.[93]

In light of what they see as "disastrous social and environmental consequences of economic globalization,"[94] they reject the worldview that "economic growth … is the central panacea for our problems … [and argue it is] actually the source of, rather than the solution to, our problems."[95] These critics dismiss outright "the preposterousness of the very idea that, on a finite earth, an economic system based on limitless growth can be supported."[96] They argue "it is impossible for the world economy to grow its way out of poverty and environmental degradation."[97] They renounce the claim that growth may somehow be transformed into sustainable behavior, simply asserting *"sustainable growth is impossible."*[98] As an alternative, they make the case for *sustainable development* without growth, which they define as "qualitative improvement of a physical economic base that is maintained in a steady state by a throughput of matter-energy that is within the regenerative and assimilative capacities of the ecosystem."[99]

Defenders of the growth imperative tend to respond with reforms they believe will make ongoing growth possible. In addition to vacuous references to "sustainable growth" as an actual option, they often suggest strategies that would permit "the use of markets and capitalist tools to protect nature"[100] under ongoing growth. A commonly suggested tool is that of incorporating the cost of externalities into market prices so consumers pay the true cost of purchased items. Under economic reasoning, the realization of market efficiencies is premised on the absence of such externalities. It is therefore assumed "that all external costs and benefits must be 'internalized' in the money price paid by whoever buys the good or service the production of which gave rise to the external cost."[101] It is suggested that if we can "make prices tell the ecological truth"[102] the marketplace will automatically redirect business activity toward "green" enterprises that respect the environment. This line of reasoning seems incapable of recognizing that such a greening of businesses merely represents a different market-expansion program, which may reduce environmental impacts in the short term but is also destined to exceed natural limits under ongoing growth. Green growth is just as unsustainable as traditional forms of material expansion. Another proffered tool for maintaining growth while protecting the environment is alternatively referred to as "eco-efficiency" or "dematerialization." This approach suggests "growth [can] be delinked from a rising consumption of energy and materials"[103] by using such inputs with ever greater efficiencies. As described by one analyst, "[e]co-efficiency … is about reducing the amount of water, energy, chemicals, and raw materials used per unit of output."[104] "It is, fundamentally, a strategy for achieving economic growth by continuously increasing the productivity of natural resources, in contrast to the present strategy of achieving growth by increasing the productivity of labor through the use of material capital and energy."[105] This train of thought seems unable to comprehend that if "the dynamics of growth are not slowed down [or stopped], the achievements of rationalization [i.e., greater realized efficiencies] will soon be eaten up by the next round of growth."[106] As one observer of recent trends recognizes, "any gains in ... efficiency are simply being swamped by the sheer scale of rising aspirations and an increasing population."[107] This preoccupation with eco-efficiency and/ or dematerialization seems incapable of recognizing that "[e]fficiency without sufficiency is counterproductive; the latter must define the boundaries of the former."[108] In the end, any attempts to reform free-market capitalism without understanding its inherent allegiance to growth, and without conceding the inherently unsustainable nature of material growth, are inevitably destined to fail.

The challenges associated with rejecting the growth imperative are compounded by the associated implication that any transition to a sustainable future will also require a rejection of one of the basic tenets of free-market capitalism: Its unwavering commitment to sustained economic growth. That commitment stems from some of the fundamental features of capitalism that make it possible to think of any national economy under capitalism as "a perpetual growth machine."[109] "A fundamental part of the modern capitalist system is the payment of interest on borrowed money."[110] So "part of the endless-economic-growth model is in place right from the beginning—without growth, you can't pay off the interest."[111] If an individual borrows $10,000 at 10 percent interest, they will have to come up with the extra $1,000 they will owe 12 months later. To avoid taking that money out of their salary or savings, they would need to invest in a business enterprise that yielded at least a 10 percent return, so they can pay the interest from the enterprise's profits. Those corporate profits come from growth, so corporations are also driven to expand their operations. Like individuals, corporations become captives of a debt-service obligation that commits them to future growth. They sell shares or borrow money to finance expansion, with loans repaid out of future profits. "To carry the debt-service load, future profits must be larger than present ones. Thus by borrowing money at fixed rates of interest, a firm stakes its actual survival on its future growth."[112] This explains the previously noted claim that the profit imperative and the growth imperative represent the most fundamental corporate drives. Higher rates of growth mean higher rates of profit, and the rate of profit matters because the "growth imperative works on Darwinian principles: it ensures that only the fastest-growing businesses ... survive."[113] Capital markets that provide money to corporations therefore represent another fundamental aspect of the capitalist system that drives ongoing growth. They provide financing on the basis of which firms promise the greatest profits. There may have been a time when merely being profitable was sufficient, but in the current era "a company's profits and stock value [have] had to increase over the next quarter or the firm was considered unworthy of investment."[114] "Corporations live or die by whether they can sustain growth. Growth determines relationships to investors, to the stock market, to banks, and to public perception."[115] The commitment to profit maximization through ongoing growth naturally leads to material expansion that by definition constitutes unsustainable behavior, but corporations under capitalism are clearly more interested in profit than sustainability. It would, therefore, be no exaggeration to claim that corporations under capitalism are addicted to growth. The marketplace of a capitalist economy therefore drives growth within the private sector in a number of distinct ways, particularly with respect to the role of interest and built-in requirements for growing profit margins. But the noted growth addiction is not limited to the private sector. "Governments are just as addicted to economic growth as is the private sector ... [because] they have made financial commitments to their present citizens—mainly social security and pensions—that can only be met out of future growth."[116] The current reality with respect to unwavering support for continued growth has been summed up aptly in the following terms: "For both firms and governments, growth of output, sales, profits, and tax revenues is necessary for financial survival. To unhook the economy from its growth fixation will be a difficult undertaking indeed."[117]

At the onset of the twenty-first century there is no evidence of a willingness to give up on the notion that economic growth represents progress. International and national initiatives continue to demonstrate the sort of singular commitment to ongoing growth that Herman Daly categorized as growthmania, i.e., the paradigm or mindset that always puts economic growth in first place. The World Bank and the International Monetary Fund continue to provide debtor countries with "standby loans" if they undergo "structural adjustment programs" (SAPs) supposedly "designed to make their economies more efficient and better capable of sustained growth."[118] These SAPs include requirements to: Remove restrictions on foreign investment, reorient an economy toward exports to earn the foreign exchange required for servicing debt, reduce wages or wage increases to make exports more "competitive," cut tariffs, devalue the local currency, privatize state enterprises, and undertake a deregulation program. The structural adjustment programs are clearly intended to further worldwide economic growth under economic globalization. Under the General Agreement on Tariffs and Trade (GATT) the World Trade Organization (WTO) has been given far-reaching power to rule against any national or local laws considered to represent trade barriers. In protecting global free trade, "GATT [has] further accelerated global economic growth and development by removing all constraints on trade, regardless of social, ecological, and moral implications."[119] In terms of national initiatives evidencing a continued fealty to ongoing economic growth, one need look no further than the "stimulus" expenditures on the part of nation states in response to the serious global recession that started in the United States during the last quarter of 2007. Countries spent trillions of dollars in efforts to jumpstart their lagging national economies, often acting in concert in an attempt to revive the global growth machine. These international and national initiatives reveal a continued unwavering commitment to further economic growth, in spite of "the incontrovertible empirical evidence that economic globalization can only increase the problems we face today."[120] The initiatives also reflect an inability "to accept that economic growth is no longer a valid public policy priority"[121] in light of mounting evidence the human enterprise has already surpassed global ecological limits to growth. They demonstrate no willingness to consider the proposition that the major problems confronting humankind at the beginning of the twenty-first century are all "intimately tied to growth,"[122] or to entertain the more radical proposition that they are all *caused* by growth. To accept that growth is actually the source of, rather than the solution to, our problems would require rejecting virtually all of the basic tenets of free-market capitalism, i.e., its association with the ideas that economic growth represents human progress, that free markets result in the most efficient and socially optimal allocation of resources, that globalization is generally beneficial to everyone because it increases economic efficiency and growth, that competitive behavior is more rational for the individual and the firm and more beneficial to society than cooperative behavior, that some of the fundamental features of capitalism like interest on borrowed money and the profit motive are socially beneficial, and so on. In short, rejection of these tenets would require what academics refer to as a revolutionary paradigm shift in traditional ways of thinking. Noted international and national initiatives reflect an ongoing commitment to the historical growth imperative rather than any sort of initiation of a paradigm shift. An understanding of the obstacles in the way of such a paradigm shift, even when it would appear to be necessary for the very survival of civilization, warrant consideration, because proponents of a no-growth imperative will have to understand the challenges associated with transitioning to a stable, sustainable future.

A social paradigm may be thought of as the collection of beliefs, values, norms, and ideals that form the worldview of a culture.[123] An earlier mention of Daniel Quinn's novel *Ishmael* noted his reference to a culture being a people enacting a story, with that story representing a culture's paradigm or mindset. As Quinn puts it:

> Given a story to enact that puts [people] in accord with the world they will live in accord with the world. But given a story to enact that puts them at odds with the world … they will live at odds with the world.[124]

At another point in his novel Quinn writes that people are "captives of a civilizational system that more or less compels [them] to go on destroying the world in order to live," and that what holds them captive is their cultural story, which they continue to enact even when they recognize the story represents "rank mythology."[125] A similar sentiment has been expressed by Herman Daly and John Cobb in their book *For the Common Good* in the following terms:

"We are living by an ideology of death and accordingly we are destroying our own humanity and killing the planet."[126] The ideology playing out across the globe that is destroying the world is the ideology of growth. "Diverse cultures around the world have incorporated the growth imperative into their own dominant social paradigms. As a result we now have what may be described as a worldwide cultural network united in its pursuit of growth."[127] The fatal shortcomings of attempting to pursue infinite growth in a finite ecological system are being revealed, particularly with respect to the pursuit of unending economic growth. It is becoming "increasingly clear that the dominant economic paradigm is making poverty, social justice, and environmental degradation worse," so much so that it is possible to assert that there is evidence of a "collapsing paradigm."[128] Mounting evidence of existent ecological limits to further growth demands a rejection of the growth imperative driving current worldwide behavior. These ecological realities suggest that "[o]ur immediate goal must be to break out of the processes of thought that imprison us."[129] Humanity is in desperate need of a new paradigm, mindset, or cultural story that no longer equates growth with progress. Ongoing growth is currently dismantling the life-support apparatus that the planet's ecosystems represent. The future of civilization and much of life depend upon ending the view of demographic, economic, and urban increases as positive occurrences. However, abandoning an existing paradigm, mindset, or cultural story ends up being an extremely challenging exercise. With respect to changing attitudes about the growth fixation embedded in free-market capitalism, it has been noted that its "tenets have become so deeply embedded within our institutions and popular culture that they are accepted by most people without question, much as the faithful take for granted the basic doctrines of their religious faith."[130] Realizing a paradigm shift to a new set of ideas to guide social behavior will undoubtedly test humanity's adaptability in unprecedented ways. The nature of the obstacles standing in the way of such a paradigm shift need to be understood by those seeking to replace the current growth imperative with a new no-growth imperative, if there is to be any hope of realizing a sustainable future. Letting go of the current pro-growth mythology will be extremely difficult, but absolutely essential if the human enterprise is to survive beyond the twenty-first century.

Some of the challenges of realizing a paradigm shift are elucidated in Simon Singh's treatment of such shifts within the sciences as part of his book on cosmology. Many of his observations certainly pertain to social paradigm shifts that have nothing to do with the natural sciences. With respect to pro-growth mythology impeding a transition to a sustainable trajectory for the human enterprise, Singh notes that myths play a critical role in explaining complicated and important aspects of the world for all cultures, and that "every myth represents the absolute truth within its society."[131] He points out that "[t]he word 'myth' is derived from the Greek word *mythos*, which can mean 'story', but also means 'word', in the sense of 'the final word'."[132] As a result, "anyone who dared to question these explanations would have laid themselves open to accusations of heresy."[133] Individuals in many cultures "would not dare to question their own mythology ... [because] each mythology [represents] an article of faith within its own society."[134] When people have spent their entire lives convinced of the truth of their culture's mythology, as in the case of the historical support for pro-growth mythology, it is understandable that they are "unable to make the intellectual or emotional leap"[135] required for the acceptance of a new paradigm that completely counters or negates their earlier cultural story. There is a "natural conservatism and ingrained respect for the existing paradigm,"[136] that serves to impede paradigm shifts even when such shifts are essential for a culture's survival.

Singh addresses the actual process of paradigm shifts by referencing Thomas S. Kuhn's treatment of these shifts in his 1962 book *The Structure of Scientific Revolutions*, in which Kuhn described the process as a "series of peaceful interludes punctuated by intellectually violent revolutions."[137] The periods of peaceful interludes represent time intervals when paradigms gradually evolve, "but every so often [under changing realities] there would need to be a major shift in thinking, known as a paradigm shift."[138] Singh points out that historically "the shift from one paradigm to another could happen only once the new paradigm was properly fleshed out and the old paradigm had been fully discredited."[139] Paradigm shifts have only occurred when "the case in favor of the new model became overwhelming, and [society] discarded its old model in favor of the new model."[140]

As for the time periods required for such revolutionary paradigm shifts, Singh suggests the path from an old paradigm to a new one may be several decades long, which he views as a comparatively short timeframe for eliminating an old paradigm that might have prevailed for centuries.[141] He even concedes a role for death as part of the process of paradigm shifts, citing the physicist Max Planck, who felt that in science important "innovation rarely makes its way by gradually winning over and converting its opponents, [instead] what does happen is that its opponents gradually die out, and the growing generation is familiarized with the ideas from the beginning."[142] Unfortunately, according to climatologists we do not have several decades to realize a paradigm shift away from the current growth paradigm's dependence upon fossil fuels and the related unending expansion of the human enterprise. A much quicker transition to a no-growth state is imperative if civilization is to avert disastrous climate change. The point illustrated previously is that international and national initiatives evidence nothing in the way of the needed paradigm shift. Subsequent descriptions of state and regional initiatives in the United States portray a similar absence of any movement toward a paradigm shift that embraces the no-growth imperative and a stable, sustainable future. With no evidence of any shift toward this new paradigm at any jurisdictional level beyond local communities, the increasing demonstration of a willingness to entertain a no-growth option within local settings suggests the needed paradigm shift might most effectively be pursued locally.

The impediment of state growth mandates

During the last decade of the twentieth century, authorities on American government linked the respective growth orientations at federal and state levels in the following terms: "Progrowth views still hold sway at the state and federal levels."[143] By the 1990s evidence of state governments' active involvement in the promotion of growth through economic development programs was being demonstrated in multiple ways. The most ubiquitous evidence appeared in virtually every state in the form of marketing efforts for economic development. Those efforts typically included promotion of a state's general image, development of tourism, advertisement of economic advantages, and creation of financial incentives packages. During the last decades of the century states seemed determined to outdo each other by providing significant incentives in terms of tax breaks and other subsidies to attract major companies.[144] In more specific terms, states revealed their pro-growth orientations via a broad array of mechanisms: Financial incentives (e.g., grants, loans, interest subsidies, etc.), tax incentives (e.g., job credits, investment credits, sales tax abatements, etc.), infrastructure development assistance (e.g., grants, loans, interest subsidies, etc.), and nonfinancial assistance (e.g., site selection, job training, business procurement assistance, etc.).[145] In short, the states clearly demonstrated pro-growth biases in multiple ways before the end of the last century. However, some of the strongest evidence of a pro-growth orientation appeared in the form of growth-promotion or growth-mandate provisions written into state-wide growth-management acts passed from the 1960s through the 1990s. As noted earlier, all of these statewide laws contain provisions to promote ongoing growth, and in eight of the 11 states the laws actually mandate ongoing growth accommodation by local governments. A quick review of some of the wording contained in those statewide laws will illustrate the extent to which these legislative enactments promote or require continued growth accommodation, and in the process erase all doubt about the nature of the pro-growth orientations in states that had passed such laws prior to 2000.

The pro-growth bias in statewide growth-management laws passed during the 1960s through the 1990s is clearly evident in specific requirements that the legislative enactments imposed on local governments. Hawaii's statute required urban districts to include "a sufficient reserve area for foreseeable urban growth."[146] Vermont's law called on planning at all local levels to provide for "reasonable expected population increase and economic growth."[147] Florida's legislation required local land-use plans to indicate the "amount of land required to accommodate anticipated growth."[148] Oregon's law required local governments to designate urban growth boundaries based on the "demonstrated need to accommodate long-range urban population growth requirements."[149] The New Jersey statute called for a state plan that would identify "growth areas" in the most densely populated state in the nation, and for local plans to be consistent with such a designation.[150] Maine's legislation required local governments to prepare plans designating "growth areas ... suitable for orderly ... development forecast for the next ten years" and a "capital investment plan ... to meet projected growth and development."[151] Rhode Island's law contained language stating the intent of the Act was to "establish a procedure in comprehensive planning at state and municipal levels which will accommodate future requirements."[152] Georgia's statewide law listed the duties of local governments, including "the development, promotion, and retention of trade, commerce, industry, and employment opportunities."[153] Legislation in the state of Washington required local governments to designate "urban growth areas" and then to revise them at least every 10 years "to accommodate the urban growth projected to occur in ... the succeeding twenty-year period."[154] Maryland's law mandated that all local plans contain a land development regulations element "which encourages ... economic growth in areas designated for growth in the plan."[155] Tennessee's 1998 act required municipalities to designate urban growth boundaries that were "reasonably compact yet sufficiently large to accommodate residential and nonresidential growth projected to occur during the next twenty (20) years."[156] Growth-promotion provisions in all of these statewide growth-management laws, and actual growth-mandate provisions in eight out of the 11 statewide enactments, offer further insights into the pro-growth orientations of state legislatures through the end of the last century. As the nation transitioned into a new millennium, states continued to evidence an ongoing loyalty to the growth imperative that was demonstrated in multiple ways.

The transition from statewide growth-management laws to statewide "smart-growth" enactments, undertaken during the last years of the 1990s and continued into the new century, reflected a continuing allegiance to ongoing growth. Earlier cited research findings indicate that these "smart-growth" bills have been "much more pro-growth and much less pro-conservation" than statewide growth-management laws passed through 1998. These "smart-growth" laws reflect nothing in the way of a recognition that growth may now represent the antithesis of societal progress. State legislatures continue to fund state economic development offices to promote ongoing growth. During the national recession that began during the last quarter of 2007, some state legislatures initiated their own state "stimulus" packages to supplement federal efforts to revive economic growth in response to state budgets that were experiencing deficits of tens of billions of dollars. Many states have, like the federal government, made financial commitments to their present citizens, as with state pension programs, that are highly dependent on future growth to meet the state's obligations. States are also subject to the financial trap driving the federal government, where the ability to fund social programs for an expanding population depends on increasing tax revenues flowing from a growing economy. In short, states, like the federal government, are captives of the growth imperative, seeing their financial survival directly tied to ongoing economic growth. With such a mindset, it is easy to understand the passage of statewide laws that promote, or actually *mandate*, continued growth by local political jurisdictions.

State laws that force ongoing growth on local governments in effect represent state mandates to continue unsustainable behavior. These laws reveal that the states are fully committed to the traditional paradigm that equates growth with societal progress. Rather than showing a willingness to reconsider the merit of further growth, the states appear wedded to the old paradigm. To maintain that loyalty they are responding to challenges to the growth paradigm by initiating "smart-growth" and/or "sustainable-growth" programs, seeking merely to reform growth as opposed to questioning it. Mounting problems associated with ecological limits will rapidly reveal the shortcomings of these programs, but in the near term they serve as serious impediments to local efforts to implement truly sustainable futures based on a no-growth path. In short, the states are effectively inhibiting a paradigm shift that embraces the no-growth imperative and opens the door to a stable, sustainable future for America's communities. As noted previously, state growth mandates put local jurisdictions in the position of having to litigate their rights to protect the health, safety, and general welfare of their citizens when they believe that further growth no longer serves the public interest. While support for a no-growth imperative therefore seems unlikely to emerge in the near future from either the federal or state governments, the possible role of regional jurisdictions or regional mindsets in affecting the needed paradigm shift seems more promising.

Beyond regionalism to bioregionalism as an organizing framework for no growth

Regional organizations have historically played a minor role within the nation's political framework. While nearly 90 percent of local governments are served by regional planning organizations, these entities have largely been powerless in terms of affecting ongoing growth. Prior to the passage of statewide growth-management laws granting some regional organizations specific roles in implementing growth-management agendas, they had largely been limited to creating regional land-use and transportation plans, providing technical assistance to local governments, and acting as forums for inter-governmental communication. The growth-management era changed this in some of the states with statewide growth-management laws by assigning regional organizations new powers. These new powers included the authority to review local plans for consistency with regional initiatives (Georgia), issue permits for all development activity over a minimum size (Vermont), appeal local development orders for developments of regional impact to a state commission where they could be vacated (Florida), and in the case of Portland's regional agency prepare and implement regional capital improvement plans and manage the region's urban growth boundary (Oregon).[157] Since state legislation awarded these new extralocal powers to regional entities, one would expect the regional organizations to be bound by the pro-growth biases of state legislatures that awarded the powers, and that has in fact been the case. As one observer has noted: "Far from stifling growth, these extralocal programs focus on the need to accommodate new development and have been shown to promote economic expansion."[158] These granted extralocal powers therefore failed to prompt any movement toward the needed paradigm shift that would replace the growth imperative with a no-growth imperative. However, some other regional initiatives carried out under state legislative enactments during the growth-management era have reflected a willingness to consider a different growth orientation in the form of significant growth controls. These examples illustrate a recognition of the need to impose substantial new controls in response to pressing threats to unique environmental resources, as when development pressures endangered the California Coastline, Lake Tahoe, and the Pinelands in New Jersey.[159]

The California Coastal Act of 1976 was adopted in response to a 1972 statewide initiative measure mandating state intervention in local coastal planning. The act established a state Coastal Commission, and six interim regional commissions, to oversee local planning and permitting activities in a designated coastal zone. Until local coastal programs were certified as being consistent with conservation and development policies set forth in the act, the regional commissions controlled the issuance of all development permits. The commissions imposed heightened standards or limitations on all development, which resulted in significant reductions in the permitted intensity of development within the coastal zone. In 1969 an interstate compact signed by California and Nevada created a bistate regional planning agency to oversee planning and regulation of development in the Lake Tahoe basin. The Tahoe Regional Planning Agency (TRPA) was established to protect the basin from environmental degradation, with a specific focus on the water quality of Lake Tahoe. Prior to adoption of the TRPA regional plan, which under the interstate compact was directed to be based on an assessment of "environmental threshold carrying capacities," interim regulation of the Tahoe basin was effected by the California Tahoe Regional Planning Agency (CTRPA). While the TRPA proved unwilling or unable to provide meaningful limits to continued growth prior to the adoption of the TRPA regional plan in 1984, the CTRPA developed a comprehensive land-use ordinance for the California side of the lake that included downzoning all residential areas not already built out. A third example of a regional body acting to significantly reduce growth options in an environmentally sensitive area was initiated by passage of the Pinelands Protection Act in 1979. The act created a regional commission with planning and regulatory authority over 55 municipalities and seven counties situated within a million acres of unique and environmentally vulnerable lands in southern New Jersey. The commission created a Comprehensive Management Plan for the Pinelands that included a "land use capability map," which indicated preservation areas slated for no development and protection areas allowing only limited development. While none of the three noted regional initiatives actually served to *stop* further growth, they all realized significant *control* of further development that closed out many growth options that had existed prior to the adoption of the regional planning and regulatory frameworks. All three initiatives reflected a recognition that environmental protection could not be effectively addressed by local jurisdictions, and instead required a regional framework to adequately address regionwide problems. The initiatives also reflected a willingness to recognize an inherent conflict between ongoing growth and environmental protection in at least some areas. As evidence builds of existent global ecological limits to further growth, these regional responses to set environmental limits suggest a possible route for effectuating a transition to stable, sustainable communities within bioregions capable of sustaining them indefinitely. The use of regional entities to implement a paradigm shift to sustainable behavior under a no-growth imperative appears possible given the former evidence of such entities having already demonstrated an ability to act on a different growth orientation. That regional bodies might possibly play such a role is strongly reinforced by a school of thought known as bioregionalism. A review of the first principles and major tenets of bioregionalism can illustrate the degree to which its principles and tenets are supportive of a societal rejection of the growth imperative and the associated adoption of a no-growth imperative.

The antecedents of bioregionalism can be traced back to the progenitors of regionalism in Europe and America during the nineteenth and twentieth centuries, when Patrick Geddes, Frederick Jackson Turner, Howard Odum, and Lewis Mumford made the case for a necessary new structural framework based on regions.[160] In this sense, bioregionalism may be "viewed as only the latest reincarnation of a centuries long effort to define how socially-just and ecologically sustainable human cultures could be created and sustained."[161] With respect to more recent antecedents, bioregionalists have been described as "heirs to the back-to-the-land and appropriate technology movements of the 1960s and 1970s."[162] However, the contemporary bioregionalism movement has its real roots in the mid-1970s, when Peter Berg and Raymond Dasmann established the Planet Drum Foundation and began a process of expounding bioregional theory and practice.[163] An extensive and rich body of literature produced since the mid-1970s has served to advance the development of a more complete framework of bioregional theory and practice. Those writings serve as a source for both the first principles of bioregionalism and its major tenets.

In terms of the first principles of bioregionalism, Kirkpatrick Sale has grouped those principles under the headings of scale (region, community), economy (conservation, stability, self-sufficiency, cooperation), polity (decentralization, complementarity, diversity), and society (symbiosis, evolution, division).[164] Bioregionalists believe we are in the midst of a "deep civilization crisis,"[165] due in large part to our estrangement from the natural world. Surviving that crisis is, in turn, assumed to involve "transformative social change" if we are to overcome the existing state of "ecological peril."[166] In this sense, bioregionalism is seen as nothing less than a "means of arresting the impending ecological apocalypse."[167] Bioregionalists advocate "a theory and practice that promises to radically change the world so that we may all survive."[168] They argue that "most of our lately-accustomed ways—of thought, perception, society, tenure, and livelihood—will have to be radically reshaped towards sustainability."[169] This radical transformation, it is assumed, "requires basic changes in present-day social directions, economics, and politics."[170] Some sense of the nature of these basic social, economic, and political changes is revealed in Sale's treatment of the above-noted first principles of bioregionalism and other related works.

In terms of implications for *social change*, bioregionalism calls for a rejection of current trends toward the creation of a global monoculture and instead proposes a process of ongoing division or differentiation based on the unique attributes of specific regions. Socially, it advocates a form of self-liberation into a closer relationship with the land and the community of a region, specifically involving communitarian values of cooperation, participation, solidarity, and reciprocity. A key part of the social transformation also embodies a shift to a speciate humility, which embodies "a profound sense of interconnectedness between individuals and nature" and produces a "way of thinking and acting that respects and cares for the natural world."[171] With respect to implications for *economic change*, bioregionalism condemns "the general transformation of community-based economies into large-scale, formal economies which support mass production and overconsumption."[172] Rejecting the quest for unending economic expansion and the associated promotion of world trade that they consider ecologically devastating, bioregionalists instead advocate for "localized and self-sufficient economies" that represent "a degree of self-reliance … summing to the carrying capacity of the region in question."[173] With the "goal of economic activity" under bioregionalism being "to achieve the highest possible level of cooperative self-reliance"[174] within all regions, bioregionalists believe trade should be limited to the exchange of true ecological surpluses between regions.[175] Under bioregional reasoning economic activity would, therefore, have to shift from its current preoccupation with exploitation and growth to a new focus on conservation and stability. As for what bioregionalism implies in terms of *political change*, its central emphasis is on the "devolution of power to ecologically and culturally defined bioregions."[176] Bioregionalists refer to a "politics of place"[177] or a "native life-place politics"[178] that makes possible the fulfillment of "a crucial bioregional value—the redistribution of decision-making to semi-autonomous territories."[179] Bioregional politics may therefore be thought of as "the politics of scale, of decentralization, the politics of cultural autonomy and *self*-government."[180] Since "[p]lace-based bioregionalists stress the importance of bottom-up, grass-roots and organic activity,"[181] they advocate replacing existing political institutions with a new, home-grown politics based on regions defined by natural boundaries.

As these descriptions of what bioregionalism implies with respect to social, economic, and political changes illustrate, the first principles of bioregional thinking represent a call for radical cultural transformation. Socially, bioregionalists envision differentiated communities governed by communitarian values (i.e., cooperation, participation, solidarity, and reciprocity) that are respectful of nature. Politically, they envisage a diverse, decentralized form of home-grown politics based on regions defined by natural boundaries. Economically, they visualize stable, localized, self-sufficient communities that exhibit a cooperative self-reliance. However, the implications for change extend beyond those noted in social, economic, and political terms. Bioregionalism also embodies a number of tenets that suggest additional radical changes as part of the envisioned cultural transformation. Those tenets are: Espousal of the primacy of sustainability; advocacy of an ecological worldview; defense of diversity; acceptance of limits to growth; adoption of a regional consciousness; endorsement of a land ethic; protection of local and regional cultures; and promotion of small communities. An overview of these tenets will further illustrate the extent to which bioregionalism affords an alternative worldview to the current growth-based paradigm, as well as reveal the value of this different mindset in attempting to envision the prospective nature of no-growth communities.

Sustainability is emphasized above all else in definitions of bioregionalism. Bioregionalists believe that "mainstream development continues down the route of unsustainability"[182] and in the process threatens the survival of both culture and nature. In response they espouse the primacy of sustainability and argue that "bioregionalism prescribes an ecologically necessary antidote to nonsustainable modern society."[183] For bioregionalists *"the* key reason for moving in a bioregional direction is to improve the interaction between humans and nature, to strive for a place in which natural and human communities are sustainable."[184] However, while "bioregionalism promotes the notion of sustainability of nature and culture over time,"[185] bioregionalists place their greatest emphasis on "ecosystem-based sustainability."[186] They concede all other forms of sustainability are dependent on "preservation and restoration of native diversity and ecosystem health."[187] For them a "sustainable future would first of all have to be based on a local commitment to restore and maintain the river, soil, forests, and wildlife that ultimately support inhabitation."[188] So for bioregionalists, it may truly be argued that "bioregionalism is about sustainability above all else,"[189] and specifically about a primary commitment to ecological sustainability.

A commitment to ecological sustainability naturally produces advocacy of an *ecological worldview*. Bioregionalism emerged as "a response to the perception that human societies were becoming alienated from the natural environment."[190] Bioregionalists believe that the current ecological crisis represented by the loss of ecosystems and biological diversity may be attributed to our alienation from the natural world, as illustrated by our "distance from nature and lack of knowledge and respect for its cycles and systems."[191] For them the only appropriate response is "a new collective renaissance grounded in ecological principles."[192] Theirs is "a call to reconstitute human society on the basis of a 'harmonization' with ecological laws of nature."[193] Bioregionalists hold the "belief that social relations ought to be derived from and governed by the local biophysical environment."[194] They believe in "the existence of ecological laws that will guide the positive transformation of bioregion-based societies."[195] For them a viable future is dependent upon people being "informed by the biological and geological truths of home places."[196] They therefore argue that "humanity needs to cultivate an ecological consciousness"[197] that will permit "the construction of an ecological identity,"[198] which will in turn produce a state "where nature is the model for culture."[199] At that point they believe it will be possible for people to develop a "deep and lasting relationship with the natural life-support systems"[200] that make human culture possible. Such a relationship with the natural world would produce "respect for the integrity of ... ecological communities"[201] and advance the "integration of human communities into their supporting ecosystems"[202] that bioregionalists consider to be so crucial to the attainment of a sustainable future. In practical terms, advocacy of an ecological worldview by bioregionalists translates into a commitment to protect the integrity of regional ecosystems.

A commitment to the integrity of regional ecosystems naturally produces a defense of biological *diversity*. Bioregionalists state the obvious when they note "that human life depends ultimately on the continuation of other life."[203] "From their biocentric viewpoint, human society is ultimately based on interdependence with other forms of life."[204] For bioregionalists human "culture is predicated upon biological integrities."[205] They therefore place great value on the maintenance and restoration of a region's biological integrity. They would have humans "include the non-human in their sense of community"[206] and have us "teach and celebrate the interdependence of human beings with other forms of life."[207] In terms of what they consider to be a requisite shift to speciate humility, they see us as "applying for membership in a biotic community and ceasing to be its exploiter."[208] With this humility they see the possibility of humans moving to a state where we "encompass a union of nature and culture in which the sacredness of all life is honored."[209] At that point bioregionalists stress the need to adopt "bioregional strategies for ... restoration of the earth's natural plant and animal diversity within a bioregional framework."[210] Justification for this emphasis is offered in terms of an ecological law that equates biological diversity with ecological stability. From the bioregionalists' perspective this case for diversity in biological terms translates into a like support for cultural diversity.[211] They advocate resistance to current trends that move all cultures toward a global monoculture, and see the task as one "of turning the whole edifice around to face in the direction of the creation of particularity of culture."[212] They would "promote the diversity of biosocial experimentation ... [because] ... in diversity is stability."[213] Based on this line of reasoning, a central goal of bioregionalism "is to sustain, protect and restore cultural and biological diversity and ecosystem integrity."[214] Diversity may therefore be recognized as one of the catchwords of the bioregionalism movement and one of its central tenets.

In the same way that different definitions of bioregionalism reveal the tenets of sustainability, an ecological worldview, and diversity, they also portray a commitment to the tenet of *limits*. Bioregionalists accept the reality of mounting evidence of existent limits to growth and lament societal denial of that reality. "Reports are published on limits to growth, on the finite carrying capacity of the Earth ... yet economic and political strategies ... continue to be based on assumptions of indefinite exploitation and continued growth."[215] At the level of local governments, bioregionalists condemn "growth-dominated municipal planning processes."[216] Bioregionalists accept that "nature sets limits"[217] and make the case for "restricting growth and development to fit the limits"[218] of specific regions. The challenge as they see it is to "decipher ecological carrying capacity" and then to foster the "evolution of lifestyles that are consciously adapted to fit the limits and opportunities of localized ecosystem processes."[219] They envision a time when "human agency is reintegrated with ecological processes, especially through careful understanding of carrying capacity"[220] and "an enlightened future where regions self-organize to live sustainably within their carrying capacities over the long term."[221] As one commentator has noted, a bioregional society would be carefully attuned to its environment and "would know its carrying capacity and the limit of the population it could sustain, and all social strictures would be bent to assure the folly of overshoot was avoided."[222] With such an emphasis on deriving limits from "the carrying capacity of land and its ecological constraints," and the primacy afforded sustainability, bioregionalists clearly believe in "limits to growth" and include an acceptance of limits among the tenets that characterize bioregionalism.[223]

Bioregionalism also embodies a commitment to the development of a *regional consciousness*. Bioregionalists express "regret, even frustration, at the rootlessness of American culture in any particular place or natural setting."[224] They believe that psychologically "we have become a social order that is fundamentally placeless,"[225] that we are, for all practical purposes, living in a placeless society. For them bioregionalism is essentially a movement "to restore a sense of place,"[226] or a "process of rediscovering human connections to the land."[227] In this sense, bioregionalism is seen "as a diverse set of notions informed above all by a sense of place."[228] Bioregionalists speak of "oneness with place,"[229] "learning to live-in-place,"[230] "understanding place,"[231] "an acute sensibility to the uniqueness of ... place,"[232] "the importance of reinhabiting one's place and earthly home,"[233] and ultimately of the need for a "place-based cultural transformation."[234] For them "reinhabitation" is seen as "the work of making oneself sustainably at home"[235] in any given place, and "creating adaptive cultures that follow the unique characteristics of climate, watersheds, soils, land forms, and native plants and animals that define these places."[236] "In bioregional thought, [this] homeplace is sacred,"[237] a locale "where people and place are delicately interwoven in a web of life."[238] Bioregionalists extol individuals to make a long-term commitment to a "homeplace" so that they can learn to live respectfully in that place, "to fit into the place, which requires preserving the place to fit into."[239] With such a "sustained relatedness to a particular area or locality,"[240] bioregionalists believe people will be able to develop a relationship with nature characterized by sparing and preserving, and thereby initiate a sustainable relationship with the natural world.

The locally oriented and place-based future envisioned by bioregionalists is seen as occurring within the context of bioregions. As originally conceived, the bioregional notion "was seen as a kind of unifying principle, a way of thinking about land and life within a regional framework."[241] These regions are viewed as places where "specific human cultures and specific landscapes ... intertwine to create distinctive places."[242] While these places are acknowledged to be "geographical province[s] of marked ecological and often cultural unity,"[243] bioregionalists stress the importance of "natural systems as a reference for human agency."[244] A key aspect of bioregionalism is a "belief in the existence of natural regions."[245] These bioregions are assumed to "represent common biotic and abiotic entities,"[246] or "geophysically and ecologically coherent areas of territory,"[247] with their boundaries determined by hydrologic, physiographic, or biotic criteria. Bioregionalists believe existing political jurisdictions based on social rather than biophysical criteria constitute artificial constructs.[248] They note that "ecological boundaries do not correspond with existing ... jurisdictions," and that the "political lines human beings have drawn separate rather than unite diverse ecosystems, and as a consequence, are dubious in terms of what diverse species and ecosystems require."[249] Successful reinhabitation of place will, they believe, require us "to organize human activity—including political jurisdictions—according to the lay of the land"[250] instead of artificial social considerations.

The advocacy of a *land ethic* represents another key aspect of bioregionism.[251] For bioregionalists "it is clear that new ethics will be required if the kind of life envisioned in the bioregional paradigm is to be realized."[252] Bioregionalists believe "[b]ecoming native to a place—learning to live in it on a sustainable basis over time—is not just a matter of appropriate technology, home-grown food, or even 'reinhabiting' the city."[253] They feel "[i]t has very much to do with a shift in morality, in the attitudes and behaviors of human beings."[254] Bioregionalists are, therefore, in essence, advocating "the regional fulfillment of Aldo Leopold's 'land ethic.'"[255] More than half a century ago Leopold expressed that ethic in the following terms:

> The land ethic simply enlarges the boundaries of the community to include soils, waters, plants, and animals, or collectively the land ... . In short, a land ethic changes the role of *Homo sapiens* from conqueror of the land-community to plain citizen of it. It implies respect for his fellow-members, and also respect for the community as such.[256]

For bioregonalists "the health of the 'land community' becomes an ethical standard for human beings everywhere."[257] As Leopold expressed it, "[a] land ethic, then, reflects the existence of an ecological conscience, and this in turn reflects a conviction of individual responsibility for the health of the land."[258] Leopold's standard for right conduct was offered in the following terms:

"A thing is right when it tends to preserve the integrity, stability, and beauty of the biotic community. It is wrong when it tends otherwise."[259] While bioregionalists hold "a profound regard for all life,"[260] the ethical responsibility they advocate encompasses more than respect for all life forms and extends to the inanimate world as well. For them bioregionalism embodies an "enfranchise-ment of other life forms and land forms, and [a] respect for their destinies as intertwined with ours."[261] Bioregionalism therefore also "has an identity as a ... contemporary land ethic,"[262] a way "of thinking and acting that respects and cares for the natural world—our home."[263] Bioregionalists speak of "an ecologically sustainable land ethic"[264] that would "be guided by an ethic of humility" and "a restoration ethic."[265] Without such an ethical base bioregionalists believe it will be impossible to respect, protect, restore, and sustain the natural world in a fashion that ensures an indeterminate future for humans.

Yet another tenet of bioregionalism consists of the high regard that bioregionalists hold for *local and regional cultures*, "which they see as the last holdout against a global monoculture."[266] They lament "the ruthless homo-geneity of national culture"[267] resulting from "the spread of a universalist European model of cultural development which succeeds in breaking down indigenous cultural structures."[268] In opposition to the ongoing homo-genization of cultures occurring in all regional settings, they insist "on the need to base cultural life on the actualities of nature in its particularities of ecology and place."[269] Since "native cultures ... [are seen] as expressing the spirit of natural regions,"[270] bioregionalists attach considerable importance "to the place-based lifestyles and practices of the original bioregionalists, the native/indigenous/tribal societies."[271] Because they believe the "human con-nection with the land is often eloquently stated by the native people"[272] a "deeply rooted respect for indigenous thinking and peoples is a tenet funda-mental to bioregionalism."[273] Bioregionalists therefore seek to both "preserve ancient and traditional forms of knowledge"[274] and to "reviv[e] historic and folk modes of understanding [a] region."[275] However, bioregionalists are more than romantics attempting to revive the past; they also value contemporary, place-based knowledge. They see the challenge as one of developing "the potential of traditional and contemporary knowledge into a regionally self-reliant entity," which they see as an "approach ... concerned with developing around local conditions and resources, taking its cue from local culture."[276] In the end, "bioregionalism specifically values the local and the regional, seeing the revitalization of local places, peoples and cultures as perhaps the only sure way of healing the planet."[277]

The final tenet of bioregionalism to be considered here is the faith that bioregionalists place in the superiority of *small communities*. Considering decentralization an "ecological law,"[278] they believe that it is only within the context of small communities, and the bioregions that house them, that "at last human potential can match ecological reality."[279] Bioregionalists empha-size the need to "confront the environmental problematic posed by megacity regions," which they argue may be attributed to "the unsustainability of modern cities."[280] Ecological footprint analyses reveal large cities to be dependent on reliable supplies of material resources and waste absorption capacity existing elsewhere in the ecosphere. Seen in this light every large city is an "entropic black hole" existing on the resources and waste sinks of a vast and scattered hinterland many times the size of the city itself.[281] In ecological terms, these large cities are modes of pure consumption existing parasitically on a resource base vastly larger than themselves. With respect to carrying capacity, they are considered major culprits in the violation of the planet's carrying capacity. A key spokesperson for the bioregionalism movement has expressed the unsustainability of large, contemporary cities in the following terms:

> Cities aren't sustainable because they have become dependent on distant, rapidly shrinking sources for the basic essentials of food, water, energy and materials. At the same time they have severely damaged the health of the local systems upon which any sensible notion of sustainability must ultimately depend.[282]

For bioregionalists, the "vast scale of ecological damage … is directly attributable to the ways cities presently function."[283] The bioregional paradigm therefore calls for either "a radical restructuring of such cities" or suggests that it is "imperative to break them up altogether."[284] In broader terms, bioregionalism seeks "to provide a clear path along which … the megacity regions and the global economic system … can be dismantled before they self-destruct."[285]

Since bioregionalists consider large, contemporary cities to be "ecologically untenable,"[286] they suggest an alternative in the form of small, sustainable communities. It has been noted that "bioregionalism is … based on ecological and perceptual scales of place."[287] This orientation produces an automatic interest in "organic forms of human relatedness and governance"[288] that bioregionalists believe can best be realized in the context of small communities. For them small communities have distinct advantages in terms of using energy, recycling wastes, reducing resource draw-downs, and adjusting to carrying capacity. "Self-reliance, appropriate technology, local control, responsible stewardship of the land, are critical props to [the bioregionalists'] philosophy,"[289] and all are assumed to be furthered in the context of small communities. Bioregionalists believe small communities will make it possible to honor the carrying capacity of individual regions, and to attain a "sustainable symbiosis of city and hinterland."[290] For them small communities are seen as "providing the operational basis for organizing and managing the relations between humans and their local environment."[291] It is assumed that it is at the scale of these communities and the bioregions that house them that "people can understand the flow of natural systems,"[292] and where "the consequences of political decisions are felt."[293] Bioregionalists feel that "[w]ithout a local population whose roots are firmly planted in the land and its history, there is no preventing the destruction of the locality for profit by extralocal forces,"[294] and that these roots are best established in the context of small communities. For them the ideal settlement of the future would be a "small scale, integrated, self-governing community, having its own identity and its own customs which are adapted to its particular place."[295] Bioregionalists believe it is only within the context of small communities subject to the control of their members that people "can make effective a proper respect for their material environment so as to defeat the ecological peril, and end the curse of alienation from life and fellowship which now afflicts millions."[296]

Taken together the noted first principles and tenets of bioregionalism suggest a truly radical shift from the growth-dominated paradigm that currently governs societal behavior in the United States. Socially, American communities reflect individuality and competition over the solidarity and cooperation favored by bioregionalists, and an exploitation of their natural environs rather than a respect for nature. Politically, our communities are often managed by homogeneous, centralized governments based on artificial boundaries, rather than the diverse, decentralized forms based on the natural boundaries of bioregions suggested by bioregionalists. Economically, our communities reflect growth and external dependency over the stability and self-sufficiency called for by bioregionalists. Most American communities evidence little or nothing in the way of an ecological worldview that recognizes the primary importance of ecological sustainability. Most reveal little or nothing in the way of acknowledging the importance of biological and cultural diversity. One would be hard pressed to identify any that exhibit an acceptance of limits to their growth. A regional consciousness based on unifying natural and cultural features, and any sense of an ethical obligation beyond the human community, are also absent from virtually all our communities. Nor do our communities tend to demonstrate any awareness of the value of local and regional cultures that have withstood the test of time, and have much to offer in terms of place-based knowledge invaluable to transitioning to sustainable behavior. And finally, American communities tend to display little or no appreciation for the ecological superiority of small communities over large cities.

At present there is little evidence of a shift toward the principles and tenets of bioregionalism in American communities. However, as the unsustainable nature of societal behavior under the current growth-dominated paradigm is increasingly revealed by mounting evidence of existent ecological limits to growth, pressure will surely build for a paradigm shift that facilitates a transition to sustainable social practices. That shift will inevitably have to include the recognition of the inherently unsustainable nature of material growth on a finite planet. With little or no evidence of such a shift being initiated by state or federal governments, and at least a tentative demonstration of a willingness to entertain a no-growth position on the part of an increasing number of citizen groups within local communities, the needed paradigm shift appears destined to be initiated by local jurisdictions. As those jurisdictions explore alternative paths to a sustainable future, the principles and tenets of bioregionalism suggest fertile ground for mining ideas appropriate to any formulation of the prospective nature of no-growth communities within a non-growing human enterprise. Bioregionalism's contribution to the nature of such communities would certainly extend beyond the needed acceptance of growth limits advocated by bioregionalists. For example, bioregionalists would point out that sustainability at the community level would depend on communities developing a sustainable relationship with the bioregions that house them, i.e., they would have no hope of being self-sufficient in the absence of the resource flows and waste sinks provided by their regions. In the end, bioregionalism suggests multiple relevant considerations for any attempt to envision the prospective nature of no-growth communities that evidence stability and sustainability. Before turning to a portrayal of likely features of no-growth communities in the last chapter of this work, the closing section of this chapter addresses the critical role of no-growth communities in any attempt to transition to sustainability in general and ecological sustainability in particular.

The role of no-growth communities in advancing sustainability

As noted in the first chapter, the world passed a milestone in 2008: For the first time in the history of humankind a majority of people lived in urban places.[297] With the world's cities and suburbs growing by some 70 million people annually, the role of urban settlements becomes progressively more dominant with each passing year. By the beginning of the twenty-first century fully 90 percent of population growth and 80 percent of economic growth in the developing world was occurring in cities.[298] Some of the greatest challenges associated with ongoing global urbanization are based in the developing world's cities, which already house more than half the planet's poor,[299] and contain "slums" that are growing by some 25 million people a year, adding to the more than 1 billion already living in such "informal settlements" worldwide.[300] The monumental nature of any undertaking to make these cities more environmentally benign, let alone sustainable, may be illustrated by pointing out that in the developing world "more than 90 percent of sewage is discharged directly into rivers, lakes, and coastal waters without treatment of any kind."[301] While cities in these contexts clearly face seemingly insurmountable obstacles to realizing urban sustainability, the United States is not exempt from having to contend with serious challenges in moving its urban settings toward sustainability. By 2010 America had chalked up two straight decades of demographic growth in excess of 3 million new residents each year. Representing the equivalent of more than 30 cities of 100,000 every 12 months, the overwhelming majority of that growth occurred within existing metropolitan areas, and served to magnify the problems associated with transitioning these large urban settings to states of sustainability. Globally, challenges associated with the pursuit of urban sustainability will be compounded by projections that have the world's urban population doubling from some 2.4 billion in 1995 to over 5 billion by 2025, taking the proportion of the world's population that is urban from 50 percent in 2008 to over

60 percent by 2025.[302] As one analyst has noted, this projected growth translates into the "need to build at least as much urban habitat as exists today"[303] by 2025 if this explosive growth continues to be accommodated rather than curtailed.

There is widespread acknowledgement that existing urban places do not constitute sustainable entities. As prominent researchers have bluntly opined: "No city today is environmentally sustainable."[304] It ought to be self-evident that "cities are by no means self-sustaining entities,"[305] and that they can only exist by drawing on areas much larger than themselves to sustain their ongoing operations. Cities all over the world now represent "the nub of overconsumption"[306] that has already collectively taken the human enterprise beyond the planet's ecological capabilities to sustain the current global urban network into the future. With an increasing awareness that the "urbanizing world must coexist with the natural world if both are to endure,"[307] it is possible to argue that the "central task of urban sustainability is effectively managing commons problems in the ecosystems that sustain cities."[308] As cities have come to dominate the global landscape, there has been a growing recognition that "cities are key to both human progress and ecological sustainability."[309] This critical relationship between urban sustainability and ecological sustainability has been acknowledged through what have become known as the Perlman Principles, which include the assertion that "[t]here can be no global environmental sustainability without urban sustainibility."[310] "The sheer size of urban populations and economies means that cities must lead the way toward more environmentally sustainable practices for the world as a whole."[311]

Although most advocates of sustainability initiatives recognize that today's cities do not represent ecologically sustainable entities, they are apt to argue that "they are potentially the most sustainable form of settlement."[312] This argument is largely based on the assertion that "cities create energy and resource efficiencies"[313] that make them potentially more efficient than any other form of settlement. Proponents of this viewpoint are likely to point to research indicating that compact cities "use approximately half as much energy on a per capita basis as sprawling, low-density cities."[314] They are also able to refer to research indicating "that low-intensity development is about 2.5 times more material-intensive than high-intensity development."[315] This line of reasoning naturally leads to favored status for large, dense urban centers, even those as large as New York City. Proponents of this viewpoint argue that on a per capita basis "the dense environment of Manhattan more than compensates for its massive, often old and inefficient buildings, making New York City one of the most resource- and energy-efficient places in the United States."[316] In David Owen's 2009 book *The Green Metropolis* he actually makes the argument that New York City is the greenest community in the United States.[317] That argument is based on the reasoning that the city's extreme compactness sharply reduces opportunities to be wasteful, permitting people to drive less, closing out options for larger homes that represent increased material and energy requirements, and eliminating such wasteful practices as maintaining lawns. While the resulting per capita impacts are undoubtedly less than those associated with suburban living, this line of reasoning conveniently ignores the cumulative impact of the larger numbers of people living in New York City.

Manhattan alone has 1.6 million people living on an island of a mere 23 square miles, representing a population density more than 800 times that of the county as a whole.[318] Because of the total number living at such a high density, "[p]er square foot, New York City consumes more energy and generates more solid waste and greenhouse gases than most comparable sized areas elsewhere in the United States."[319] Although the city's per capita consumption may be less than comparably sized areas elsewhere in the country, the city still epitomizes lifestyles based on consumerism. That reality is clearly revealed by the fact that some 600 rigs are needed to move garbage from New York City daily, with these tractor-trailers forming a convoy nearly 9 miles long, hauling garbage to landfill sites in New Jersey, Pennsylvania, and Virginia, sometimes to sites as far away as 300 miles.[320] Merely attempting to make such consumerism more efficient in its exploitation of resources and energy fails to address the disconcerting fact that "consumption-oriented societies are not sustainable."[321] Ecological "[f]ootprint analysis shows that total consumption levels had already exceeded the planet's ecological capacity by the late 1970s or early 1980s."[322] The challenge is clearly much greater than simply perpetuating and extending a consumer society through an ongoing quest to realize continued consumption growth through ever-greater efficiencies.

The absurdity of attempting to rationalize the possibility of continuing down a consumer-society path may be illustrated by the implications associated with an ongoing expansion of motor-vehicle ownership. By the end of the first decade of the twenty-first century the global total for motor vehicles had already exceeded 900 million.[323] Over 250 million of those vehicles were in the United States, driving over a national network of more than 4 million miles of roads and streets, and in the process consuming more gasoline annually than the next 20 countries combined.[324] With just over 4 percent of the world's population situated in the United States, the material and energy implications of attempting to replicate such a system of private transportation globally defy comprehension. If the current count of more than 900 million vehicles where lined up bumper to bumper along the earth's equator they would circle the planet more than 100 times, and yet this imposing number of vehicles is expected to double by 2030.[325] As noted in the first chapter, if all people on the planet were to own motor vehicles at the ratio of Americans the total number would increase to over 5.6 billion, a 6-fold increase over the number on roads worldwide in 2010. The embedded materials and energy in a fleet of vehicles that size, as well as in the infrastructure needed globally to provide the energy to fuel that fleet, plus that required for creation and maintenance of the road network to accommodate that number of vehicles, would require a level of ecological capacity that no longer exists on the planet.

Current fantasies regarding prospects for such options as "green vehicles," "zero-emission vehicles," and "environmentally benign vehicles" must be recognized for what they are: Illusions or chimeras. These impossible or foolish fantasies are simply not in accord with the fact that irrespective of the fuel source that might power a global fleet of over 5 billion vehicles, the embedded material and energy in creating those vehicles, fueling them, and providing roadways for them, represent unrealizable ends in a world that has already surpassed ecological limits to further growth. The inherent fallacy, or outright deception, associated with the term "green vehicles" has been recognized in Norway, where advertising guidelines "include a ban on advertising cars as 'green,' 'clean,' or 'environmentally friendly.'"[326]

Any attempt to extend motor vehicle ownership globally epitomizes an expansion in consumerism that is inherently unsustainable. Further growth in vehicle ownership would also increase prospects for low-density development patterns, creating built environments where "resulting patterns are highly unsustainable."[327] If urban places are to realize a true state of sustainability, "there is likely to be no alternative to a politically-unpopular solution: to find ways of restraining car ownership and use."[328] True urban sustainability will ultimately require recognizing that there "is an inherent conflict between the automobile and the city," that part of this conflict includes facilitation of unsustainable mobility and settlement patterns, and that achieving sustainability will ultimately require "redesigning cities for people, not for cars."[329] "Earth cannot provide enough for today's global population to live like the average American, or even the average European."[330] Cars must quickly come to be recognized as the quintessential expression of a consumer society that is simply not transferable to all nations across the globe. Any hope of realizing true urban sustainability will ultimately depend on rejecting lifestyles based on consumerism, including a specific rejection of automobile ownership as one of the clearest embodiments of those unsustainable lifestyles. In all national settings, including America, cities seeking to establish sustainable and self-reliant relationships with the bioregions that house them will have to abandon the idea of being able to realize that end under automobile ownership. Bioregions are clearly incapable of providing the ongoing material and energy flows for their urban centers that would be required to sustain lifestyles based on cars. Bioregions could, on the other hand, conceivably support cities designed to realize sustainable mobility and settlement patterns based on pedestrian, bicycle, and public transportation options.

The overwhelming majority of current sustainability initiatives place their primary emphases on attempts to advance the single end of *efficiency*. This pursuit of efficiency is, in turn, motivated by an interest in being able to maintain ongoing growth as the primary social objective. Smart-growth initiatives are largely based on the rationale of realizing more efficient use of land as cities grow, under the assumption that moving from dumb, low-density sprawl to smart, high-density urban living will permit ongoing urban growth to be sustained. Eco-efficiency initiatives, in turn, are predicated on the view that possible efficiency improvements in the material and energy inputs per unit of output will permit ongoing economic growth to be sustained. Another perceived avenue for being able to sustain growth consists of initiatives to improve the efficiency of technology. These technical adaptations, as illustrated by ongoing fantasies about technologies that would permit zero-emission cars and zero-emission pollution flows, suggest prospects for being able to extend consumer lifestyles in ways that would even permit demographic growth to be sustained. In the end, these smart-growth, eco-efficiency, and technological initiatives all represent efforts to put off or sidestep any consideration of the contentious issue of limits to growth. They also represent an inability or unwillingness to confront the reality that material increases represented by demographic, economic, and urban growth are inherently unsustainable. Finally, these initiatives uniformly overlook the fact that any efficiency gains are destined to be negated by ongoing growth, e.g., having material, energy, and pollution reductions of 50 percent negated by the next doubling of an economy. Any attempt to maintain fealty to the current growth imperative in spite of these uncomfortable realities suggests a form of collective denial regarding the actual implications of ongoing growth. Defenders of the growth imperative ignore the sobering reality "that the limited gains made since 1992 in shifting toward more-sustainable patterns of consumption and production have been largely overwhelmed by the continued global growth of the consumer society."[331] In a related vein, "any gains in technological efficiency are simply being swamped by the sheer scale of rising aspirations and an increasing population."[332] Among technological optimists there is little recognition that the "wiser use of technology can only buy time—and precious time it is—to bring consumption and population growth down to sustainable levels."[333] Ultimately, the current ignorance or denial of existent ecological limits to growth successfully impedes any recognition of the fact that the challenge presently confronting humankind is much greater than simply seeking to grow more efficiently.

The prevalent quest to realize urban sustainability via efficiency initiatives is understandable. It has, for example, been noted that "[e]co-efficiency is the easiest component of the transition to sustainability to implement."[334] However, none of the efficiency initiatives constitute sufficient responses to current ecological realities. More efficient urban settlement patterns, economic production processes, and technological adaptations will only serve to slow down the ongoing ecological degradation attributable to continued demographic, economic, and urban rates of exponential growth. Having already surpassed global ecological limits to growth, necessary responses are far more profound than simply realizing greater efficiencies in urban growth, economic production processes, and consumer-oriented lifestyles through technological innovations. These efficiency initiatives can only be expected to realize urban sustainability if they are preceded by the attainment of a state of no growth in urban centers. Under continued demographic, economic, or urban growth, any realized efficiency gains will simply be lost to ongoing growth rather than serving to reduce the unsustainable ecological footprints of today's cities.

Once growth has been stopped in America's urban centers, communities could begin to address the daunting task of downsizing to ecologically sustainable levels. In most communities, historic violations of local ecological carrying capacities will require achieving and then maintaining a period of negative growth until these centers scale back their impacts to levels that can be maintained indefinitely (sustained) without impairing the functional integrity or productivity of their local ecosystems.[335] Shutting down growth would obviously play a large part in helping communities transition to ecologically sustainable levels, as revealed by one calculation "that *about 55 percent of the energy we consume is required by the economic growth process itself.*"[336] Similarly large initial reductions in materials usage and pollution levels could be expected by stopping growth, which would then collectively set the stage for efforts to downsize communities to ecologically sustainable levels. These initiatives to downsize communities to levels determined by their ecological carrying capacities would include a quest for efficiency gains pursued through redesigned land-use patterns, eco-efficiency initiatives, and technological adaptations. Under this suggested scenario true urban sustainability would ultimately depend on three successive actions: Shutting down the demographic, economic, and urban growth that constitutes inherently unsustainable behavior; downsizing communities to levels approximating their ecosystems' capabilities to sustain them without violating the ecological integrity of the bioregions that house them; and implementing efficiency initiatives that permit the ecological footprints of communities to be reduced to sustainable levels.

Shutting down the growth of America's communities clearly represents an intimidating undertaking in light of the historical attitude toward growth in the United States. Downsizing local communities to ecologically sustainable levels set by the capacities of their respective bioregions will represent an even more daunting task than stopping growth, because in many communities the attainment of such levels will require periods of negative growth to realize ecological sustainability. Efficiency initiatives may, in turn, be thought of as instruments to be used in conjunction with downsizing undertakings intended to reduce community ecological footprints to sustainable levels. With mounting evidence that the human enterprise has already surpassed global ecological limits to growth, merely pursuing more efficient growth strategies must quickly come to be recognized as an insufficient response to current ecological realities. Efficiency initiatives will only realize expected payoffs if they are implemented under states of no growth as part of concerted efforts to downsize communities to ecologically sustainable levels. In the case of large urban centers and their associated metropolitan agglomerations that have already grown far past the ecological capabilities of their bioregions, efficiency initiatives alone will be insufficient to transform them to sustainable states. In these contexts absolute downsizing via periods of negative growth coupled with efficiency initiatives will be required to realize urban sustainability. In communities that still retain excess ecological capacity, or have not significantly exceeded the ecological capacities of their bioregions, efficiency initiatives may suffice to continually reduce their ecological footprints. However, in light of the fact that global ecological limits to growth have already been surpassed, growth must be rejected as a policy option in all of America's political jurisdictions. The global challenge is one of reducing the scale of the human enterprise to a level capable of being sustained indefinitely by the planet's ecosystems.

No-growth communities clearly have a large role to play in advancing sustainability gains in America and globally. With the growing dominance of urban places around the world, if cities cannot be made sustainable there can be no hope of realizing planetary sustainability. Cities will be unable to achieve true sustainability if they cannot let go of the growth that represents inherently unsustainable behavior. The quest for urban sustainability will therefore ultimately depend on whether future urban development will be guided by a no-growth imperative or today's dominant growth imperative. No-growth communities directed by a no-growth imperative arguably represent an indispensable avenue for realizing sustainable patterns of living in all national settings. In the United States, these communities represent vehicles for reinventing and redesigning some of the most unsustainable urban environments on the planet, in terms of outsized ecological footprints, into sustainable entities.

5   Envisioning no-growth communities

It is not economic globalization that we should aim for but the reverse: *economic localization*.

Edward Goldsmith[1]

The salient fact about life in the decades ahead is that it will become increasingly and intensely local and smaller in scale ... The downscaling of America is the single most important task facing the American people.

James Howard Kunstler[2]

American communities are captives of a cultural story that equates growth with progress. The ongoing enactment of that story is dismantling the ecological life-support structures and their associated life-support services that sustain communities across America's landscape and represent the very foundation of the country's civilizational complex. This current cultural story based on an ideology of growth therefore needs to be rejected on ecological grounds if American communities are to experience an indeterminate future. There also appear to be sufficient economic and social grounds for rejecting the growth imperative driving current behavior. The phenomenal economic growth in America during the last half of the twentieth century also produced increasing income and wealth inequalities, as well as an expanding sense of economic insecurity. "Most Americans, and not just the poor in the ghetto, are facing lives characterized by growing economic insecurity."[3] The benefit of ongoing economic growth during recent decades has also been questioned by claims that "growth now makes us poorer by increasing costs faster than it increases benefits."[4] Better measures of economic welfare than GDP that incorporate social and ecological costs reveal a declining level of prosperity in America since the mid-1970s.[5] This case for the "uneconomic" nature of growth has been building for decades and suggests strong grounds for rejecting the merit of further economic expansion. Even by the traditional measure of household income adjusted for inflation, American generations born since 1955 have been losing ground financially rather than replicating the income growth of previous generations.[6] Social grounds for renouncing the merit of further growth appear in the form of lists of the social ills that characterize America in spite of, or perhaps because of, its dramatic former growth: "Among industrialized countries we have the highest rates of teenage pregnancy, abortion, infant mortality, divorce, single-parent families, murder and rape, drug consumption, imprisonment, air pollution, and toxic waste production."[7]

If enactment of the current cultural story is failing America's communities ecologically, economically, and socially, it is time to acknowledge the desperate need for a new cultural story, mindset, or what academics refer to as a social paradigm, that no longer equates growth with progress. This new mindset would recognize demographic, economic, and urban growth as the *cause* of, rather than the *solution* to, our collective societal problems. Acknowledgement of that reality would permit the critically needed paradigm shift that would replace the current growth imperative with a new no-growth imperative. That shift would in turn permit American communities to reinvent themselves in ways that enabled them to advance the primary goal of sustainability in general, and ecological sustainability in particular. Some likely features of such stable, sustainable, no-growth communities are explored below. The first three sections of the chapter are designed to convey likely characteristics of no-growth communities, under the assumption that no-growth advocates will have to provide a plausible alternative if local residents are to be expected to abandon their historical support for the dominant, pro-growth paradigm that still rules most local jurisdictions. The final section of the chapter offers observations on likely prospects for realizing no-growth communities in the United States in spite of the demonstrated inertia of the growth imperative in virtually all local settings.

Likely economic features of no-growth communities

The greatest challenge associated with attempting to portray prospective features of no-growth communities is envisioning viable local economies based on stability rather than growth. Historically, the discipline of economics has provided little guidance for those seeking to depict the likely characteristics of practicable no-growth communities. Traditional economics, with the business enterprise representing the basic unit of analysis under microeconomics, and the nation being the basic unit of analysis under macroeconomics, has largely overlooked the matter of *community economics*.[8] Attempts to address community economics have belonged to a "subterranean tradition of organic and decentralist economics whose major spokesmen include Prince Kopotkin, Gustav Landauer, Tolstoy, William Morris, Gandhi, Lewis Mumford, and, [more] recently, Alex Comfort, Paul Goodman, and Murray Bookchin."[9] That tradition of addressing community economics within the context of a libertarian political economy distinguished itself from orthodox socialism and capitalism by insisting that *scale* and *place* had to be treated as independent and primary considerations in any discussions of economics. This tradition has treated both bigness and the absence of place-based economics as the nemeses of the community economics it has espoused. Associating bigness with impersonality, insensitivity, and a concentration of abstract power, these advocates of community economics have lauded smallness; associating it with freedom, efficiency, creativity, enjoyableness, and prospects for endurance. These proponents of an economics for community have also extolled the virtues of "a new economics that takes into account the critical importance of place,"[10] arguing that it is only in the context of local communities that one can hope to shift attention from such traditional goals as profitability and growth to new ends like economic security, community stability, and ecological integrity. This attention to place is predicated on the belief that it is only in such place-based contexts that people can be expected to care about their neighbors, community institutions, and ecological heritage.

In 1973 E. F. Schumacher drew renewed attention to the subject of community economics with his treatment of a "Buddhist" economics centered on people and nature in his book *Small is Beautiful*. In that work Schumacher revealed his affinity for the thinking embodied in Gandhi's proposal to stabilize and enrich village life in India through labor-intensive manufacture and handicrafts implemented under decentralized economic decision making. Schumacher shared Gandhi's view that people have an innate desire to be self-determining, and criticized aid to poor countries that pushed "the adoption of production methods and consumption standards which destroy the possibilities of self-reliance and self-help."[11] Schumacher's interest in self-reliance would portend an ongoing fascination with self-reliant communities in subsequent writings on the economics of community. Other important works addressing community economics followed: *Neighborhood Power: The New Localism* (1974), by David Morris; *Steady State Economics* (1977), by Herman Daly; *Human Scale* (1980), by Kirkpatrick Sale; *Self-Reliant Cities* (1982), by David Morris; *Cities and the Wealth of Nations* (1984), by Jane Jacobs; *The Living Economy* (1986), edited by Paul Ekins; *Environmental Protection and Economic Well-Being* (1988), by Thomas Michael Power; *For the Common Good* (1989), by Herman Daly and John Cobb, Jr.; *Short Circuit* (1996), by Richard Douthwaite; and *Going Local* (1998), by Michael Shuman. While these books covered diverse perspectives and recommendations, they all reflected faith in the importance of one central concept: *Community self-reliance.*[12] During the opening decade of the twenty-first century an increasing number of individuals appeared willing to accept this idea of self-reliance as one of the core principles of community economic development.[13]

By the end of the twentieth century American advocates of community economics increasingly made the case for community self-reliance on the basis of the belief that it represented an antidote to growing economic insecurity associated with globalization. From their perspective the free trade and economic growth at the heart of globalization initiatives since the end of the Second World War were increasingly serving to destroy American families, communities, and their vitally important local ecosystems. For them "a spreading culture of insecurity"[14] appeared directly attributable to inherent features of a global economy based on free trade and economic growth. Global free trade, as noted previously, is based on David Ricardo's concepts of specialization and comparative advantage, which encourage nations to specialize in producing those things for export in which they have the greatest comparative advantage and to import everything else. This focus on an export-oriented development model that encourages intensive specialization in what countries can produce most efficiently for sale to others is assumed to increase productivity, further growth, and enhance prosperity among all nations. However, proponents of community economics see a downside to continuously increasing efficiency and productivity, pointing out that closure of "inefficient" workplaces displaces workers, as does the ongoing quest to increase productivity via technological changes that reduce the need for workers. They believe that "[s]pecialization inevitably leads to chronic unemployment and to lower wages"[15] and are able to cite research showing that under globalization developed countries are experiencing declining wages and lost jobs in both the manufacturing and services sectors.[16] These proponents of community economics view the growing number of Americans "who see their livelihood destroyed or their businesses impoverished"[17] as clear evidence of increasing economic insecurity attributable to globalization. They also attribute that insecurity to the globalization push for large-scale efficiencies and ever-greater specialization that result in "increasing integration and interdependence" and in turn yield "increasing vulnerability to systemic failure."[18] While advocates of community economics clearly attribute much of this increasing insecurity and vulnerability to the export-oriented development model associated with globalization, their criticism of development biased in favor of exports extends to local development efforts with a similar export bias.

Local governments in America have demonstrated near-universal fealty to an "economic base" model to guide their economic development initiatives. That "economic base model is nearly always used to support an export-based development policy," because the model treats "production for export as the 'base' or driving force of economic development, and production for the local market as derivative and dependent on export production."[19] The model "emphasizes that it is the extent to which a city can command income from beyond its border which is the key element in its growth,"[20] with those export dollars representing new money that can both bring further expansion capacity in "basic" activities and provide the foundation for growth in "non-basic" or "service" activities. Proponents of community economics are just as likely to associate such an emphasis on export activity at the local level with prospects for insecurity and vulnerability as a national emphasis on exports. They see any shift away from local production for local consumption to production directed at external markets as diminishing local control over a community's economic future, opening it up to external decisions to close or relocate local businesses, outside price fluctuations for exports that undercut local "basic" activities, and possible interruptions in the flow of imports no longer produced locally that make communities incredibly vulnerable to events beyond their control. In response to this sense of growing insecurity and vulnerability within local communities, advocates of community economics repeatedly call for a shift to greater community self-reliance or self-sufficiency.

Associating the specialization, efficiency, productivity, and growth required by the export-oriented development path with insecurity and vulnerability, proponents of community economics suggest an alternative development model based on import substitution intended to realize local production of necessities.[21] They argue that "[d]evelopment led by import-replacement rather than export-promotion diversifies, stabilizes, and strengthens the local economy."[22] This import-replacement model argues that communities should "[s]top trying to expand economic activity through exports, and instead strive to eliminate dangerous dependencies by creating new import-replacement businesses that meet people's basic needs."[23] Proponents of community economies envision such a "needs-driven economy" in terms of "a network of locally owned and operated corporations which [take] care of most of [a community's] needs for energy, food, water, housing, and clothing."[24] Such a move towards community self-reliance in meeting essential needs is seen as fundamental to overcoming the insecurity and vulnerability associated with the export-oriented development model. "Dependencies on necessities from outside the community means that a remote crisis can reverberate into a local one" and the "more essential an item is for our survival, the more dangerous it is to depend on someone outside the community selling it to us."[25] As one advocate of community economics suggests, the "long-term benefit of weaning the community away from depending on outsiders is that the community reduces its vulnerability to events outside its control."[26] However, the interest in having communities become more self-sufficient and less dependent on imports ends up being based on much more than just lessening the growing economic insecurity and vulnerability associated with relying on a limited number of export firms to support a local economy.

Proponents of community economics believe that a diverse set of local import-replacement businesses directed at meeting essential needs would accomplish much more than simply trying to realize greater local employment security or lessen vulnerabilities to external economic forces. The needs-based economic orientation structured on a diverse set of local import-replacement businesses suggests some of the radical economic changes envisioned by proponents of community economics. A focus on needs, rather than on artificially created wants, implies a dramatic departure from current economies driven by consumers pursuing an ever-expanding array of wants. The focus on diverse import-replacement businesses meeting local needs, rather than a few export businesses intended to bring in outside dollars to drive further local growth, implies another radical departure from the behavior of most current local economies. Proponents of community economics "make the meeting of the basic needs of human beings and ecological sustainability the starting point for the economic system."[27] For them an economics of community "aims at sufficiency of goods for the sake of community well-being, and not at the endless growth of production and consumption."[28] While they believe in the possibility of communities being relatively "self-sufficient in necessities"[29] under the constraints of ecological sustainability, they reject prospects for realizing ecological sustainability under "the tremendous waste of energy, raw materials, and resources that now go toward the production of superfluous goods simply to maintain 'effective demand' and to keep the monstrous economic machine going."[30] In this respect, they condemn the "aggressive want-stimulating advertising" that stands in the way of "distinguishing 'needs' from extravagant luxuries or impossible desires"[31] and serves to impede consideration of what is ecologically possible on a finite planet. In the end, their focus on a needs-based economic orientation within the limits set by ecological sustainability leads proponents of community economics to reject the growth required by export-oriented development. Their rejection of growth as the ultimate end opens the door for advocates of community economics to take a number of other positions that differ dramatically from current precepts associated with the conventional economic development path of endless growth.

With an orientation that values sustainability over growth, sufficiency of goods over endless increases in production and consumption, a needs-based over a wants-based economy, economic stability over economic expansion, self-reliance or self-sufficiency over external dependency, and development based on diversification over enlargement, advocates of community economics clearly espouse an economic orientation diametrically opposed to that held by neoclassical growth economists. Community no-growth economists carry their critique of conventional economics even further by challenging other aspects of reasoning traditionally heralded by growth economists. They value "community well-being" over an "unlimited quest for personal gain."[32] They prize "societal durability" over "economic efficiency."[33] They favor "community stability" over "business profitability."[34] They side with "jobs and security" over "income and wealth."[35] They endorse "labor-intensive" businesses over "capital- and energy-intensive" enterprises.[36] They support economic activities based on "cooperation" over "competition" within local economies.[37] They advocate economic practices that "conserve" resources and ecosystems over those that "exploit" these vital underpinnings of local economies.[38] Taken together these values produce a critical view of traditional, growth-obsessed capitalist economies along the following lines: "The marketplace of our traditional capitalist economy, with its emphasis on competition, exploitation, and individual profit, needs to be phased out."[39] Proponents of community economics suggest an alternative system based on acceptance of the need to quickly transition to a sustainable state of no growth, because in their view "[m]arket economics simply does not reflect the real—ecological—world."[40] The nature of the alternative community-based economics they envision is suggested by advocates of these new local economies.

The key features of community economics championed by advocates of this alternative paradigm are implied by their espousal of stable, self-reliant, sustainable local economies based on a diverse set of locally owned and operated corporations that make communities relatively self-sufficient in necessities. Interest in *diversity* and *stability* has its origins in the disciplines of biology and ecology, where practitioners understand "that the most powerful survival principle of life is *diversity*."[41] "Diversity confers resilience, adaptability and the capacity for regeneration."[42] These traits are in turn linked to ecosystem stability, and diversity is thus valued because it is believed to represent "the basis of ecological stability."[43] Proponents of community economics extend this logic to their call for a diverse set of local import-substitution businesses along the following lines: "Like a well-balanced ecosystem, this kind of diversified economy [is] not easily vulnerable to outside events."[44] Associating economic growth with "social and environmental instability,"[45] proponents of community economics suggest an alternative orientation based on diversity and stability realized through a diverse set of local, import-replacement corporations meeting essential needs.

An interest in *self-reliance* and *self-sufficiency* directly links proponents of community economics to proponents of bioregionalism. "Self-reliance ... at the regional level, is ... inherent in the bioregional concept."[46] Bioregionalism "advocates economies of self-sufficiency within naturally articulated 'bioregional' boundaries."[47] Bioregionalists recognize that communities would be unable to realize a state of self-sufficiency with respect to meeting such basic needs as water, food, clothing, building materials for housing, and energy without drawing on the resources and ecosystems in their bioregions. Proponents of community economics acknowledge that "cities are by no means self-sustaining entities" and of necessity "rely heavily on rural areas for resources" required to meet their essential needs.[48] This advocacy of self-reliance or self-sufficiency in meeting basic needs within delimited bioregions naturally suggests a conservational orientation toward natural resources and ecosystems expressed along the following lines:

> A bioregional economy would seek ... to maintain rather than use up the natural world, to adapt to the environment rather than exploit it or manipulate it, and to conserve not only the resources but also the relationships and systems of the natural world.[49]

"Similarly, a community committed to self-reliance will be mindful not to foul its own nest" if it depends on its own bioregion for such essential needs as water and food, which makes it possible to consider self-reliance as "a tool for ecological protection and restoration."[50] This conserver posture toward resources and ecosystems naturally infers an interest in *sustainability*, because "a community that relies exclusively on its own forests, rivers, and farms—and doesn't see the use of outside resources as either necessary or desirable—will take special care to safeguard its natural resources for future generations."[51] In the end, the bioregionalists' tenets of sustainability, an ecological worldview, diversity, limits, and a land ethic all find expression in the position taken by advocates of community economics toward resources and ecosystems.

Proponents of community economics point out that the "market has no built-in tendency to grow only up to the scale of aggregate resource use that is optimal (or even merely sustainable) in its demands on the biosphere."[52] While neo-classical growth economists tend to overlook or discount resource or ecological limits to growth, advocates of community economics recognize those limits and seek to address matters of optimum or maximum scale of local economies relative to the potentialities of their bioregions. They believe that within these limits "[m]any regions within the United States could become relatively self-sufficient."[53]

The interest that proponents of community economics have in self-reliance or self-sufficiency finds its strongest expression in their call for agricultural self-sufficiency. This line of reasoning concludes that "[i]f economics is reconceived in the service of community, it will begin with a concern for agriculture and specifically for production of food."[54] Such a conclusion represents the devolution of a national stance on food production to local communities, with the national position being that "[t]here can be no effective national economy if a people cannot feed themselves and otherwise meet their essential needs."[55] Similarly, proponents of community economics believe dependency on outsiders for a fundamental requirement such as food weakens a community, hence they consider the matter of "how and where food is grown [as] foundational to an economics of community."[56] They see relative self-sufficiency in local food production as an essential step in moving communities away from external dependencies and having them gain effective local control over their economic destinies. However, their support for relative agricultural self-sufficiency extends far beyond assumed reductions in external dependencies and enhanced local economic control. For them a central "aim of an economics of community is that the self-sufficiency of agricultural production should be indefinitely sustainable."[57] For proponents of community economics, realistic prospects for such sustainable agricultural practices are dependent on the development of "local land-based economies,"[58] where farmers develop "mutually beneficial relationships with a community of consumers" through a "Community Supported Agricultural" (CSA) movement.[59]

Under this model of local food production for local consumption, consumers pay a share of the costs in early spring that meet the farmer's operating expenses for the upcoming season. By paying in advance they allow the farmer to raise interest-free operating capital, and in dealing directly with the farmer the need for marketing is eliminated, as is the middleman to mark up prices, which in total makes it possible to deliver products at below market prices. But the suggested benefits of the CSA model are assumed to extend beyond lower prices. Members have the option of contributing work, but even when they forgo this opportunity "CSA connects consumers with the landscape in which their food is grown and the people (and animals) that produce it."[60] That connection produces a natural interest in organic food production and sustainable practices on CSA farms. The benefits of CSA also extend to its role in reestablishing a sense of community in locations where it has been seriously eroded by making it possible for "farmers and consumers to create social relationships in their communities."[61] Proponents of community economics see additional prospects for furthering a sense of community through local food production for local consumption in the farmers markets that tend to accompany any revival of local agriculture. They are able to point to research on shopping behavior indicating "that consumers have *ten times as many conversations* at farmers' markets as they do at supermarkets."[62] That research reveals that a "simple change in economic life—where you shop—produces an enormous change in your social life."[63] Instead of being a mere consumer at farmers markets, citizens become participants in a community process that allows them to express their preferences and in the process expand their sense of belonging to a community. For proponents of community economics "the orientation of agriculture to local needs, local possibilities, and local limits is simply indispensable to the health of both land and people."[64]

Support for agricultural self-reliance among proponents of community economics is further justified on the basis of claims it can dramatically reduce material and energy inputs in food production. This position on resource and energy inputs derives from an asserted need to stabilize world climate by drastically reducing greenhouse gas emissions, which they believe is "only feasible if the global economy is replaced by a localized economy with its vastly reduced energy and resource requirements."[65] With respect to localized food production, proponents of community economics point out that "the further food is transported, the more waste is created—in terms of fuel, packaging, refrigeration, and spoilage."[66] In terms of the energy implications of industrialized food production for a global market, they note that "[b]etween production, processing, distribution, and preparation, 10 calories of energy are required to create just 1 calorie of food energy."[67] Even when the energy for processing, distribution, and preparation are excluded, critics claim that in our conventional system "three times as much energy is employed to grow 1 calorie of food energy" as that required by a "small-scale CSA approach."[68] Just "[p]rocessing, packaging, and distributing food around the nation and the world consumes four times again as much energy" as that utilized on the farm in producing the food.[69] The implications for greenhouse gas emissions and associated global warming are significant, because "compared with regional and local food systems, our national and international model releases five to seventeen times more carbon dioxide into the atmosphere."[70]

In light of these realities, proponents of community economics argue for moving toward "smaller-scale food networks."[71] They condemn a food system that has the average food item on American plates traveling more than 1,500 miles,[72] where "25 percent of the food produced never makes it to the table due to spoilage during transportation or in the grocery bins."[73] By way of comparison, they point to research indicating that "the farthest distance food travels in a North American CSA is 200 miles"[74] and in terms of the average distance, much less. In defense of smaller-scale food networks, they point out that "large-scale, centralized systems … are almost without exception more stressful to the environment than small-scale, diversified, locally adapted production."[75] They also cite research revealing that small farms produce more food per acre than large-scale industrial farming operations.[76] In terms of addressing the energy implications of current agricultural practices, they argue that small-scale operations can be far less energy intensive than agribusiness, and that local production for local consumption can help resolve any future energy crisis by reducing energy needs for transportation, processing, and packaging.[77] With respect to sustainability, they see far greater prospects for advancing that end under localized food production than under a large-scale food production process where "[a]bout three [to four] times as much energy is consumed in ... off-farm activities as is used in the nation's farms."[78] All in all, proponents of community economics believe there are multiple compelling reasons for quickly moving toward a system of local food production for local consumption that enhances self-reliance or self-sufficiency within the context of bioregions. For them "[r]eplacing corporate products with local produce on the dinner plate is a small first step in relocalizing the economy."[79]

Proponents of community economics also offer descriptions of the likely nature of the diverse, needs-based, import-substitution businesses they believe should represent the very foundation of local economies. As noted previously, conventional, for-profit corporations are driven by growth and profit imperatives, and as a result they demonstrate what has been described as "an inexorable, unabatable, voracious need to grow and expand."[80] Since advocates of community economics value stability and sustainability over growth, and favor a needs-based economy guided by the principle of sufficiency of goods over an endless increase of production and consumption under a wants-based economy, they naturally make the case for alternatives to for-profit corporations. Since the suggested alternative orientations would be completely antithetical to the ideology of for-profit corporations, proponents of community economics suggest a local business structure based largely on nonprofits, cooperatives, and public enterprises.[81] One advocate of community economics refers to these alternative businesses as *community corporations*, with their primary characteristic consisting of being anchored to the community through ownership.[82] Reasoning has it that national and multinational firms have no community loyalties, and that economic well-being in communities can only be realized "when ownership, production, and consumption become intimately connected with place."[83] The quest would be to move control of businesses from the boardrooms of distant, national and multinational, for-profit corporations back to community corporations representing "locally owned businesses which use local resources sustainably, employ local workers at decent wages, and serve primarily local consumers."[84]

The envisioned community corporations would not be driven by the same growth and profit imperatives of for-profit corporations. Nonprofits, cooperatives, and public enterprises are capable of surviving at marginal rates of return. A proponent of community economics notes that "if a company only needs to achieve a positive rate of return (whereby revenues exceed costs) rather than a maximum rate of return, many more goods and services can be made and sold locally than are today."[85] These increased prospects for import-substitution firms are seen as strengthening a local economy by increasing the economic multiplier represented by dollars staying within a community to be recirculated on subsequent expenditures rather than being lost to external markets in paying for imports. "As the variety of goods and services produced locally expands, the richer commercial economy attracts and holds more of the residents' dollars."[86] Local dollars that would otherwise have flowed out of the local economy stay put. "Every [local] expenditure cascades into a larger number of transactions that enrich the community. Once the multiplier leaves the community, the benefits of subsequent transactions are lost."[87] In keeping with this line of reasoning, proponents of community economics believe that the "primary virtue of import substitution, community corporations, and local investment is that these strategies increase the likelihood of the economic multiplier staying at home."[88] However, in contrast to conventional economic reasoning, proponents of community economics do not view such an increase in a local economic multiplier as a way of ensuring the demographic and economic growth of a community. Instead, they view multiplier benefits associated with import substitution as a way of enhancing the employment prospects of a community's existing residents. As a proponent of community economics put it, a "community committed to import substitution ... [actually] ... aims to *minimize* population growth. The goal is to expand the quantity and quality of jobs without drawing new people."[89] The noted emphasis changes from merely seeking job growth as a way of fueling ongoing economic growth to moving local communities as close to a practicable state of full employment as is possible. In addition, proponents of community economics address the nature of desired jobs under such a full employment ideal. "The goal of an economics for community is as much to provide meaningful and personally satisfying work as to provide adequate goods and services."[90] This quest for a new form of work typically includes a condemnation of "the alienating and dehumanizing character of much of the labor required in modern business and industry" that is attributable to "the inherent drive of the system toward productivity through specialization."[91] Advocates of a new and meaningful form of future employment point to what they consider to be "an inherent tension between humanly satisfying work and the quantity of production per worker."[92] As a result, they open the door to the possibility of a renewed role for artisans in relocalized economies of the near future, suggesting that "[i]n a decentralized economy with high energy costs, artisans will be able to compete with factories better than at present."[93] In the end, the portrayal of these respective stances toward full employment and the appropriate nature of work present additional dramatic contrasts with conventional economic reasoning. That dominant neoclassical reasoning discounts the possibility of realizing anything approaching full employment, favors technological changes that reduce the need for labor and thereby increase productivity, and even "warns against policies that would artificially attain full employment now at the expense of curtailing growth"[94] because inflated labor costs under full employment are assumed to divert capital from investments necessary for ongoing growth.

The case that proponents of community economics make for favoring locally owned businesses over national and multinational corporations is usually reinforced by specific references to the ways in which these corporations harm local communities. Wal-Mart typically serves as the quintessential scapegoat for illustrating the extent to which large, non-local, for-profit corporations negatively affect America's communities. By the 1990s Wal-Mart was the world's largest retailer and America's third-largest corporation, and was opening a new store somewhere in North America every three days.[95] Critics argue that Wal-Mart uses "a variety of tactics ranging from low-wage part-time employment, misleading advertising, predatory pricing, competition law violations, and coercive sourcing from suppliers ... to force local merchants out of business."[96] They note that "study after study confirms what hundreds of American towns learned the hard way: Wal-Mart leads to a net loss of jobs, decreased income for the community, and a decline of central shopping areas."[97] With respect to the loss of jobs, they are able to cite studies showing "that for every job created by Wal-Mart, as many as 1.5 jobs are lost."[98] A study in Iowa showed that over the course of a few years when Wal-Mart was expanding rapidly "the state lost 555 grocery stores, 298 hardware stores, 293 building supply stores, 161 variety shops, 158 women's clothing stores, and 116 pharmacies."[99] The replacement jobs provided by Wal-Mart tend not to pay the living-wage salaries paid by displaced stores, tend to provide minimal benefits, and tend to drive down wages and benefits across entire regions as employers try to compete with Wal-Mart's prices. As a result, incomes decrease across communities affected by new Wal-Mart superstores. A 2004 study in Pennsylvania revealed that the presence of Wal-Mart "unequivocally raised family poverty rates in the U.S. counties during the 1990s relative to places that had no such stores."[100] That study showed that all counties with Wal-Mart stores have grown poorer than surrounding counties without such stores, and that the more Wal-Mart stores they had the more quickly they became poorer. Proponents of community economics extend their criticism of Wal-Mart further by pointing to research indicating that "a dollar spent on a locally owned business has four to five times the economic spin-off of a dollar spent at Wal-Mart."[101] Rather than sending local expenditures to externally located corporate headquarters in the manner of Wal-Mart operations, locally owned businesses tend to recirculate their earnings and thereby strengthen local economies.

Proponents of community economics do not limit their criticisms of national and multinational corporations to Wal-Mart. They extend criticism of Wal-Mart's practice of exporting local expenditures to all businesses that siphon dollars out of local economies. They are able to point, for example, to research indicating that three-quarters of consumers' expenditures at

McDonald's restaurants are exported.[102] This stands in stark contrast to expenditures at local businesses, where the majority of expenditures stay within local communities. Under this line of reasoning, economic development "rooted in local ownership ... has clear benefits in terms of stopping economic leakage, a term that refers to community income that is spent outside the local economy."[103] That leakage occurs when locally generated incomes are spent outside a community on non-local purchases or on products produced outside the community but consumed locally. Both forms of leakage represent an economic loss to local communities. Proponents of community economics are able to point to studies showing "that local businesses yield two to four times the multiplier benefit compared with non-local businesses."[104] This positive impact is attributable to local businesses spending more on management, business services, advertising, and investments within their communities than national or multinational corporations. Spending on these four items can constitute one-third or more of total expenditures.[105] In sharp contrast to local businesses, national and "multinational chain stores siphon revenues out of communities through economic leakage."[106] Advocates of community economics respond to this perceived shortcoming by making the case for purchases from local businesses along the following lines: "Local purchasing is the primary means both of supporting existing businesses and of increasing the economic multiplier, resulting in a more efficient, self-reliant, economically resilient community."[107] In addition to local purchasing, another suggested strategy for stopping economic leakage from communities consists of the creation of "local currencies" or "Local Exchange Trading Systems" (LETS) to supplement national money.[108] "About four thousand 'complementary currency' schemes are in operation around the planet,"[109] including some "[t]wo dozen communities in the United States [that] promote local trade through ... local money,"[110] utilizing such varied mechanisms as "HOURS" in Ithaca, New York, "Bread" in Burlington, Vermont, and "Berk-shares" in Western Massachusetts. Since such alternative currencies can only be spent in jurisdictions that issue them, "consumers and producers know that *any* purchase or sale within the money system helps the local economy"[111] by avoiding losses associated with economic leakage.

Those making the case for community economics also tend to emphasize the importance of recycling finance locally in any attempt to realize economic self-reliance.[112] They believe that for-profit commercial banks are unlikely to finance the needs-based businesses that represent the foundation of local, self-reliant economies. They point out that the envisioned "needs-based businesses ... tend to be small and ... looking for start-up loans on the order of thousands of dollars rather than millions ... [while] commercial banks do not regard the high administrative costs associated with processing these loans as worth the interest payments."[113] Since proponents of community economics are unable to conceive of their called-for community corporations being formed without new infusions of capital, they are apt to suggest "that the starting place for restructuring the local economy needs to be the financial sector."[114] In this respect proponents of community economics harken back to a time of community banking, when a bank "raised most of its funds through local deposits and made most of its loans to local borrowers."[115] In those banks the "money was local, it was loaned locally, and the commercial bank evaluated its loan opportunities relative to other local borrowers."[116] Under current commercial banking, banks have largely abandoned such community-based financial dealings in favor of seeking out profitable loan opportunities in a global banking context. Advocates of community economics argue the case for reestablishing community-based financial institutions with place-based loyalties to local communities. For these advocates a "way to finance community corporations ... is to open a new bank with an unequivocal mission to invest locally."[117] Hundreds of these community-development financial institutions exist in the United States, and "their ranks include commercial banks, thrifts, place-based credit unions, and community-development loan funds."[118] Among these institutions proponents of community economics emphasize the potentially positive role of credit unions. As community-based, nonprofit financial institutions that are cooperatively owned and controlled by their members, "credit unions ensure that financial investments are not only economically successful but also in line with the broader social objectives and values of the communities in which they operate."[119] As cooperative institutions, their policies are designed to benefit their memberships as a whole, and those benefits are capable of being envisioned as more than just financial returns. Not driven just by profit maximization in the manner of traditional banks, credit unions are in the position of being able to entertain dramatically lower interest rates than commercial banks for loans that benefit a community. Providing low financing costs for local needs-based businesses is perceived as essential for making the transition from growth to economic development. Proponents of community economics argue that local businesses will only be able to make the shift to strengthening and diversifying a local economy if they are able to avoid having to grow and maximize profits to cover the high financing costs of their loans.

Proponents of community economics also shed light on the nature of likely prospects for the needs-based industries they believe should provide local communities with basic necessities like water, food, clothing, building materials for housing, and energy, as well as describing the probable nature of any goods produced by these industries. With respect to the possible viability of local needs-based industries, they challenge the prevailing wisdom among economists and businesspeople that effective industrial production can only occur under large economies of scale. They argue that "[f]or basic necessities, economies of scale appear to be shrinking to the point where hundreds or even thousands of U.S. communities could move toward self-reliance."[120] They claim that "[r]ecent breakthroughs in technology, workforce organization, and resource management are enabling local entrepreneurs to provide food, water, wood, energy, and materials in cost-effective ways."[121] In terms of a specific example, they are able to point to "energy-service companies" that have succeeded in moving into small-scale energy production.[122] Proponents of community economics additionally offer suggestions as to the likely nature of any goods or products that would be generated by a needs-based economy. They clearly envision a dramatic reduction in the number of items produced under a transition from a wants-based consumer society to a needs-based conserver society. They see a sustainable world as "one in which products are made to serve a real human need and incorporate principles of durability, recyclability, and low energy and ecological cost."[123] With respect to products genuinely required to satisfy real needs, they suggest that our relationship to these products ought to be governed by three *R*s—reduce, reuse, recycle— with the need to reduce being by far the most important precept, followed by a need to favor the reusable over the recyclable.[124] This proposed relationship to goods or products suggests a very different future than the universal material affluence pursued under conventional economic reasoning.

In short, the economic future advanced by proponents of community economics bears little resemblance to today's economic system. In sharp contrast to the current push for unending economic growth via globalization under neoclassical reasoning, community economics calls for a localized, self-reliant, stable economy that recognizes ecological limits to growth based on the carrying capacities of bioregions. Admittedly, not all advocates of community economics reject the merit or possibility of further growth under localized self-reliance. One supporter of localized, self-reliant economies admits to being "a strong believer in economic growth"[125] and opines that "[a]chieving community self-reliance in basic necessities hardly precludes further opportunities for economic growth."[126] However, most proponents of community economics extend their line of reasoning to encompass an acceptance of limits to economic growth based on the ecological capabilities of the bioregions that house local communities. They reason that realizing and then maintaining a state of self-sufficiency within a bioregion requires sustainable behavior that respects the limits of local ecosystems and pro- tects their abilities to provide basic life-support necessities over time. This general acceptance of limits to growth among proponents of community economics suggests that this school of thought might provide guidance to those seeking to envision the economic nature of no-growth communities that evidence stability and sustainability. Table 5.1 compares and contrasts some of the key precepts of neoclassical economics with those of community economics.

Table 5.1 Neoclassical (growth) economics versus community (no-growth) economics

Neoclassical economics	Community economics
Sanctifies the primacy of economic growth	Sanctifies the primacy of ecological sustainability
Idealizes an ideology of growth and wealth	Idealizes an ideology of stability and sufficiency
Considers economic growth to represent the central panacea for societal problems and the primary indicator of societal progress	Considers economic growth to represent the source of societal problems and the antithesis of societal progress

Table 5.1 (continued)

Neoclassical economics	Community economics
Values specialization, efficiency, and productivity in pursuit of material affluence	Values diversity, resilience, and durability in pursuit of community well-being
Champions the merit of individuality and competition in economic decision making and behavior	Champions the merit of solidarity and cooperation in economic decision making and behavior
Celebrates capital- and energy-intensive enterprises as a way of increasing productivity via reduced labor inputs	Celebrates labor-intensive businesses as a way of advancing local employment security and moving toward full employment
Sanctions the exploitation of resources and natural systems in furtherance of economic growth	Encourages the conservation of resources and natural systems in furtherance of ecological sustainability
Serves a wants-based consumer society guided by the postulate of non-satiety concerning goods	Serves a needs-based conserver society guided by the principle of sufficiency of goods
Suggests individual well-being is best served by commodity-intensive lifestyles realized under consumerism	Suggests individual well-being is served by the furtherance of community well-being under conserver lifestyles
Touts the advantages of economic globalization without place-based loyalties	Touts the advantages of place-based economies with place-based loyalties
Makes a case for the advantages of economic integration and interdependence in a global marketplace	Makes a case against external dependencies and for local self-sufficiency
Favors an export-oriented development model where a few, large-scale firms with comparative advantages gain external dollars to fuel further growth	Favors an import-substitution development model where a diverse set of small-scale businesses meet essential needs within a stable economy
Endorses national and multinational, for-profit corporations capable of realizing economies of scale in furtherance of increased production for a global market	Endorses local, nonprofit community corporations producing local goods for local consumption in furtherance of making communities self-reliant in necessities
Promotes national and multinational, for-profit financial institutions capable of funding ongoing economic expansion	Promotes local, nonprofit financial corporations capable of funding local businesses without the inordinate finance charges that force further growth
Argues for the desirability of "sustained growth" and the possibility of "sustainable growth"	Argues for the desirability of "sustainable development" and the impossibility of "sustainable growth"
Discounts or rejects the idea of limits to economic growth based on unlimited prospects for substitutability, eco-efficiency, and human ingenuity	Accepts the idea of limits to economic growth based on the limited ecological capabilities of bioregions and existent ecological limits globally
Evidences uncompromising loyalty to the growth imperative	Evidences uncompromising fealty to the no-growth imperative

In terms of the quintessential difference between the two, their respective stances on growth lie at the very core of their visions of alternative economic futures. However, other precepts of community economics suggest additional prospective economic features of communities under a realized state of no growth. Communities seeking to stop economic growth could advance that end by implementing the noted precepts of community economics, as they undertake a transition from neoclassical growth economics to community no-growth economics. That transition will surely encounter substantial challenges, but the current reality of existent ecological limits to growth necessitates confronting those challenges and undertaking the admittedly daunting task of devising local, no-growth economies. The community economics movement has advanced prospects for envisioning such local, no-growth economies by challenging the "prevailing myth … that in order to foster economic development a community must accept growth."[127] Proponents argue for an alternative position in the following terms: "The truth is that growth must be distinguished from development: growth means to get bigger, development means to get better—an increase in quality and diversity."[128] In terms of development options, they suggest that "[t]wo alternatives for development without growth are supporting existing businesses and increasing the number of times a dollar is spent in the community."[129] In short, they have broken ground on the daunting task of attempting to conceptualize the nature of local, no-growth economies by first suggesting the possibility of such entities and then identifying some of their likely characteristics.

Likely social and political features of no-growth communities

Some of the likely *social features* of no-growth communities are implied by the nature of the formerly surveyed economic features that are apt to be demonstrated by such communities. As noted above, these localized, self-reliant, stable economies would consist of diverse, needs-based, import-substitution businesses focused on meeting essential local needs. This needs-based economic orientation predicated on realizing sufficiency of goods for the sake of community well-being obviously infers very different social characteristics than a wants-based economic orientation based on maintaining endless growth in incomes and material affluence via continual increases in production and consumption. A shift from a wants-based consumer society to a needs-based conserver society would, above all else, infer a dramatic reduction in the number of goods produced, which would, in turn, suggest different social behaviors and values. This reduced emphasis on the role of consumption under a needs-based orientation would, for example, permit producers and consumers to create social relationships that could be expected to expand feelings of belonging to a community. A shift from a primary focus on personal gain to one directed at community well-being, and an accompanying interest in jobs and security over income and wealth, would infer additional social features of no-growth communities. These attributes could, for example, be expected to lead to a shift from competition to cooperation. A focus on employment security would, in turn, result in an interest in meaningful and personally satisfying work as an alternative to the alienating and dehumanizing jobs associated with industrial positions driven by considerations of efficiency and productivity. In short, likely economic features of no-growth communities suggest dramatically different social arrangements and characteristics than those typically associated with communities driven by their loyalty to the growth imperative.

Under the dominating influence of the growth imperative "[e]ndless economic growth driven by unbridled consumption has been elevated to the status of a modern religion."[130] In the conventional view, the recipe for progress is simple: "the more people consume, the happier they will be."[131] However, research examining the hypothesis that happiness or life satisfaction is linked to income growth that enables increased consumption does not support this conventional view. Such research shows that any correlation between more income and happiness disappears after people attain annual per capita income levels somewhere between $10,000 and $15,000.[132] In the United States, for example, while real income per head has tripled since 1950, the percentage of people reporting themselves as very happy has declined since the mid-1970s.[133] With a growing awareness that income and associated consumption growth no longer translate into increased happiness beyond a discernable level of wealth, "the growth mandate is giving way in some quarters to a new focus on development."[134]

"Development is ultimately about improving human well-being—meeting fundamental human needs for food and shelter, security, good health, strong relationships, and the opportunity to achieve individual potential."[135] Such a "transition to an economic system where progress is measured by improvements in well-being rather than by expansion of the scale and scope of market economic activity"[136] would represent a fundamental paradigm shift in economic thinking. This paradigm shift is supported by

> [a]n increasingly large and robust body of hedonics research [that] confirms what people know intuitively: beyond a certain threshold, more material wealth is a poor substitute for community cohesion, healthy relationships, a sense of purpose, connection with nature, and other dimensions of human happiness.[137]

Additional support for the paradigm shift can be found in research suggesting "a negative correlation between materialistic attitudes and subjective well-being," where findings indicate that "people who define and measure their own worth through money and material possessions ... report lower levels of happiness."[138] In the end, "[t]he single most common finding from a half century's research on the correlates of life satisfaction ... is that happiness is best predicted by the breadth and depth of one's social connections."[139] Those calling for a "shift from an emphasis on consumption to an emphasis on well-being"[140] are largely motivated by the belief that "happiness depends ... on intimate human relationships."[141] Proponents of this point of view argue that "well-being depends critically on family stability, friendship, and strength of community."[142] They "believe time spent with those we love, sharing conversations, companionship and activities, is far more pleasurable than the fleeting enjoyment of possessing a novelty item."[143] While this belief that the real sources of human happiness reside in family, friends, and community[144] may be comforting in its suggestion of an alternative to consumerism for realizing personal happiness, life satisfaction, and well-being, it must contend with disconcerting research showing that social connections have "eroded steadily and sometimes dramatically over the past two generations."[145]

Research has shown that *social capital*, which refers to connections among individuals, declined significantly over the course of the last third of the twentieth century. That research reveals that "beginning in the 1960s and 1970s and accelerating in the 1980s and 1990s ... the fabric of American community life [began] to unravel."[146] Over that time period Americans became increasingly disconnected from family, friends, neighbors, and community social structures like the church, clubs, and political parties. "The sharp, steady declines in club meetings, visits with friends, committee service, church attendance, philanthropic generosity, card games, and electoral turnout have hit virtually all sectors of American society over the last several decades and in roughly equal measure."[147] Evidence suggests that "the last several decades have witnessed a striking diminution of regular contacts with friends and neighbors," and that "[w]e know our neighbors less well, and we see old friends less often."[148] Over roughly the last third of the twentieth century the number of times the average American entertained friends at home declined by 45 percent, their readiness to make new friends declined by nearly one-third, and their social contacts with neighbors fell by about one-third.[149] "By some surveys, three-quarters of Americans confess that they don't know their next-door neighbors."[150] Connections within families also suffered during this time period, as the average American employee added the equivalent of five 40-hour weeks to their annual work schedules.[151] These additional hours spent working have come at the expense of time spent with spouses and children, with the latter confirmed by surveys showing that the "amount of time parents spend with their children has steadily decreased."[152]

Research clearly shows the loss of family, friend, and community connections comes at a very real cost. Social capital represents "social networks and norms of reciprocity [that] can facilitate cooperation for mutual benefit."[153] This capital may be thought of as a form of "social potentiality sufficient to the substantial improvement of living conditions in the whole community."[154] Social capital represents a system of good will, fellowship, sympathy, social intercourse, and good neighborliness that benefits all our lives. It is "good for undergirding specific reciprocal and mobilizing solidarity" that, in turn, "allow citizens to resolve collective problems more easily."[155] At the community level it is capable of generating such positive consequences as mutual support, cooperation, trust, and institutional effectiveness.[156] At the personal level family, friends, and community institutions can be thought of as "social safety nets"[157] that help people survive life's challenges. "Where once we could fall back on social capital—families, churches, friends—these are no longer strong enough to cushion our fall."[158] As social capital connections weaken people are naturally apt to feel more vulnerable and insecure. "In measurable and well-documented ways, social capital makes an enormous difference in our lives."[159] Research shows that it affects outcomes across child welfare and education, the health and productivity of neighborhoods, economic prosperity, health and happiness, and democratic citizenship and government perform-ance. It is possible to "present evidence that social capital makes us smarter, healthier, safer, richer, and better able to govern a just and stable society."[160] There is "hard evidence that our schools and neighborhoods don't work so well when community bonds slacken, that our economy, our democracy, and even our health and happiness depend on adequate stocks of social capital."[161] With respect to individuals, research has shown "that social connectedness is one of the most powerful determinants of our well-being ... [revealing that] the more integrated we are with our community, the less likely we are to experience colds, heart attacks, strokes, cancer, depression, and premature death of all sorts."[162] "As a rough rule of thumb, if you belong to no groups but decide to join one, you cut your risk of dying over the next year *in half*."[163] Related research has show "that *people who are socially disconnected are between two and five times more likely to die from all causes, compared with matched individuals who have close ties to family, friends, and community*."[164] And as noted previously, personal happiness also ends up being best predicted by the breadth and depth of one's social connections. The ongoing erosion of social capital is therefore disturbing and finds expression in the following terms: "Our growing social-capital deficit threatens educational performance, safe neighborhoods, equitable tax collection, democratic responsiveness, everyday honesty, and even our health and happiness."[165] Attributing such importance to social capital naturally produces an interest in understanding the causes of its decline over the course of the past couple of generations.

Research has identified the following explanations for the erosion of social connections in the United States: Pressures of time and money, including the special pressures of two-career families; suburban sprawl (which consumes time for commutes, increases social segregation in ways that reduce civic involvement, and disrupts the well-defined and bounded communities that foster involvement); electronic entertainment (which has privatized leisure time); and generational changes in values (which have replaced an unusually civic generation with several generations that are less embedded in commu-nity life).[166] Research exploring the related matter of a steady decline in life satisfaction among adult Americans over the course of past decades has found that "[r]oughly half of the decline in contentment is associated with financial worries, and half is associated with declines in social capital: lower marriage rates and decreasing connectedness to friends and community."[167] These findings reveal that various forms of economic determinism play a part in explaining the declines in both social capital and personal contentment. Pressures of time and money that have played a part in the erosion of social capital can be linked to the need to work additional hours for the income necessary to maintain consumer lifestyles driven by the motivation to keep up with the Joneses. The decline in contentment attributable to financial worries can, in turn, be linked to an accelerating nationalization and globalization of economic structures that increase individuals' economic vulnerabilities and insecurities. In the American context this naturally raises the question as to what degree ongoing declines in happiness, contentment, and well-being can be attributed to inherent features of an economic system based on free-market capitalism. This question raises the troubling possibility that some of the features of capitalism that are necessary to maintain growth prospects may simultaneously erode social relationships.[168] Among the features of capitalism that might be subject to such a criticism are its endorsement of "a culture of economic individualism,"[169] its support of personal freedom expressed through privatism, autonomy, and mobility, and its praise of economic self-reliance. While these features may, as will be noted, be linked to furtherance of consumerism, they can be criticized for their corrosive affects on social connectedness.

An ongoing social contest between individualism and community has a long and rich tradition in the United States, as expressed in the following terms: "Community has warred incessantly with individualism for pre-eminence in our political hagiology."[170] "Liberation from ossified community bonds is a recurrent and honored theme in our culture," and in spite of the undeniable reality that much of what has been accomplished in America could not have taken place without networks of civic engagement, "the myth of rugged individualism continues to strike a powerful inner chord in the American psyche."[171] This contest between individualism and community was extended into the realm of economics by social critics who argued "that capitalism would undermine the preconditions for its own success by eroding interpersonal ties and social trust."[172] Noted theorists like Georg Simmel and Karl Marx "argued that market capitalism had created a 'cold society,' lacking the interpersonal warmth necessary for friendship and devaluing human ties to the status of mere commodities."[173] However, these criticisms did not stop defenders of capitalism from arguing that people pursuing their own interests in a free-market society represented the best possible route for facilitating the pursuit of wealth by individuals and nations. Nor did it stop them from defending the merit of personal freedom via support for laissez-faire principles, under which individuals ought to be free to act in their self-interest without governmental interference, with everyone standing to gain as they freely compete in an unregulated marketplace. Support of personal freedom extended to a defense of the merit of personal mobility, under the reasoning that the ongoing "creative destruction" of businesses in pursuit of ever-greater efficiencies necessitated a view of workers as exchangeable units of production capable of freely relocating to newly created workplaces. As sold to workers, mobility was said to represent an avenue for pursuit of ever-higher incomes as workers moved to take advantage of better remuneration. Defenders of capitalism have also espoused the virtue of economic self-reliance, arguing that individual responsibility for one's own economic circumstances represents the only reasonable path for continual improvements in the collective economic status of any country. The classic argument claims that social welfare programs undermine the personal initiative necessary for collective economic gains. If these defining features of capitalism have combined to further the pursuit of national material affluence via ongoing increases in production and consumption embodied in the extreme consumerism of American lifestyles, this reality still begs the question of why these gains have failed to advance individual states of happiness, life satisfaction, or well-being.

The favored status of individualism as an operational principle of capitalism has increasingly resulted in a "world [that] is composed, more and more, of individuals in isolation from each other, each following his or her own path."[174] In the United States this has produced a society of "hyper-individualists"[175] who have largely lost sight of the value of family, friends, and community in determining prospects for individual well-being. The "powerful myth of the primacy of the individual, free to act and move as an independent entity" has produced a sort of myopia regarding the unassailable fact that "[w]e are profoundly social animals, not atomized individuals moving freely and separately from all else."[176] As individuals have played out their assigned social roles as producers and consumers under capitalism, research findings suggest that their unending pursuit of personal affluence and associated consumer lifestyles has increasingly alienated them from their families, friends, and communities. In an ultimate twist of irony, it has been suggested that in attempting to respond to this alienation, and its associated loneliness and emptiness, we have collectively turned to increased consumption to provide relief from the very alienation produced by consumer lifestyles in the first place.[177] Far too few have been willing to consider the possible role consumerism has played in severing social connections, as reflected in the following observation: "Longer working hours, higher levels of stress, failing families, drug addiction, children at risk—these may be to some extent the pathology of consumerism."[178] This viewpoint raises the troubling question of whether "an ever larger pile of stuff" actually "undermines community."[179] If individualism, driven singularly by economic considerations of personal wealth and consumer lifestyles, has failed to deliver on promises of personal happiness, contentment, and well-being, one can readily understand why some critics have been inclined to make a case for the essential role of community in shaping prospects for individuals. In the opinion of one critic, the appropriate social response "should concentrate on creating and sustaining strong communities, not creating a culture of economic individualism."[180]

Capitalism's support of personal freedom as expressed through privatism, autonomy, and mobility also raises questions of community, particularly with the association of the term autonomy with the independence of, and the absence of control over, the individual. Privatism, in turn, represents a concern only with personal involvements and a disregard for public affairs, while mobility represents an independence from social ties that might serve to bind individuals to communities. Taken collectively, these expressions of personal freedom clearly discount the value of community. In a similar vein, capitalism's support of economic self-reliance also suggests a possible personal independence from community. This view of self-reliance assumes that if individuals become economically self-reliant they will naturally realize personal states of happiness, contentment, and well-being. However, the noted research indicates that neither personal freedom nor economic self-reliance represent avenues for realizing these states, and that instead their realization ultimately depends on the social connections of family, friends, and community. This awareness produces a natural skepticism about the respective merits of economic individualism, personal economic freedom, and economic self-reliance. Skeptics argue that instead of economic individualism, what we really need is "a shift to an economy that connects us more closely."[181] With respect to personal economic freedom expressed through privatism, they argue we need to "break the spell of privateness" and recognize our inherent desire "to be a part of something larger than ourselves."[182] Offering a different take on freedom, they suggest we might have something to learn from the higher regard for community among many Europeans, who tend to "define freedom in community—in belonging, not belongings."[183] These skeptics also offer a critical take on the idea of economic self-reliance that touches on yet another aspect of freedom, suggesting that community economies might offer "relative freedom from the uncertainty of the global economy and market forces."[184] This view of economic self-reliance in an age of increasing nationalization and globalization emphasizes the role that any pursuit of self-reliance by individuals plays in creating personal economic insecurity. Critics point to our "ever-present need to feel secure,"[185] asserting that "[s]ecurity is as basic a human need as there is, and [that] its lack is already the defining feature of our age."[186] As an alternative, they call for collective recognition of the fact that the "knowledge that you matter to others is a kind of security that no money can purchase."[187] The resulting rejection of economic individualism, personal economic freedom, and economic self-reliance as possible routes to personal fulfillment naturally suggests an alternative vision with very different social characteristics.

Critics of the social outcomes associated with the current capitalistic economic system call for nothing less than a paradigm shift capable of producing completely different social relationships than those that dominate the current era. At the most basic level they call for a "transition from self-interest to social behaviors"[188] and an associated community engagement that builds solidarity with neighbors.[189] They argue that it is the local community "which provides individuals and families with a sense of place and belonging, fellowship and support, purpose and meaning."[190] For these critics "[s]table communities and neighborhoods are a prerequisite for happiness, for productive and rewarding lives, for a crucial sense of security and belonging."[191] These critics emphasize that "a community suggests a group of geographically rooted people engaged in relationships with each other."[192] They therefore argue that people need to forsake personal mobility in pursuit of higher incomes to support further consumption in favor of place-based, geographical commitments that will engender community. In this regard it is of interest to note recent data indicate that people are changing addresses less often and thereby reversing a former, long-term trend, with one in five moving annually during the 1970s and only one in seven moving each year in 2007, the lowest rate since the census started tracking movement in 1940.[193] Believing the current "hedonic treadmill" of rising income and increasing consumption to be quite simply unsustainable,[194] proponents of an alternative economic and social future tend to believe that "the key to human survival will probably be the local community ... [represented] by vibrant, increasingly autonomous and self-reliant local groupings of people that emphasize sharing, cooperation and living lightly on the Earth."[195] Living lightly would consist of sharply reduced personal consumption as part of a shift from a wants-based economy to a needs-based economy, and afford producers the opportunity to develop interpersonal connections with consumers as they began to "shop locally, eat locally and seasonally, hire locally, work locally, [and] play locally."[196] Goods associated with meeting such basic needs as clothing, building materials for homes, and local energy generation would be characterized by their "[d]urability, repairability, and 'upgradability' [so as to] lessen the environmental impact of consumption,"[197] which under the latter two attributes would further increase prospects for building social connections.

Shifting away from consumer lifestyles, sometimes called "downshifting" in discussions of trends toward broader attempts to simplify lifestyles, evokes aspects of a rapidly emerging voluntary simplicity movement.[198] Members of this movement clearly favor personal time over more money and additional consumer goods, which suggests a quest for individual fulfillment via an alternative route to that represented by consumer lifestyles. In this regard, the suggested social reforms call for "redefining prosperity to emphasize a higher quality of life rather than the mere accumulation of goods."[199] In sum total, the prior survey infers that no-growth communities would be very different social entities than those represented by today's growth-fixated communities, with inhabitants reflecting the following preferences: Social relationships over consumer goods; voluntary simplicity lifestyles over consumer lifestyles; community well-being over personal economic gain; fellowship over individualism; belonging over autonomy; community self-reliance over personal self-reliance; place-based loyalty over mobility; cooperation over competition; job satisfaction over higher incomes; time over money; happiness over wealth; and social interaction over privatized entertainment. These preferences demonstrate a clear bias toward communitarian values (i.e., cooperation, participation, solidarity, and reciprocity) that contrast sharply with the values of individualism (i.e., competition, autonomy, self-reliance, and self-serving behavior) that characterize today's American landscape. Taken together these social characteristics of no-growth communities would represent a new commitment to the development of community ties that might be expected to enhance individual prospects for happiness, self-satisfaction, and well-being.

Any attempt to envision the likely *political features* of no-growth communities is compounded by having to address both the internal politics of these communities and the politics of their bioregions. As noted formerly, local communities have no hope of becoming stable, self-reliant, sustainable entities in the absence of reciprocal relationships with their bioregions. It is only in such regional contexts that local communities can hope to become self-reliant with respect to fulfilling their basic needs for such essentials as water, food, energy, and building materials. While bioregionalists argue the case for a form of decentralized politics based on regions defined by natural geophysical boundaries, any transition to such an ideal would have to contend with the current political boundaries of local communities. In this context, the entity closest to the political regions envisioned by bioregionalists would be some of today's counties that encompass geographical areas large enough to meet their communities' basic needs. Some of the political features of emerging no-growth communities could be demonstrated by cities, while other features might be revealed through the reciprocal relationships cities develop with the counties within which they are located.

Politics at the city level would take on an entirely different tenor than that displayed currently if urban places were to adopt no-growth stances. Rejection of further growth would mean that cities would no longer function as the "growth machines" characterized by Harvey Molotch. Their politicians would, in turn, reflect an allegiance to a far broader raison d'être than merely serving to increase land values through an ongoing intensification of land use. These politicians would cease to be defenders of an outdated and irrelevant set of pro-growth myths, and would instead help cities undergo a transformation to stable, self-reliant, sustainable communities. Their decisions would serve to increase the *use* values of local properties rather than their *exchange* values in the prospective manner outlined by Molotch. Decisions of no-growth politicians would also reflect a deliberate process of transforming local economies from their current wants-based orientations to new needs-based alignments that emphasize relative self-reliance. In this respect their decisions would support local import-substitution businesses over the export orientation traditionally supported under pro-growth rationales. Some other aspects of a no-growth, decision-making orientation were addressed in the former treatment of strategies for stopping growth in local communities. Local elected officials committed to no-growth would eliminate all public subsidies for the infrastructure improvements that enable further growth. They would also eliminate an array of growth subsidies and incentives that have traditionally been used to recruit new firms. In this respect politicians would establish entirely new relationships with their Chambers of Commerce, only providing funding allocations for programs intended to diversify and strengthen the local economy, not grow it. In a similar vein, they would completely redefine the role of local economic development agencies, also requiring those agencies to focus on development rather than growth. They would additionally modify local plans and associated land-use regulations so as to close out options for further growth. However, options for helping local economies transition to stability, self-reliance, and sustainability under a state of no growth are not limited to these types of local political decisions.

Politicians shaping the future of a local community have the power to "mobilize *all* its legal powers of investment, purchasing, contracting, hiring, and taxation"[200] in ways that can just as effectively *suppress* growth as those powers have traditionally been used to *promote* growth. They could, for example, take the economy in a new direction "by awarding subsidies, investments, contracts, and purchases primarily to community corporations"[201] committed to diversifying and strengthening, rather than growing, the local economy. In terms of specifics they could give hiring preferences to local citizens and locally owned firms, conduct local purchasing for any municipal needs, help create community currencies, contract with local firms in any privatization of public functions, and create tax and fee structures that favor community corporations.[202] While some critics would contest the ability of local governments to enact local laws favoring community corporations, citing such obstacles as the Commerce Clause of the U.S. Constitution, it is possible to argue that local laws may infringe on commerce if their purpose can be directly linked to community health, safety, and welfare.[203] Under a liberal interpretation of such local latitude to freely regulate on general welfare grounds, it is possible to make the case that any "local government with competent counsel which can make a credible case about how a proposed law will serve public 'health, safety, and welfare' can pretty much legislate as it pleases."[204] There seems little doubt that local politicians have the power to direct local economies in ways that would allow them "to generate their own electricity, grow their own food, recycle water and wood, fabricate local assets into clothing and shelter, [and] create viable service economies"[205] in the course of creating self-reliant economies that meet local needs without growth. To help meet the important goal of self-reliance with respect to local food production, local decision makers could make public properties available for farmers' markets and community gardens, as well as having local government serve as a clearing house for community supported agriculture initiatives. It would appear that prospects for local political decision making in support of stable, self-reliant, sustainable communities would be virtually unlimited once local politicians decided to shift the emphasis of community engagement from growth promotion to sustainable development. Local politics directed at making communities *better* rather than *bigger* would demonstrate a range of political characteristics distinctly different from the features typically associated with cities operating as growth machines. These new characteristics might be expected to include the following preferences on the part of local politicians: Support of use values over exchange values for community properties; approval of import-substitution businesses over export-oriented businesses; funding for improvements of existing infrastructure over that for new infrastructure supporting further growth; allocation of monies for programs to diversify and strengthen the local economy over those intended to expand it; a preference for the downzoning of land over upzonings that create growth prospects; and the application of all available local legal powers to enhance the status of existing local needs-based businesses over non-local, wants-based businesses.

Additional likely political features of no-growth communities could be expected to emerge from their relationships with their bioregions—the geographical areas that serve as both sources of essential resources and waste sinks for their cities. In a small minority of situations the relationships of urban centers with their broader hinterlands has been ordained by federal and state legislation, often in response to pressing environmental problems brought on by growth. The noted cases of laws passed to protect the California coastline, Lake Tahoe, and the Pinelands in New Jersey represent examples of such legislated relationships between urban centers and their broader regions. In other geographical settings statewide growth-management laws have mandated reciprocal relationships between cities and larger geographical areas, sometimes involving regional commissions or agencies created to address development that entails regional impacts, but more typically these laws have imposed reciprocal relationships between cities and their counties. Under the statewide law in the state of Washington, for example, cities are directed to contain future growth within so-called urban growth areas, while counties are required to maintain rural areas and to adopt regulations to conserve agricultural, timber, and mineral resource lands.[206] This conservation of resource lands outside urban centers would obviously constitute an essential prerequisite to cities being able to achieve and maintain sustainable, self-reliant states of no growth within the productive capacities of their surrounding resource lands. A likely political feature of no-growth communities could therefore be expected to consist of contractual agreements between cities and their counties specifically intended to protect the long-term viability of the resource lands needed to sustain urban centers. It is of particular interest to note that these contractual agreements would not be dependent upon the prior passage of statewide growth-management laws. In Washington State, for example, such a statewide law was not passed until 1990, but the absence of that law did not stop the cities of Lacy, Olympia, and Tumwater, and the county of Thurston from entering into a memorandum of understanding in 1988 intended to contain sprawl and conserve rural resource lands.[207] Under the existing governmental framework of cities and counties across America's landscape, these sorts of agreements might be expected to become common political features of local communities attempting to ensure their long-term viability as self-reliant, no-growth entities.

Likely physical features of no-growth communities

There can be little doubt that "a community manifests its values through its physical design."[208] Over the course of the latter half of the twentieth century and the opening decade of the twenty-first century a built environment emerged in the United States that clearly manifested American values. A preference for lower-density living reduced the average population density of all urbanized areas dramatically, from some 10 persons per acre in 1920 to about four persons per acre by 1990, and developments built after 1960 averaged only a little over two persons per acre.[209] This preference for lower densities resulted in an impressive jump in the amount of land being urbanized, as illustrated by a 47 percent increase between 1982 and 1997, whereas the nation's population only grew by 17 percent during that period.[210] During this period the conversion of rural land into developed land increased from 1.4 million acres per year in the 1980s to 2.2 million acres per year in the 1990s, representing, as noted previously, the conversion of an area the size of Vermont about every 2.5 years.[211] A preference for ever larger houses was also demonstrated during this period, with the median size of new single-family homes rising 39 percent, from 1,520 square feet in 1982 to 2,114 square feet in 2002.[212] An associated preference for private transportation, which pushed the number of registered vehicles past the number of licensed drivers in 2003,[213] made access to these ever-larger houses at more dispersed locations possible. As a result, vehicle miles traveled per capita increased from 3,979 in 1960 to 9,220 in 1995, and jumped to nearly 13,000 by 2004.[214] These ongoing increases in land conversion, the size of residences, and per capita miles driven have served to continuously increase the ecological footprints of American communities. That continuing expansion represents movement toward less sustainable states rather than a shift toward ever-greater sustainability. With the average ecological footprint of individual Americans already at over 20 acres, while the planet only contains some 4 acres of ecologically productive space per capita that is being continuously reduced by ongoing population growth and ecological degradation,[215] the current challenge is one of dramatically reducing the footprints of individuals and communities. Merely slowing the rate of an ongoing increase in these footprints via efficiency measures will not suffice to bring about the desperately needed transition to sustainable, no-growth communities.

The former survey of likely economic, social, and political features of no-growth communities suggested dramatic changes in each of these realms in order to be able to realize states of no growth in American communities. Economically, communities would have to undergo transformations from wants-based to needs-based economies. Socially, their residents would have to forego consumer lifestyles in favor of enriched social connections in order to experience gains in happiness, self-satisfaction, and well-being. Politically, communities would have to abandon their historical roles as growth machines, with their elected officials working to advance *use* values instead of *exchange* values of local properties. The likely physical features of no-growth communities would undoubtedly reflect similarly striking changes in their built environments. As noted previously, typical American communities have already outgrown the ecological support capabilities of their bioregions. In the case of large cities and their associated metropolitan complexes, they have radically surpassed the abilities of their ecosystems to sustainably support them. In these settings communities will actually have to undergo periods of negative growth until their populations and economies reach levels capable of being maintained indefinitely (sustained) without impairing the functional integrity and productivity of their ecosystems. Having exceeded ecological limits to growth within their bioregions, they now face the challenge of downsizing and redesigning themselves to levels that are ecologically sustainable within the capabilities of their respective bioregions. From the perspective of bioregionalists, the appropriate response to the current unsustainable state of most cities is "a radical restructuring"[216] directed at realizing a "sustainable symbiosis of city and hinterland."[217] In essence, at least some bioregionalists believe there are possibilities of downsizing and redesigning even large cities and their associated metropolitan complexes into sustainable frameworks comprised of "communities of communities,"[218] if their ecological footprints are significantly reduced both by periods of negative growth and radical redesign.

A case for the inherently unsustainable nature of virtually all of today's American cities may be made in two distinct ways. First, American cities represent the focal points of resource consumption and waste generation that produce a national ecological footprint for the United States that far exceeds the country's available ecological capacity.[219] America's cities have to rely on other nations to produce the resources they consume and assimilate the wastes they generate, making them major importers of ecological capacity. Collectively, their reliance on ecological capacity outside the United States makes it possible for the "country in effect to exceed its domestic and regenerative and absorptive limits by 'importing' those capacities from other countries."[220] This "sort of global transfer" makes it possible for "countries to live beyond their ecological means."[221] However, not all countries are capable of living beyond their ecological means without destroying the planet's ecological capital. Mounting evidence of the collective human enterprise having already exceeded global ecological limits to growth suggests that continued reliance on ecological capacities outside the United States no longer represents a viable policy option. American cities relying on ecological capacities outside their bioregion's capabilities are therefore engaged in inherently unsustainable practices. The current unsustainable nature of most American cities is also demonstrated by the extent to which they typically continue to degrade their local ecosystems in spite of their reliance on areas outside their respective bioregions. Current ecological realities therefore suggest that any meaningful shift to local urban sustainability will require dramatically scaling back the ecological footprints of individual communities to levels capable of being sustainably supported by their own bioregional capacities. American communities will only realize sustainable states when their operations no longer degrade global or local ecosystems.

If all American communities lived within the ecological capabilities of their bioregions, their individually sustainable behaviors would collectively amount to national sustainability for the United States. At that point the nation's ecological footprint would no longer exceed its available ecological capacity and America would no longer be degrading global ecosystems in order to sustain its citizens. To realize that state the first challenge confronting American communities is that of stopping growth. With ecological footprints that surpass their bioregions' capacities in virtually all cases, the foremost response necessarily requires shutting down any further increases in their ecological footprints. As noted formerly, that end will not be achieved by merely increasing the efficiency of further growth. *The absolutely essential first step in making a transition to urban sustainability will of necessity require shutting down the material increases that are inherently unsustainable, i.e., stopping demographic, economic, and urban growth.* Under estimates that growth is responsible for some 50 percent of annual energy consumption, and one might assume of equally significant percentages of annual resource demands and pollution emissions, shutting down growth would produce significant reductions in the ecological footprints of American communities immediately. However, with most communities having exceeded their ecological capabilities by wide margins, merely stopping future growth would represent an insufficient response. *Communities would also have to downsize to levels capable of being supported indefinitely by the capacities of their respective bioregions.* As part of this second response to advancing urban sustainability, local communities could undertake studies needed to determine their bioregions' sustainable ecological footprints. *Concurrent with initiatives to downsize American communities, local governments could initiate a broad spectrum of efficiency initiatives to help reduce their ecological footprints to sustainable levels.* Those initiatives could be expected to include programs to redesign and then redevelop land-use patterns that further urban sustainability. Some of the likely physical features of the no-growth communities that would emerge from stopping growth, downsizing existing urban centers, and adopting efficiency initiatives that include the creation of new land-use patterns, are logical outcomes of the likely economic, social, and political features of no-growth communities surveyed previously.

Any shift from a wants-based economy to a needs-based economy would imply significant reductions in the amount of land devoted to superfluous commercial and industrial enterprises. A corresponding shift from consumer-based lifestyles to community-based lifestyles could be expected to produce neighborhood designs intended to foster social connections, such as pocket parks and community gardens to facilitate social interaction. Politically, having locally elected officials shift their primary focus from enhancing *exchange* values of real estate to enhancing *use* values of community properties would expand the scope of political decision making beyond its current focus on mere intensification of land use to the design of land-use patterns that help build community. These shifts would cumulatively serve to create land-use patterns representing a very different built environment to the one that currently dominates the American landscape. As noted above, some bioregionalists believe today's large cities and their associated metropolitan complexes would have to be radically restructured into "communities of communities" in order to realize sustainable states. That restructuring process might be expected to include two distinct elements. First, as part of their downsizing initiatives, communities would be able to return significant portions of their landscapes to natural areas capable of carrying out essential ecological functions. The greatest change embodied in realizing such a new land-use pattern would be the former acceptance of the inherently unsustainable nature of automobile ownership within bioregions committed to self-sufficiency. Any recognition "that most of the world's people are not likely to ever own automobiles can lead to a fundamental reorientation of transport system planning and investment."[222] That reorientation would free up large portions of the landscape, because physical features of transportation systems based on cars and trucks claim "about one-third of the land mass of cities."[223] The rejection of private transportation on sustainability grounds will mean that the "automobile age as we have known it will be over,"[224] and the large areas within metropolitan areas currently occupied by freeways, state highways, and major arterials will be available for uses far better adapted to an age of sustainability. These linear networks could be transformed into interurban rail lines, urban farms to support agricultural self-reliance, and natural areas performing essential ecological functions. While any wholesale rejection of an automobile-based urban transportation system would undoubtedly require the involvement of the federal and state governments, local governments are active participants in a national system that provides hundreds of billions of dollars of annual subsidies to ensure the solvency of private transportation in the form of cars.[225] "If U.S. citizens had to pay the true costs of personal vehicles, they would not be able to afford them."[226] Federal and state governments could follow the lead of European countries in moving toward true cost pricing for automobiles. In Belgium and the Netherlands, for example, they have imposed excise and sale taxes that have increased the purchase price of cars to two or three times that of manufacturers' suggested sticker prices, and throughout Europe countries have imposed sales taxes on gasoline that has produced prices typically four or five times that paid in America. However, even in the absence of actions by federal or state governments, local communities could induce a rapid shift away from cars simply by cutting their infrastructure subsidies to local street systems, while at the same time rejecting any further offers of state or federal monies to support automobile infrastructure development or maintenance. These initiatives would permit expenditures to be diverted to interurban public transport systems that would free up land currently used for interurban highways and arterials and allow it to be transformed into more sustainable uses. These alternatives to highways and streets could effectively serve to separate urban communities from one another, and also help transform today's amorphous metropolitan masses into distinct and differentiated urban communities.

The second element of restructuring large cities and their associated metropolitan complexes into sustainable entities would consist of efficiency initiatives in the newly differentiated urban communities. These initiatives would focus on reassembling existing low-density development patterns into more efficient, higher-density patterns designed for people instead of cars. The newly created centers of higher-density development might be expected to draw on some of the tenets of new urbanism and "smart growth," such as a focus on public transit and nonmotorized forms of transportation represented by walking and biking, mixed-use development, a variety of housing types, commercial, and civic uses, and useable public spaces. The reassembly of low-density patterns into higher-density nodes would free up land for reintegrating such natural amenities as urban forests, wetlands, and wildlife habitats into urban communities, as well as creating space for agricultural operations within communities that would further the end of realizing agricultural self-sufficiency. While American cities tend to meet little if any of their own food needs, "cities worldwide already produce about one third of the food consumed by their residents on average."[227] The possibility of urban food production in North American cities is illustrated by Vancouver, Canada's largest West Coast city, where 44 percent of residents produce some of their own food.[228] If urban communities reassembled portions of their low-density suburban landscapes into higher-density centers, parts of the freed-up landscape could be converted to community gardens capable of meaningful contributions to local agricultural self-sufficiency. The feasibility of actually eliminating significant portions of low-density suburbia in American communities would appear to be enhanced by the near-term inevitable arrival of the "global oil peak"[229] and the high oil prices that are certain to follow. "Isolated by high oil prices, sprawling suburbs may prove to be ecologically and economically unsustainable."[230]

As James Kunstler has noted, "America finds itself nearing the end of the cheap-oil age having invested its national wealth in a living arrangement—suburban sprawl—that has no future."[231] The likely outcome has been suggested by Thomas Wheeler in the following terms: "There will eventually be a great scramble to get out of the suburbs as the world oil crisis deepens and the property values of suburban homes plummet."[232] If these prognostications are correct, urban communities are apt to encounter little resistance to converting unsustainable suburban patterns into more viable, pedestrian-oriented living arrangements. In suburban areas that might offer some resistance to taking part in a needed rearrangement of the built environment, local communities could take advantage of the 2005 *Kelo* ruling by the U.S. Supreme Court that sanctioned the use of the power of eminent domain to take single-family, suburban properties as part of local economic development programs.[233] However, local communities have other available approaches to realize a sustainable, built environment short of utilizing the controversial power of eminent domain. They could, for example, employ the tool of "transferable development rights" to achieve the reassembly of low-density, suburban development into more sustainable, pedestrian-oriented centers. That tool would use density incentives to encourage the purchase and transfer of development rights from sending zones (i.e., the suburbs) to receiving zones (i.e., the new centers) as part of an overall community planning effort intended to redesign the landscape. As part of this effort, many existing suburbs would come to be viewed as "the salvage yards and mines of the future,"[234] where suburban houses, malls, and chain-store franchises are exploited to obtain resources needed to rebuild the landscape into sustainable living patterns.

While transforming today's dominant suburban landscape into a new, land-use pattern based on people-oriented centers undoubtedly represents a significant social challenge, gaining public acceptance of the inherently unsustainable nature of automobile ownership within bioregions committed to self-sufficiency comprises an equally daunting undertaking. Designing the new centers for people, instead of cars, would negate a need for private transportation within these higher-density, pedestrian-oriented environments, while a need for cars outside these centers would also be eliminated if centers were effectively linked by public transit systems. Growing recognition that an automobile-based future for cities is simply not sustainable has found expression in calls for "making public transportation the centerpiece of urban transport, and augmenting it with sidewalks, jogging trails, and bikeways."[235] Advocates of such an urban transport system argue that "a combination of rail lines, bus lines, bicycle pathways, and pedestrian walkways offer the best of all possible worlds in providing mobility, low-cost transportation, and a healthy urban environment."[236] However, some sustainability advocates believe that the need to redesign the landscape goes beyond the technological adaptation of making public transportation the center of urban transport. These advocates suggest the newly designed landscape would of necessity entail more than a shift from cars to public transport, and instead create "daily environments that will have to be much more defined by walking distances."[237] In short, these advocates call for putting pedestrians at the very center of sustainable urban transport systems, not public rail lines. They believe "the transportation picture in the mid-twenty-first century will be very different from the fiesta of mobility we have enjoyed for the past fifty years."[238] For them, the "twenty-first century will be much more about staying put than about going to other places."[239] They argue that "[d]ensities in central cities, regional centers, and neighborhood centers need to increase so that whatever [transportation] mode people choose they can travel less."[240] A critical part of redesigned landscapes would therefore consist of the creation of "pedestrian cities—communities designed so that people do not need cars because they can walk wherever they need to go or take public transportation."[241] To the extent that these newly created communities still required public transport systems to supplement their pedestrian-oriented landscapes, they would include networks of electric trolleys characteristic of a former era in America. It has been noted that "[f]rom 1890 to about 1920, American localities managed to construct hundreds of local and interurban streetcar lines that added up to a magnificent national system."[242] Recreating such a system would obviate a need for much of the current urban street networks and associated parking lots, permitting communities to replace streets and parking lots with community gardens, parks, greenways, and a system of natural places capable of providing vital ecosystem services. The possibility of such a pedestrian- and trolley-based transportation system is evident in much of Europe, where "[s]cores of cities are declaring car-free zones"[243] and many have extensive networks of electric streetcars. Beyond changes in transportation infrastructure, another significant difference likely to be found in no-growth communities would undoubtedly consist of local networks of renewable-energy facilities. These decentralized solar and wind facilities would represent highly visible features of local communities, helping them realize energy self-sufficiency through a mix of these neighborhood energy facilities supplemented by energy sources drawn from their greater bioregions.

Lesser-sized urban centers could be expected to undergo a similarly radical physical transformation to that described for large cities and their associated metropolitan complexes. They too would have to abandon car-based landscapes in favor of pedestrian- and trolley-based development patterns to realize sustainable urban states. In their push to create sustainable, no-growth communities, smaller urban centers would also need to redesign and redevelop their landscapes to realize environments built for people instead of cars. Their reclaimed streets and parking lots would also be transformed into open spaces, parks, and natural landscapes. In contrast to the challenge of creating "communities of communities" within metropolitan areas, they would transform themselves into "communities of neighborhoods." These neighborhoods might be expected to reflect many of the same characteristics of the rearranged urban landscapes within metropolitan complexes, i.e., higher densities, mixed-use developments, variety in commercial and civic uses, and useable public spaces. As with larger urban centers, the reassembly of their unsustainable suburban land-use patterns into more viable, higher-density, pedestrian-oriented living arrangements would free up land for reintegrating such natural amenities as urban forests, wetlands, and wildlife habitats into these newly reconfigured communities. To realize agricultural self-sufficiency, they would likely contain significant areas devoted to public gardens, urban farms, and farmers markets, in addition to being surrounded by permanent greenbelts that protect the agricultural capabilities of their bioregions. These lesser-sized urban centers could also be expected to reflect an interest in energy self-sufficiency along the same lines demonstrated by larger centers, with decentralized, renewable-energy facilities evident in all neighborhoods. As one observer has noted: "Cities could become free of cars and could generate a significant portion of their energy and even their food by harnessing their rooftops and green spaces for solar arrays, wind turbines, and gardens."[244]

As the survey of likely physical features of no-growth communities reveals, American communities "will have to reorganize physically as well as socially and economically"[245] if they are to have any hope of realizing sustainable states. The suggested physical changes required for achieving urban sustainability are admittedly dramatic: Creation of a balance between built environments and natural areas capable of carrying out essential ecological functions; reassembly of existing, low-density development patterns into more efficient, higher-density, mixed-use patterns designed for people instead of cars; development of pedestrian- and trolley-based, community transport systems that negate the need for cars; reservation of agricultural spaces intended to further agricultural self-sufficiency; and construction of neighborhood-based solar and wind facilities intended to further energy self-sufficiency. The challenge of transitioning to sustainable, no-growth communities ends up being even more daunting when the economic, social, and political changes required to realize sustainable urban states are added to the mix, e.g., abandonment of a wants-based economy in favor of a needs-based economy, adoption of lifestyles guided by communalism rather than individualism, and a reorientation of political decision making from quantitative increases to qualitative improvements of communities. Taken together, the necessary economic, social, political, and physical changes required to realize sustainable, no-growth states in local communities represent nothing less than a total paradigm shift.

The implied new set of ideas, beliefs, values, and norms would represent a dramatic departure from today's dominant cultural paradigm. Virtually every aspect of current American behavior would have to change in order to stop demographic, economic, and urban growth as necessary prerequisites to achieving sustainable local communities. Housing arrangements would be radically altered. People's dietary habits would be completely revamped. Mobility patterns would be significantly curtailed. Economic activity would largely be relocalized. The nature of work would be reinvented both in terms of duration (taking productivity gains in terms of time off rather than increased income) and emphasis (shifting from wants-based employment to needs-based jobs, work directed at yielding durability rather than planned obsolescence, etc.). Attitudes toward residences would change from houses representing exchange values to be exploited to homes expressing use values to be protected. Individual reproductive behaviors would change to reflect a level of ecologically sustainable childbearing. And these changes only begin to scratch the surface in terms of how societal behavior would have to be radically altered in order to realize sustainable, no-growth communities. All of which raises the question of whether there are realistic, near-term prospects for achieving states of no growth in American communities.

Prospects for realizing sustainable, no-growth communities

A mounting global ecological crisis is increasingly being recognized as a threat to human civilization.[246] Some elements of that crisis are demonstrating an accelerating rate of deterioration over time, as illustrated by the examples of biodiversity loss, ocean acidification, and climate change. In 2001, data indicated that the species extinction rate attributable to anthropogenic causes was "at least 1,000 times higher than the background rate."[247] By 2008 a researcher was able to conclude that the "loss of biodiversity is tremendous and disturbing, and it continues to grow at an exponential rate."[248] In that same year, the International Union for Conservation of Nature issued a press release warning that an "extinction crisis" was underway and acknowledging the increasing role of climate change in exacerbating that crisis.[249] With respect to ocean acidification, a 2008 study reported that carbon dioxide was raising ocean acidity at least 10 times faster than previously thought, with clear negative effects on shellfish species.[250] As for evidence of an accelerating rate of climate change, it "is now clear that the speed, scale, and duration of climate change are at or beyond the worst-case scenarios of even a few years ago."[251] Researchers have reported that ice loss from Greenland in the summer of 2008 was nearly three times greater than in 2007.[252] "A May 2009 study that used the Integrated Global Systems Model of the Massachusetts Institute of Technology found that unless significant action is taken soon, median temperature increases would be 5.1 degrees Celsius by 2100, more than twice as much as the model had projected in 2003."[253] These accelerating rates of biodiversity loss, ocean acidification, and climate change are undermining the ecological systems that support humanity and the rest of the community of life on the planet. The resulting degradation and loss of ecosystems and their associated life-support services are seen as constituting the noted threat to civilization that appears to quickly be intensifying.

Evidence of the escalating rate of unsustainable demands on the planet's ecosystems has recently appeared in the form of updated data from the Global Footprint Network. In 2006 the Network reported that global demands on ecosystems exceeded the capacity of those systems by an estimated 25 percent, but in 2009 the Network suggested the planet's ecological carrying capacity was being overshot by some 40 percent.[254] By 2010 the World Wildlife Fund reported humanity's collective ecological footprint exceeded Earth's biocapacity by 50 percent. There is, in short, a growing understanding that people are using more of the Earth's ecological capacity than is available, and that in doing so they are quickly "undermining the resilience of the very ecosystems on which humanity depends."[255] This awareness has led one observer to assert that "there is no legitimate question that the human presence in nature is increasingly precarious and that the biosphere is uncomfortably close to the threshold of irreversible changes in Earth systems."[256] To date the response to this growing awareness of serious ecological problems and an associated "dialogue about sustainability has been almost exclusively focused on how to arrest environmental deterioration."[257] Those efforts have tended to rely on technological, market-price, and eco-efficiency adaptations to maintain pro-growth loyalties.

Technological optimists appear unable to recognize that a meaningful shift toward sustainability will involve "something more fundamental than the adoption of new technologies,"[258] and that while new technologies have a role to play in helping realize a sustainable future "they are only a part of what's needed for long-run sustainability—necessary change, but not sufficient."[259] Market-place loyalists, in turn, seem unable to recognize that sustainable behavior will involve more than merely getting prices to tell the ecological truth. The challenge is greater than the prevailing focus on "consumption shifting" to green purchases, and actually requires "consumption reducing" actions to realize genuinely sustainable patterns of consumption.[260] Eco-efficiency advocates similarly appear unable to recognize that "eco-efficiency is not improving fast enough to prevent impacts from rising,"[261] as reflected by data showing that "[d]espite a 30-percent increase in resource efficiency, global resource use has expanded 50 percent over the past three decades."[262] So while eco-efficiency clearly represents a key element of necessary change, it also represents an insufficient response to current ecological realities. Humankind finds itself in the position of having to "solve the largest threat humanity has ever faced: unsustainable practices undermining the very [ecological] systems people depend on."[263] Continuation of current unsustainable behavior is only made possible through "the short-sighted conversion of ecosystems into resources at the expense of both human communities and the Earth community" under a development paradigm where "ecological degradation masquerades as economic development."[264] The ecological dilemma arising from having surpassed existent ecological limits to growth "can be traced back to one overarching problem: we have failed to adapt our current socioecological regime from an empty world to a full world."[265] Mere technological innovations, price adjustments, and eco-efficiency adaptations do not constitute adequate responses to current ecological limits to further growth. The reality of existent ecological limits to growth suggests that a "dramatic shift in the very design of human societies will be essential."[266]

Evidence of a willingness to entertain a dramatic shift in the nature of the human enterprise currently dismantling global ecosystems is suggested by recent calls for the need to quickly transition "from cultures of consumerism to cultures of sustainability."[267] The Worldwatch Institute's *2010 State of the World* report, which focuses on this necessary transition, acknowledges in its foreword that "[n]o culture in history has achieved a cultural transformation as sweeping as the one called for [in the report]."[268] In that report dozens of contributing authors examine the cultural roots of the world's accelerating ecological crisis, identifying different aspects of consumer cultures "that have allowed human societies to outgrow their environmental support systems."[269] The common theme throughout the report is one of having to reject the cultural orientation of consumerism in favor of a new cultural framework based on sustainability, and that "[p]reventing the collapse of human civilization requires nothing less than a wholesale transformation of dominant cultural patterns"[270] based on consumerism. Under the viewpoint that the ecological crisis is also a crisis of culture, contributors to the Worldwatch report alternatively call for a new cultural mindset, story, paradigm, or worldview capable of prompting a rapid transition to "planetary lifestyles."[271]

These contributors uniformly believe in a pressing need for new "values, attitudes, practices, habits, and lifestyles that promote sustainability."[272] Individually, they call for a broad array of changes necessary to successfully transition from cultures of consumerism to cultures of sustainability, including: Environmentally sustainable childbearing; sustainable agriculture; sustainability education; sustainable work schedules and business practices; governmental sustainability policies; reorientation of media to broadcasting sustainability; social sustainability movements; and sustainable consumption and production processes. With respect to the consumerism paradigm, one contributor to the report cites environmental scientist Donella Meadows in identifying assumptions that need to change, including "that more stuff makes people happier, that perpetual growth is good, that humans are separate from nature, and that nature is a stock of resources to be exploited for human purposes."[273] Taken together, the suggested changes required to transition from a culture of consumerism to a culture of sustainability clearly represent a dramatic paradigm shift. Most of those changes represent significant challenges, but none more so than the call to abandon the idea "that perpetual growth is good."

The 2010 Worldwatch report acknowledges the challenge presented by the current growth imperative driving social behavior in virtually all national contexts. One contributor to the report acknowledges the existence and significance of "a simple economic law that might be called the growth imperative"[274] underlying continued growth. Another calls for shifting societal goals "from maximizing growth of the market economy to maximizing sustainable human well-being."[275] In a similar vein, another addresses "delinking growth from well-being."[276] Yet another comments on "the absurdity of the concept of infinite economic growth,"[277] and laments the fact that when the global economic recession accelerated in late 2009 "wealthy countries did not see this as an opportunity to shift to a sustainable 'no-growth' economy."[278] Even though these authors recognize the obstacle that growth represents to any possible transition to a culture of sustainability, their contributions to the Worldwatch report did not succeed in shifting the focus from consumerism to growth itself as the central problem of the current era. One of the authors concedes that "instead of becoming outmoded, the perpetual growth model is now spreading worldwide,"[279] yet the report centers on the need to "challenge consumerism and create post-consumer cultures"[280] rather than on a full frontal assault on growth as the ultimate evil confronting humankind. The report demonstrates the view that the primary challenge is one of awakening people "from the spell of the false promises of consumerism"[281] and recognizing that "[i]n an increasingly 'full world' in which human numbers and appetites press against natural limits, introducing an ethic of limited consumption is an urgent task."[282] Nowhere in the Worldwatch report is there any concession that realizing a sustainable future will require a cessation of any further demographic, economic, and urban growth. Nor does the report identify the pressing need to replace today's dominant growth imperative with a no-growth imperative as the primary prerequisite to advancing the end of sustainability.

Failure to address the inherently unsustainable nature of material increases in any and all forms, both within the report and within society at large, demonstrates the tremendous hold the growth imperative still exerts in the present era. If one concedes the continued dominant influence of pro-growth attitudes globally and nationally within the United States, this might raise serious doubts about prospects for stopping growth in American communities and transforming them into sustainable, no-growth entities. However, prospects for stopping growth in local communities are not as dismal as they may initially appear.

For decades evidence has been building in the United States of both a new attitude toward growth and an interest in an alternative to continued adherence to the growth imperative. With respect to the emergence of a new social view of growth in America during the last two decades of the twentieth century, the third chapter cited surveys that showed a majority of residents in rapidly growing areas were supportive of public actions to slow or stop growth. That anti-growth attitude continued to be revealed by survey findings during the first decade of the twenty-first century. In 2000 a poll indicated that more Americans had a greater concern about sprawl and traffic congestion than with crime, jobs, or education, which had been the traditional issues of primary concern.[283] The third chapter also cited findings from Virginia, Maryland, California, and Washington State polls during that decade indicating that a majority of citizens no longer equate growth with progress. Many local residents are continuously reminded of such an alternative position on growth by the opposition that regularly surfaces to many proposals for any form of new development. All of these examples reveal that it is no longer public opinion that drives continued growth, but rather pro-growth coalitions that represent minority instead of majority opinions. Actual public sentiment on growth suggests very real prospects for the emergence of no-growth coalitions to redirect local communities toward a sustainable, no-growth development path.

Realizing the critically needed paradigm shift to a new no-growth imperative will undoubtedly be a daunting undertaking. Growth-imperative loyalists can be expected to argue that further growth is inevitable, possible, necessary, and even desirable. Their assertions of its inevitability would likely make note of the power of so-called "demographic momentum" to drive further population growth, the economic momentum associated with underdeveloped countries seeking to attain developed-country status, and a claim of governments being unable to control urban growth. Their protestations of the possibility of further demographic growth are apt to emphasize technological advances capable of supporting more people, eco-efficiency gains enabling further economic growth, and smart-growth initiatives creating prospects for additional urban growth. Their assertions of its necessity might be expected to cite a need for demographic growth to support aging populations, economic growth to address current income inequities, and urban growth to maintain competitiveness in a global economy. As for its desirability, they might be expected to point to increased prospects for human ingenuity under an expanding population, reduced prospects for addressing social ills in the absence of economic growth, and expanded opportunities and choices in larger urban settings.

The challenge for those coming together to form no-growth coalitions will be one of providing effective counter arguments to these claims. Since demographic, economic, and urban growth represent inherently unsustainable phenomena, the most effective counter to assertions that further increases in any of these terms is inevitable would simply be a refusal to accept the premise that ongoing unsustainable behavior is inevitable. The most direct counter to assertions that further material increases are possible would be represented by the mounting evidence that former expansion has already taken the human enterprise beyond ecological limits to growth. Assertions of the necessity of further growth are capable of being countered by alternative formulations of likely economic, social, political, and physical features of no-growth communities surveyed previously, which collectively suggest viable options for American communities in the absence of growth. Finally, counter arguments as to the desirability of further growth in local communities are capable of being effectively framed in terms of deliberate efforts to debunk pro-growth myths, and by references to research findings that ongoing growth is undermining the social, economic, and ecological viability of America's communities. Based on these counter claims as to the merit of continued allegiance to the growth imperative, and polls showing majority support for an alternative stance on growth, it would appear that prospects for realizing sustainable, no-growth communities are considerably greater than skeptics might concede.

Prospects for realizing no-growth communities may also be inferred from a rapidly expanding base of interest in an alternative to continued adherence to the growth imperative. Since the 1970s several movements have demonstrated a willingness to transition from a cultural story wedded to the growth imperative and move on to a story guided by a no-growth imperative. As revealed by the former survey of the contemporary Bioregionalism Movement that has its roots in the mid-1970s, bioregionalists embody a mindset centered on considerations of sustainability, an ecological worldview, and growth limits that provide an alternative to the current growth-based paradigm. Drawing on ancient idealizations of lifestyles based on voluntary poverty and voluntary simplicity, another movement emerged during that same time period. Fueled by such works as Goldian VandenBroeck's anthology *Less is More: The Art of Voluntary Poverty* published during the 1970s, and the release of *Voluntary Simplicity* by Duane Elgin and *Simple in Means, Rich in Ends* by Bill Devall during the 1980s, the Voluntary Simplicity Movement quickly attracted the loyalties of an increasing number of adherents. Participants in that movement demonstrate attitudes and behaviors based on a few key tenets that reflect the essence of voluntary simplicity: Material frugality, personal growth, and ecological modes of living. These participants view excesses in material possessions as encumbrances, suggest our lives would be enhanced if we were less burdened by possessions, and believe prospects for realizing personal freedom depend upon drastically limiting material possessions. They see the endless stream of material goods associated with meeting frivolous wants as a principle indicator of a dysfunctional society. For them living a materially simpler life has intrinsic value, but it is also valued for its ties to the tenets of personal growth and ecological modes of living. They believe that material simplicity advances psychological and spiritual aspects of living that can translate into personal growth. The reflective consciousness associated with such personal growth is, they believe, capable of promoting an ecological orientation toward all life on the planet. For them a personal consciousness opens the door to an ecological consciousness that motivates one to live more simply so as to be able to live in harmony with the vast ecology of all life. Among proponents of voluntary simplicity the escalating nature of ecological crises mandates new approaches to living if we are to live sustainably. The resulting mindset among these advocates of a materially simpler life suggests a direct rejection of the growth-based story that currently drives American cultural behavior. "Today voluntary simplicity has become a movement for sustainability and happiness in a post-consumer society."[284] Members of the Voluntary Simplicity Movement clearly demonstrate a mindset willing and able to let go of the growth imperative in favor of a no-growth imperative. For participants in the movement, "[i]t's about 'less is more'—more tranquility, more joy, more happiness."[285]

In the same era a number of other movements joined the Bioregionalism and Voluntary Simplicity Movements in calling for radical changes in what may alternatively be thought of as our current growth-based cultural story, mindset, or social paradigm. In 1986 a Slow Food Movement was born in Italy in response to "the erosion of the local, sustainable, and healthy food culture in Italy."[286] That movement quickly spread to other countries, including America, with the specific mission of reconnecting producers and consumers, promoting culinary diversity, protecting biodiversity, networking artisanal producers, enhancing traditional production to make it economically viable, and ensuring the availability of healthy, tasty food on a local scale. "Throughout the movement's activities, the emphasis is on making gastronomic pleasure and ecological responsibility inseparable."[287] The nature of concerns addressed by the Slow Food Movement suggests a preference for qualitative considerations over quantitative growth ends, which can readily lead to the conclusion that the movement is "playing an important role in facilitating a shift to sustainable cultures."[288] By the 1990s an Ecovillages Movement joined the former movements and began to demonstrate "innovative experiments in post-consumerist, community-based living."[289] These experiments with intentional, human-scale settlements demonstrate a strong focus on sustainability, delinking growth from well-being, reconnecting people with the place where they live, and affirming indigenous values and practices.[290] Ecovillages tend to emphasize relative self-reliance in food production, community-owned renewable energy facilities, community currencies and investment, cooperation and solidarity in community undertakings, and design features that reduce energy and materials intensity. Again, like the former noted movements, the Ecovillages Movement suggests a further option for viable, sustainable future living based on stability rather than growth.

During the opening decade of the twenty-first century other movements broadened the realm of alternatives to growth-based lifestyles. Emergence of a Take Back Your Time Movement has served to promote efforts "to trade advances in labor productivity for free time instead of additional purchasing power."[291] Proponents of this viewpoint identify numerous benefits associated with shorter working hours, including "more time for connection with friends and family, exercise and healthy eating, citizen and community engagement, attention to hobbies and educational advancement, appreciation of the natural world, personal emotional and spiritual growth, conscientious consumer habits, and proper environmental stewardship."[292] With respect to sustainability considerations, less work time directly translates into reductions in energy use, pollution, and carbon and ecological footprints for both individuals and communities. The expressed preference for time over money by individuals in this movement again indicates a willingness to consider decoupling well-being from growth, and infers a corresponding willingness to entertain limits to necessary future productivity increases once people have met their basic material needs.

In 2005 a Transition Town Movement originated in the United Kingdom and quickly began spreading around the world, with some 200 communities recognized as official Transition Towns by 2010.[293] This movement seeks to respond to the challenges of Peak Oil and Climate Change by building "resilience" in communities. Many of the initiatives undertaken by participants in this movement parallel those in the Ecovillages Movement, but the overriding focus of the Transition Towns Movement is on reducing communities' dependency on oil. Initiatives include various approaches to reduce oil use (e.g., shopping and eating locally, gardening, etc.) and institute behaviors based on sharing (e.g., car sharing, tool exchanges, community gardens, community-supported agriculture, etc.). As one observer noted: "Transition Towns are based on preparing for resource scarcity and climate change by building communities that are both socially and economically resilient, where the focus is on improving quality of life for the inhabitants while living sustainably."[294] This movement represents yet another example of people connecting on the basis of a belief in an alternative future driven by something more than the pursuit of endless material growth. Whether motivated by an acceptance of limits to growth, or a questioning of the desirability of further growth, these movements all exhibit a growth orientation that rejects allegiance to the growth imperative.

While all of the former movements represent attempts to transition to sustainability, as well as the noted interest in a new growth orientation, none identify growth as the central problem of the current era. None of them emphasize the inherently unsustainable nature of demographic, economic, and urban growth, or assert that realizing a state of sustainability will require a cessation of growth in each of these terms. Nor do any of those movements suggest that replacing the current dominant growth imperative with a no-growth imperative represents the primary prerequisite to advancing sustainability. However, failure to address this principal obstacle to transitioning to a sustainable future may finally be overcome by the emergence of a new political movement in Europe that has made growth its central focus. During the opening decade of the twenty-first century a Degrowth Movement gained increasing traction in countries like France, Italy, and Spain, with the subsequent formation of degrowth political parties in France and Italy.[295] Those parties have developed political platforms that envision degrowth societies centered on sustainability and relocalized production and consumption. The publication *La Decroissance* (*Degrowth*) is available across newsstands in France as well as in the rest of the francophone world, spreading the word about the need to rethink the role of growth at all governmental levels. This degrowth political movement is disseminating a degrowth vision as part of "an important effort to remind people that not only can growth be detrimental, but sometimes a sustainable decline is actually optimal."[296] *The revolutionary leap from simply questioning the merit of further growth, to actually recognizing the need for a period of negative growth to bring the human enterprise back into balance with the ecological capabilities of the planet's ecosystems, represents the true nature of the challenge confronting humankind at the beginning of the twenty-first century.* If the Degrowth Movement were to spread to the United States, it would dramatically enhance prospects for realizing no-growth communities in America by jumpstarting the process of reassessing the role of growth and the barrier growth presents to transitioning to states of true sustainability.

The role of social movements in bringing about dramatic social change has been acknowledged in the following terms: "Throughout history, social movements have played a powerful part in stimulating rapid periods of cultural evolution, where new sets of ideas, values, policies, or norms are rapidly adopted by large groups of people and subsequently embedded firmly into a culture."[297] In the past those movements have, for example, succeeded in liberating states from colonial rule, abolishing slavery, securing women's suffrage, and ending apartheid. However, according to prominent scientists the ecological crisis confronting humankind today calls for far quicker resolution than the time periods that were required to realize the former social gains. In addition, the sweeping nature of the cultural paradigm shift required to realize sustainability implies far greater social change than even the sum total of the noted examples. The required Cultural Revolution "implies a serious rethinking of people's current concepts of reality and significant imagination, but the shifting ecological realities are sure to provide the necessary inspiration."[298] An example of dramatic social change from the past that occurred within a relatively short time period, and which could be cited as support for the possibility of pulling off the needed transition to sustainability, would be the post-war transformation that "created a radical reversal of thrift values and an explosion of consumerism that ignited in the United States in the 1950s and spread around the world."[299] In less than a decade, the combined influences of government policies and corporate marketers did away with a thrift-based value system that had gotten Americans through decades of war and economic depression and remade the social landscape into a culture of consumerism. If the public and private sectors were able "to motivate a massive reorientation of cultural values and behaviors in relatively little time" in the past, one would hope they could do it again and bring about "a new set of values and political changes necessary to confront today's ecological crises."[300] The formerly surveyed social movements might be considered as having played a part in laying the foundation for the dramatic cultural changes needed to realize a state of ecological sustainability and thereby guarantee an indeterminate future for humankind on earth. While the necessary cultural changes cover an extensive array of social, economic, and political shifts far removed from current practices, and also entail a complete redesign and physical transformation of the built environment, *the central argument made in this work has been that sustainability gains made on any of those fronts will be for naught if they are not proceeded by deliberate actions to stop any and all further growth in demographic, economic, and urban terms.*

Having surpassed global ecological limits to growth the challenge is now much greater than simply making a transition to more efficient ongoing growth. The actual need is one of first stopping further growth in demographic, economic, and urban terms, and then instituting periods of negative growth in those terms in virtually all geographical contexts. Realizing these ends will require a prior rejection of such fatuous and vacuous terms as "smart growth" and "sustainable growth." In order to make meaningful headway on transitioning to a state of ecological sustainability, the moronic oxymoron of "sustainable growth" must be widely exposed as a serious impediment to realizing a state of sustainability. To advance sustainability the historical idea of growth representing progress will have to be abandoned in favor of a new recognition that growth represents inherently unsustainable behavior. The required transformation will also entail acceptance of the fact that under existent ecological limits further growth now represents the central problem of the current era. *And finally, and most significantly, the needed metamorphosis will require replacing the growth imperative that drives present social behavior with a no-growth imperative as the essential prerequisite to advancing a multitude of other sustainability ends.* In light of the profound nature of required changes associated with transitioning to sustainability, the prospects for realizing no-growth communities in America might appear to be slim at best. However, a different take on the prospects for realizing no-growth communities in the United States may be deduced from surveys indicating that a majority of Americans no longer consider growth within their communities to represent progress. With respect to an earlier admission that no-growth advocates would have to provide a plausible alternative paradigm if local residents are to be expected to abandon their historical support for the dominant, pro-growth paradigm, alternative formulations of likely economic, social, political, and physical features of no-growth communities surveyed previously collectively suggest viable options for American communities in the absence of growth. Similarly, the overview of social movements reflecting an interest in an alternative growth orientation suggests that the shift away from a cultural allegiance to the growth imperative and toward a no-growth imperative is already underway. In the end, prospects for realizing no-growth communities in America would appear to hinge on little else than the willingness of progressive communities to adopt the rationales and strategies for stopping growth laid out in the third chapter of this work. Options for ongoing growth will likely be severely curtailed in any case in the near future by mounting ecological crises, so the wise course would appear to be one of rejecting further unsustainable growth-driven behavior in favor of realizing a sustainable state of stability under no-growth. The transition from a culture dominated by the growth imperative to one guided by a no-growth imperative would represent the abandonment of an increasingly obsolete and lethal ideology in favor of a life-affirming ideology based on qualitative improvements rather than quantitative increases. Making America's communities better instead of bigger would represent a key turning point in implementing sustainability in the local settings that Americans call home, and nothing could advance that sustainability end more meaningfully than putting an end to the growth that represents inherently unsustainable behavior. Viewed in these terms, prospects for realizing no-growth communities in progressive local settings appears to represent such a positive new policy path that the near-term likelihood of witnessing the emergence of such stable, sustainable communities is highly probable. In such progressive settings local politicians might be surprised to discover the extent of public support for rationales and strategies intended to stop growth. The stage appears to be set for realizing stable, sustainable local communities, and the transformation is apt to take on surprising speed once a few communities demonstrate that the no-growth option is in fact a viable path for local governance.

With more than 80 percent of Americans living in metropolitan areas comprised of suburban and urban communities, there can clearly be no hope of achieving national sustainability unless these communities are transformed into sustainable entities. That transformation will ultimately depend on the ability of Americans to shift their loyalties from today's dominant growth imperative to a new no-growth imperative. Letting go of the traditional idea that demographic, economic, and urban growth represents progress will not be easy, but any pursuit of sustainability will require the prior recognition that these forms of material increases represent inherently unsustainable behavior. Rather than representing solutions to today's problems, growth in these terms represents the central problem of the current era. With the human enterprise having already surpassed global ecological limits under prior centuries of exponential growth, ongoing growth represents the single greatest threat to an indeterminate human future. It also represents the primary obstacle to advancing sustainability in local community contexts. If America's communities cannot shut down the unsustainable growth they presently exhibit, they can have no hope of realizing sustainable states. Ongoing growth will inevitably exhibit the pernicious attribute of negating any efficiency gains associated with sustainability initiatives. The quest for community sustainability must come to be recognized as being dependent on a prior rejection of any further material increases. *The growth imperative must be replaced with a no-growth imperative for America's communities to realize sustainability.* Current ecological realities demand that communities across the American landscape stop their unsustainable growth trends and implement stable, sustainable states of no growth.

Epilogue

10 difficult personal actions needed to save the world

The emergence of an environmental movement during the latter 1960s and early 1970s was prompted by a growing awareness of purported environmental crises. By the 1990s an increasing number of publications suggested the real concern had shifted to a range of ecological crises. Responses often appeared as lists of so-called simple things or easy steps that individuals could do to help save the Earth. These lists continued to be promulgated by environmental organizations during the opening decade of the twenty-first century, as illustrated by the World Wildlife Fund's list of "10 Simple Things YOU Can Do to Help Save the Earth!" With the primacy of global warming as the critical issue of the current era, the Environmental Defense Fund responded with a list of "10 Easy Steps to Fight Global Warming!" What these lists held in common was the claim that individuals could successfully mitigate environmental and ecological crises with easy or simple personal actions, such as recycling purchased products, adjusting thermostats, turning off lights, installing low-flow shower heads, replacing standard light bulbs with compact fluorescent bulbs, washing clothes in cold water, plugging air leaks in doors and windows, etc. The argument advanced in this work is that while these easy or simple steps may be necessary, they are insufficient to address the actual environmental and ecological crises presently confronting humankind. Those crises are all capable of being traced back to the continued exponential growth of the human enterprise, and challenges associated with stopping the demographic, economic, and urban increases dismantling the planet's ecological life-support systems represent difficult rather than easy personal actions. The following list of "10 Difficult Personal Actions Needed to Save the World" is intended to serve as a counterpoint to the lists of easy personal actions that are insufficient to address the current ecological dilemma. None of the lists of easy or simple steps to save the Earth acknowledge the essential need to shut down the inherently unsustainable demographic, economic, and urban increases as essential first steps in transitioning to a state of ecological sustainability. Personal actions needed to stop these forms of growth will be anything but easy, and yet the challenges they represent need not be viewed as insurmountable.

Action 1: Form a no-growth community coalition focused on shutting down urban growth within your political jurisdiction

Traditional pro-growth coalitions have historically succeeded in pressuring local politicians to support the further intensification of development that enhances the exchange values of real estate in America's communities. These coalitions have also co-opted most environmentalists and community activists with effective sales pitches for "smart growth" and "sustainable growth," garnering support for ongoing growth if it is expressed through ever-more-efficient land development. No-growth coalitions would have to challenge pro-growth mythology, and convince local politicians that the majority of residents are more interested in the community's use values of land than in making money off increasing exchange values of land. These no-growth coalitions would focus on stressing the inherently unsustainable nature of urban increases, and on conveying the essential message that stopping urban growth represents an indispensable prerequisite for realizing stable, sustainable communities. Members of these coalitions would consistently oppose the fallacious idea of "smart growth" representing a legitimate response to current ecological limits, and uniformly condemn any references to "sustainable growth," pointing out the moronic nature of that oxymoron given the impossibility of material growth ever representing a sustainable phenomenon. As an alternative to the delusional ideas of "smart growth" and "sustainable growth," no-growth coalitions would champion the merits of shifting to a "better not bigger" focus, with the objective of creating stable, localized, self-reliant, no-growth communities that value quality over quantity.

Action 2: Become an outspoken advocate for ecologically responsible childbearing, advancing the argument that "One or None" represents the necessary reproductive response to an overpopulated world where humans have surpassed the planet's ecological limits

Past approaches to addressing runaway population growth have emphasized the need to shift to a replacement fertility rate of 2.1 births per woman, with the goal of stabilizing the human population. That replacement fertility rate represents an insufficient response to the reality of humans having already surpassed ecological limits on two principal grounds. First, until human populations are evenly distributed across age cohorts the replacement fertility rate fails to achieve an immediate stabilization of population. Where population distributions are skewed toward large numbers that have yet to reach reproductive ages, the replacement rate will continue to generate population increases over a subsequent generation. Second, merely stabilizing human populations at current levels fails to address mounting evidence that humans have already exceeded the planet's ecological limits to growth. The actual challenge is one of reducing human numbers rather than merely stabilizing them. To immediately realize that end would require an average number of births in the range of "one or none" per woman. Individuals could further that outcome by joining the national organization Negative Population Growth, Inc. and establishing a local chapter to lobby for the "One or None" reproductive behavior that represents ecologically responsible childbearing under current ecological realities.

Action 3: Take up the position of a local advocate of ecologically responsible consumption intended to shut down the exponential economic growth that represents inherently unsustainable behavior

Some 70 percent of America's economic activity is attributable to the con-spicuous consumption of private households. That consumption drives the inherently unsustainable economic growth of America's national economy. Existent ecological limits to growth demand an end to that unsustainable growth, and the adoption of a new economic orientation based on stability rather than growth. Research findings confirm that conspicuous consumption is uncorrelated with feelings of personal well-being or happiness once basic needs have been met. That research clearly shows that individual well-being and happiness are more dependent on the social connections of family, friends, and community, than on the ongoing consumption and possession of addi-tional novelty items. Ecologically sustainable consumption will require a dramatic reduction in personal consumption guided by the three Rs of recycle, reuse, and reduce, with the most important precept being the need to reduce, followed by the need to favor the reusable over the recyclable. To the maximum feasible extent possible this new consumption orientation would be guided by a deliberate attempt to boycott the acquisition of new items whenever possible.

Action 4: Assume the role of a local champion of ecologically responsible immigration reform, which would reduce immigration to the point where it makes no net contribution to national population growth

Immigration has become the main driver of U.S. population growth. Over the four decades prior to 1965 some 200,000 immigrants were allowed into the county annually, but from 1965 to 1990 immigration reform increased that number to an average of 1 million people each year. Since 1990 the number has increased to about 1.5 million annually (1 million legal and half a million illegal), to the highest rate in history.[1] A 1998 assessment concluded that up to 70 percent of the next 100 million people added to the U.S. would be immigrants and their descendants.[2] The current rate of population growth will produce the next 100 million Americans in a mere 30 years. Such population growth is incompatible with sustainability. Lost biodiversity and stressed ecosystems reveal that the United States is overpopulated at its current level of more than 300 million people, and permissive mass immigration policies only enable continued ecological irresponsibility.[3] According to the doctrine of "competitive exclusion" articulated by conservation biologists, one species can benefit only at the expense of some other, and in an ecologically full world there is increasing evidence that humans can only expand at the expense of other species and the ecosystems that house them. Americans cannot have their cake and eat it too in the form of both continued population growth and realizing sustainability. Proponents of immigration restrictions may be labeled as xenophobes or racists by social justice advocates, but current unsustainable immigration rates will continue to drive population increases that doom any and all sustainability initiatives.

Action 5: Make a personal shift from private to public transportation, adopting a "One or None" ownership stance on private vehicles per household

In 2003 for the first time the United States recorded more registered motor vehicles than licensed drivers. That level of vehicle ownership and use plays a large part in generating an average American ecological footprint at least five times the ecologically productive space available on a per capita basis across the Earth. At about 4 percent of the world's population, Americans may temporarily be able to inequitably live beyond the planet's ecological capacity, but such behavior is simply not possible or sustainable for the more than 7 billion people presently on the planet. An attempt to replicate the American ratio of motor vehicle ownership globally would require a 6-fold increase in vehicles, from some 900 million today to over 5.6 billion. The material and energy implications of creating, fueling, and providing roadways to accommodate those vehicles represent unrealizable ends in a world that has already surpassed ecological limits to further growth. Private motor vehicles represent the quintessential expression of conspicuous consumption that currently drives unsustainable behavior. True sustainability will ultimately depend on rejecting lifestyles based on consumption, including a specific rejection of automobile ownership as one of the clearest embodiments of unsustainable consumerism. Automobile dependency must quickly give way to mobility based on public transportation, and a corresponding shift to pedestrian and bicycle options for most trips, if American communities are to successfully transition to stable states of sustainability. Individuals can lead the way in this needed transformation by making a personal shift away from automobile ownership and use.

Action 6: Reject mobility for economic gain in favor of a place-based geographical commitment

Rebuilding community as an alternative to the hyper-individualism of today's consumer culture represents an essential prerequisite to fashioning sustainable living arrangements. Living responsibly on the land, and being accountable to neighbors and the ecosystems that house us, require the re-creation of place-based communities that respect the ecological limits of their bioregions. Bioregionalists extol the importance of individuals making a long-term commitment to a "homeplace" so people can learn to live respectfully in that geographic space. They argue that people need to fit into the places where they live, which naturally requires preserving their "homeplaces" to have the locales to fit into. Successful reinhabitation of place-based environments requires development of an ecological conscience and a conviction of individual responsibility for the health of the land that can only occur when individuals come to know an area intimately. The transition to sustainable communities will require individuals to develop that intimate understanding via long-term residence. Such place-based commitments will enable individuals to create the communities needed to support sustainable lifestyles.

Action 7: Eat lower, much lower, on the food chain, shifting to "One or None" meat meals per day

Almost 20 percent of greenhouse gases are produced by livestock raised to meet humanity's growing demand for meat.[4] According to a recent UN report, livestock produce more greenhouse gases than all of the world's transport combined.[5] A significant shift away from meat-based diets would not only reduce individual carbon footprints, it would also produce additional environmental benefits, including preservation of natural habitats, ecosystem services, clean water, and healthy topsoil. In terms of direct human health benefits, reduced meat consumption would lower the fat content of diets and thereby address the obesity epidemic confronting America. With respect to psychological benefits associated with reduced meat consumption, any cutback in demand for meat would permit a shift away from the inhumane industrialized factory farming of meat that brutalizes animals during the course of meeting an ever-increasing demand for meat. A shift to sustainable agricultural systems represents an essential element of realizing sustainable living practices, and those systems appear unlikely to emerge without a significant move away from meat-based diets.

Action 8: Become a locavore, eating regionally, seasonally, and organically whenever possible

Eating locally, seasonally, and organically will amplify the benefits of reduced individual carbon and ecological footprints associated with personal shifts away from meat-based diets. With respect to greenhouse gases, the national and international agricultural model of today produces up to 17 times the carbon dioxide emissions of regional and local food systems.[6] Localized food production would dramatically reduce energy needs for transportation, processing, refrigeration, and packaging, and in the process avoid much of the

25 percent presently lost to spoilage under today's model. The small-scale, diversified, locally adapted food production processes associated with regional food systems would be less stressful to the environment than the agro-business processes that dominate the national and international model. Eating seasonally would radically reduce the energy and resource requirements associated with global distribution systems that do not honor seasons in determining food availability. Eating organically would further responsible production processes designed to continue indefinitely under respectful farming operations. The role of regional, seasonal, and organic food systems appears indispensible to realizing sustainable agriculture as the very foundation of sustainable local economies.

Action 9: Oppose water conservation initiatives unless the conserved water is committed to ecosystem restoration

Few environmental initiatives are as counterproductive as those directed at conserving local water resources. The conserved water typically enables continued growth by freeing up water shares to support further development in local communities. Such growth is apt to result in further environmental degradation as additional built environments replace natural ecosystems and their services. Hence, water conservation initiatives should be treated as suspect and only supported when conserved water shares are specifically committed to restoring the natural hydrologic functions of local and regional ecosystems. Environmentalists and community activists tend to automatically lend their support to water conservation programs under the assumption that such programs represent environmentally responsible behavior. Opposing these programs on environmental grounds will challenge conventional wisdom within most local jurisdictions, but any local actions that facilitate further growth must be contested if there is to be any hope of realizing sustainable communities.

Action 10: Challenge environmental management approaches to addressing our relationships to the natural world, insisting instead on the management of human behaviors as the most pressing unmet need of the current era

Environmental disciplines tend to accept a management approach to dealing with the natural world. That approach typically argues that environmental systems have been so radically modified by human activities that they can only be expected to function naturally if they are intensively managed. In reality, those systems are more than capable of managing themselves if they are simply afforded the space to carry out their traditional ecosystem functions absent from human interference. That space is now being continuously eroded by the ongoing expansion of the human enterprise. If ecosystems are to have any hope of continuing their essential historical functions across the American landscape into the foreseeable future, growth of the human enterprise will have to be managed in a manner that shuts down the unsustainable demographic, economic, and urban growth that characterizes virtually all human behavior in the current era. The real challenge is one of managing human behaviors, rather than nature's ecosystems.

All of the proposed actions represent unconventional behaviors that will put their practitioners well outside the mainstream of current American beliefs and practices. Urban growth is still widely accepted as representing social progress. Births are still celebrated within the context of most extended families. Conspicuous consumption continues to be portrayed as the route to individual happiness and societal economic well-being. It is politically incorrect to challenge the wisdom of the current level of immigration in most social settings. Discussions of transportation options neglect to consider the unsustainable nature of private transportation during attempts to envision sustainable cities. Most Americans are not apt to be introduced to any questioning of the social merit of personal mobility. Nor are they likely to be challenged by public policy debates that point out the shortcomings of meat-based diets or nonlocal food production systems. Few will experience a portrayal of water conservation initiatives as representing a wrongheaded approach to protecting the natural world, or encounter the argument for the superiority of a human-management approach over an environmental-management approach. In short, individuals pursuing the proposed actions will be placing themselves so far outside the mainstream they will probably find themselves marginalized or ostracized. Advocacy of the paradigm shift embodied in the above actions will undoubtedly be difficult, but the alternative is the unacceptable option of continuing the unsustainable behaviors associated with the growth imperative that drives the American socioeconomic system. The inherently unsustainable demographic, economic, and urban growth that characterizes most American communities will have to be stopped if local jurisdictions are to succeed in realizing stable, sustainable, no-growth states. All 10 of the noted actions are indispensible to achieving such states of sustainability.

Notes

1 Requiem for the growth imperative

1 Lester R. Brown, *Plan B 3.0: Mobilizing to Save Civilization* (New York: W. W. Norton, 2008), 6.
2 Christopher Flavin, "Preface," in Worldwatch Institute, *State of the World 2008: Innovations for a Sustainable Economy* (New York: W. W. Norton, 2008), xix.
3 Donella H. Meadows, Dennis L. Meadows, and Jørgen Randers, *Beyond the Limits: Confronting Global Collapse, Envisioning a Sustainable Future* (Post Mills, Vermont: Chelsea Green Publishing Company, 1992), 22.
4 Ibid., 44.
5 Donella H. Meadows, Jørgen Randers, and Dennis L. Meadows, *Limits to Growth: The 30-Year Update* (White River Junction, Vermont: Chelsea Green Publishing Company, 2004), 17.
6 Ibid., 2.
7 Ibid., 138.
8 Meadows *et al.*, op. cit. note 3, xv–xvi.
9 Paul R. Ehrlich and Anne H. Ehrlich, *Healing the Planet: Strategies for Resolving the Environmental Crisis* (New York: Addison-Wesley, 1991), 216.
10 Meadows *et al.*, op. cit. note 5, 119.
11 Meadows *et al.*, op. cit. note 3, 130.
12 Meadows *et al.*, op. cit. note 5, 48.
13 Ibid., 203.
14 Ibid., 175.
15 Donella H. Meadows, Dennis L. Meadows, Jørgen Randers, and William W. Behrens III, *The Limits to Growth* (New York: Universe Books, 1972).
16 Gabor Zovanyi, *Growth Management for a Sustainable Future: Ecological Sustainability as the New Growth Management Focus for the 21st Century* (West Port, Connecticut: Praeger Publishers, 1998).
17 A survey of the historical rationales used to support population, economic, and urban growth appears in Gabor Zovanyi, *Toward a No-Growth Urban Planning Philosophy* (University of Washington Doctoral Dissertation, 1981) and in Zovanyi, op. cit. note 16, 3–7.
18 Alfred Sauvy, *Zero Growth* (New York: Praeger Publishers, 1976), 3.
19 The First Book of Moses, called *Genesis, Chapter IX, Verse 1*.
20 Norman B. Ryder, "Two Cheers for ZPG," *Daedalus: The No-Growth Society*, vol. 102, no. 4 (1973), 59–60.
21 See Wilfred Beckerman, "Two Cheers for Economic Growth," *Lloyds Bank Review* (October 1972), 52.
22 See David T. Bazelon, "The New Factor in American Society," in William R. Ewald, ed., *Environment and Change: The Next Fifty Years* (Bloomington, Indiana: Indiana University Press, 1968), 269.

23 Bill McKibben, *Deep Economy: The Wealth of Communities and the Durable Future* (New York: Holt Paperbacks, 2007), 7–8.

24 A description of the transformation of GNP into GDP as the primary indicator of economic progress appears in Ted Halstead and Clifford Cobb, "The Need for New Measurements of Progress," in Jerry Mander and Edward Goldsmith, eds., *The Case Against the Global Economy: And a Turn Toward the Local* (San Francisco, California: Sierra Club Books, 1996), 205, who point out that under the old GNP the profits of multi-nationals were attributed to the nation in which the corporation was based, whereas under GDP those profits are included in the GDP of the nation where the profits are generated, even if those profits eventually return to the nation housing the corporation.

25 Barbara Ward and René Dubos, *Only One Earth* (New York: W. W. Norton, 1972), 120.

26 See the interview with Margaret Mead, in William L. Oltmans, ed., *On Growth* (New York: Capricorn Books, 1974), 21, for such an identified link between material and spiritual well-being.

27 Brown, op. cit. note 1, 192.

28 See Niles M. Hansen, *Intermediate-Size Cities as Growth Centers* (New York: Praeger Publishers, 1971), 68; Albert O. Hirschman, *The Strategy of Economic Development* (New Haven, Connecticut: Yale University Press, 1958), 183–84, 187; and Lloyd Rodwin, *Nations and Cities: A Comparison of Strategies for Urban Growth* (Boston, Massachusetts: Houghton-Mifflin, 1970), 25, for expression of such an acceptance.

29 Meadows *et al.*, op. cit. note 15, 87.

30 Ibid., 91, 142.

31 Ibid., 145, 154.

32 Ibid., 29.

33 For sources of the cited demographic figures and associated growth rates see Zovanyi, op. cit. note 16, 8–10, 14–16.

34 UN Population Division, *World Population Prospects: The 2006 Revision Population Database*, updated 2007. Online. Available HTTP: www.unpopulation.org (accessed September 26, 2008).

35 Sources for the cited changes over time in annual increases to total global population appear in Zovanyi, op. cit. note 16, 8–9, 13–14.

36 John A. Palos, *Innumeracy: Mathematical Illiteracy and Its Consequences* (New York: Hill and Wang, 1988).

37 Lester R. Brown, *Eco-Economy: Building an Economy for the Earth* (New York: W. W. Norton, 2001), 228.

38 Gary Gardner and Thomas Prugh, "Seeding the Sustainable Economy," in Worldwatch Institute, *State of the World 2008: Innovations for a Sustainable Economy* (New York: W. W. Norton, 2008), 2, 5.

39 Brown, op. cit. note 37, 5.

40 The 2006 global output figure appears in *The World Factbook 2007* (Washington, D.C.: Central Intelligence Agency, 2007).

41 Cited figures on changes in motor vehicle production and total numbers of vehicles appear in Zovanyi, op. cit. note 16, 16–18; Michael Renner, "Vehicle Production Continues to Expand," in Worldwatch Institute, *Vital Signs* (New York: W. W. Norton, 2008), 64–65; Michael Renner, "Vehicle Production Rises, But Few Cars Are 'Green'," at Worldwatch Institute, *Vital Signs* Online. Available HTTP: www.worldwatch.org/node/5461#notes (accessed October 16, 2010).

42 Brown, op. cit. note 1, 43.

43 Ibid., 192.

44 UN Population Division, *World Urbanization Prospects: The 2005 Revision Population Database*, electronic database, updated 2006. Online. Available HTTP: www.unpopulation.org (accessed October 8, 2008).

45 UN Habitat, *State of the World's Cities 2010/2011: Bridging the Urban Divide* (Sterling, Virginia: Earthscan Publishing, 2008), 42.

46 Natural Resources Conservation Service, *National Resources Inventory, 2001 Annual NRI: Urbanization and Development of Rural Land* (July 2003). Online. Available HTTP: www. nres.usda.gov (accessed August 10, 2004).
47 See Lester R. Brown, *Building a Sustainable Society* (New York: W. W. Norton, 1981); Paul R. Ehrlich and Anne H. Ehrlich, *The Population Explosion* (New York: Simon and Schuster, 1990); Ehrlich and Ehrlich, op. cit. note 9; Lester R. Brown *et al.*, *State of the World 1994* (New York: W. W. Norton, 1994); Brown, op. cit. note 37; Brown, op. cit. note 1.
48 Ransom A. Myers and Boris Worm, "Rapid Worldwide Depletion of Predatory Fish Communities," *Nature*, vol. 432 (15 May 2003), 280–83.
49 UN Food and Agriculture Association, *The State of World Fisheries and Aquaculture 2006* (Rome: FAO, 2007), 29.
50 Such descriptions of the life-support services provided by ecosystems appear in Ehrlich and Ehrlich, op. cit. note 9, 15–37; Gretchen C. Daily (ed.), *Nature's Services: Societal Dependence on Natural Ecosystems* (Washington, D.C.: Island Press, 1997), 3–4; and Meadows *et al.*, op. cit. note 5, 83–86.
51 Ehrlich and Ehrlich, op. cit. note 47, 134.
52 Jane Lubchenco *et al.*, "The Sustainable Biosphere Initiative: An Ecological Research Agenda," *Ecology*, vol. 72, no. 2 (1991), 377.
53 Union of Concerned Scientists, *World Scientists' Warning to Humanity* (1992). Online. Available HTTP: www.ucsusa.org/about/1992-world-scientists.html?print=t (accessed February 20, 2012), 1.
54 Ibid., 1.
55 Ibid., 2.
56 Ibid., 3.
57 Ehrlich and Ehrlich, op. cit. note 9, 366; Edward O. Wilson, *The Diversity of Life* (Cambridge, Massachusetts: Harvard University Press, 1992), 424.
58 Millennium Ecosystem Assessment, *Ecosystems and Human Well-Being: Synthesis* (Washington, D.C.: Island Press, 2005). Online. Available HTTP: www.millenniumassessment.com (accessed February 20, 2012), 4.
59 World Wildlife Fund International, *Living Planet Report 2010: Biodiversity, Biocapacity and Development* (Gland, Switzerland: World Wildlife Fund, 2010). Online. Available HTTP: www.panda.org (accessed February 20, 2012), 12.
60 Ibid.
61 Mathis Wackernagel *et al.*, *Ecological Footprints of Nations? How Much Do They Use? How Much Do They Have?* (Toronto: International Council for Local Environmental Initiatives, 1997), 64.
62 Mathis Wackernagel *et al.*, "Tracking the Ecological Overshoot of the Human Economy," *Proceedings of the National Academy of Sciences*, vol. 99, no. 14 (9 July 2002), 9, 266–71; Global Footprint Network, WWF, and Zoological Society of London, *Living Planet Report 2006* (Oakland, California: Global Footprint Network, 2006), 14.
63 L. Balmford *et al.*, "Economic Reasons for Conserving Wild Nature," *Science*, vol. 297, no. 5583 (2002), 1–8.
64 World Wildlife Fund International, *Living Planet Report 2004* (Gland, Switzerland: World Wildlife Fund, 2004). Online. Available HTTP: www.panda.org (accessed June 10, 2005).
65 Millennium Ecosystem Assessment, op. cit. note 58, 1.
66 Millennium Ecosystem Assessment, *Living Beyond Our Means: Natural Assets and Human Well-Being*, Statement from the Board. Online. Available HTTP: www.millenniumassessment.com (accessed February 20, 2012), 5.
67 The noted findings are available online at www.conservation.org under Hotspots Revisited, Key Findings (accessed 5 July 2006).
68 Johan Rockström *et al.*, "A Safe Operating Space for Humanity," *Nature*, vol. 461 (24 September 2009), 472–75.
69 Ibid., 472.

70 World Wildlife Fund International, op. cit. note 59, 8.
71 William Rees, "Toward a Sustainable World Economy," Institute for New Economic Thinking Annual Conference, Bretton Woods, New Hampshire (April 2011), 12.
72 Ibid.
73 Intergovernmental Panel on Climate Change (IPCC), "Summary for Policymakers," in *Climate Change 2007: The Physical Science Basis* (Cambridge: Cambridge University Press, 2007). Online. Available HTTP: www.ipcc.ch (accessed August 3, 2012).
74 IPCC, *Climate Change 2001: Third Assessment Report* (New York: Cambridge University Press, 2001).
75 W. L. Hare, "A Safe Landing for the Climate," in Worldwatch Institute, *State of the World 2009: Into a Warming World* (New York: W. W. Norton, 2009), 17.
76 Thomas Lovejoy, "Climate Change's Pressures on Biodiversity," in ibid., 67.
77 Christopher Flavin and Robert Engelman, "The Perfect Storm," in ibid., 7.
78 The reported doubling appears in "State of the World: A Year in Review," in Worldwatch Institute, op. cit. note 2, xxiv.
79 Stephen Pacala and Robert Socolow, "Stabilization Wedges: Solving the Climate Problem for the Next 50 Years with Current Technologies," *Science*, vol. 305 (13 August 2004), 968–72.
80 James Hansen *et al.*, "Dangerous Human-made Interference with Climate: A GISS Model Study," *Atmospheric Chemistry and Physics*, vol. 7, no. 9 (2007), 2287–2312.
81 See Hare, op. cit. note 75, 17–18.
82 Ibid., 19.
83 James Hansen *et al.*, "Target Atmospheric CO_2: Where Should Humanity Aim?" *Open Atmospheric Science Journal* (2008).
84 Nicholas Stern, "Opinion: Decision Time," *New Scientist*, vol. 201, no. 2692 (24 January 2009), 26.
85 See Brown, op. cit. note 1, 50.
86 Ibid., 57.
87 Ibid.
88 Ibid., 56.
89 A. Sterl *et al.*, "When Can We Expect Extremely High Surface Temperatures," *Geophysical Research Letters* (19 July 2008).
90 See Brown, op. cit. note 1.
91 Ibid., 63.
92 See Lovejoy, op. cit. note 76, 69.
93 Ibid., 19.
94 Daniel G. Boyce, Marlon R. Lewis, and Boris Worm, "Global Phytoplankton Decline Over the Past Century," *Nature*, vol. 466 (29 July 2010), 591–96.
95 C. L. Sabine *et al.*, "The Ocean Sink for Anthropogenic CO2," *Science* (2004), 367–71.
96 UN Food and Agriculture Organization (FAO), High-Level Expert Forum, *How to Feed the World in 2050* (2009). Online. Available HTTP: www.fao.org/wsfs/forum 2050/wsfs-forum/en (accessed February 20, 2012).
97 As cited on the United Nations Environment Programme/GRID-Arendal website, under "Impacts from Intensification of Croplands." Online. Available HTTP: www.grida.no/publications/rr/food-crisis/page/3569.aspx (accessed February 20, 2012).
98 FAO, op. cit. note 96, Executive Summary, 2.
99 UN Food and Agriculture Organization (FAO), *State of the World's Land and Water Resources for Food and Agriculture* (2011). Online. Available HTTP: www.fao.org (accessed February 20, 2012).
100 As cited on the United Nations Environment Programme/GRID-Arendal website, under "Environmental Costs of Conventional Intensification and Expansion of Food Production," op. cit. note 97.
101 Ibid.
102 World Wildlife Fund International, op. cit. note 59, 58–59.

103 Johan Rockström *et al.*, op. cit. note 68, 474.
104 Millennium Ecosystem Assessment, op. cit. note 58, 17.
105 UN Food and Agriculture Organization (FAO), op. cit. note 96.
106 James Hansen *et al.*, "Climate Change and Trace Gases," *Philosophical Transactions of the Royal Society A*, vol. 365 (2007), 1925–54.
107 Johan Rockström *et al.*, op. cit. note 68, 473.
108 Ibid.
109 Millennium Ecosystem Assessment, op. cit. note 58, 17.
110 James Lovelock, "The Earth is About to Catch a Morbid Fever that May Last as Long as 100,000 Years," *The Independent* (16 January 2006). Online. Available HTTP: www.jameslovelock.org/page 10.html (accessed March 12, 2009).
111 M. Pagani, Z. Liu, J. LaRiviere, and A. C. Ravelo, "High Earth-System Climate Sensitivity Determined from Pliocene Carbon Dioxide Concentrations," *Nature Geoscience*, vol. 3 (2010), 27–30.
112 Jeffrey Park and Dana L. Royer, "Geologic Constraints on the Glacial Amplification of Phanerozoic Climate Sensitivity," *American Journal of Science*, vol. 311, 1–26.
113 Brown, op. cit. note 1, 105.
114 United Nations, *World Population Prospects: The 2010 Revision*. Online. Available HTTP: www.unpopulation.org (accessed May 4, 2011).
115 The reported global GDP growth rates for 2010 and 2011 appear in the Central Intelligence Agency's *The World Factbook*. Online. Available HTTP: www.cia.gov/library/publications/the-world-factbook/geos/xx.html (accessed February 20, 2012).
116 The World Bank's projections of likely global economic growth were presented to the FAO Expert Meeting in 2009, and appear in the report from that meeting, op. cit. note 96.
117 Millennium Ecosystem Assessment, op. cit. note 58, 2.
118 Rees, op. cit. note 71, 12.
119 Justin Gillis, "Global Carbon Dioxide Emissions in 2010 Show the Biggest Jump Ever Recorded," *The New York Times* (5 December 2011), A4.
120 United Nations, *World Urbanization Prospects: The 2009 Revision*. Online. Available HTTP: www.unpopulation.org (accessed March 25, 2010).
121 William Rees and Mathis Wackernagel, "Urban Ecological Footprints: Why Cities Cannot be Sustainable—and Why They Are a Key to Sustainability," *Environmental Impact Assessment Review*, vol. 16 (1996), 245.
122 Ibid., 223, 237.
123 United Nations Human Settlements Programme (UN-HABITAT), *State of the World's Cities 2010/2011: Bridging the Urban Divide* (London: Earthscan Publications, 2008), 42.
124 Millennium Ecosystem Assessment, op. cit. note 58, 13.
125 World Wildlife Fund International, op. cit. note 59, 83.
126 Millennium Ecosystem Assessment, op. cit. note 58, 11–12.
127 Robert J. Diaz and Rutger Rosenberg, "Spreading Dead Zones and Consequences for Marine Ecosystems," *Science*, vol. 321 (2008), 926.
128 World Commission on Environment and Development, *Our Common Future* (Oxford: Oxford University Press, 1987).
129 E. Holden and K. Linnerud, "The Sustainable Development Area: Satisfying Basic Needs and Safeguarding Ecological Sustainability," *Sustainable Development*, vol. 15, no. 3 (2007), 175.
130 World Commission on Environment and Development, op. cit. note 128, 8, 40.
131 Ibid., 16.
132 Ibid., 15, 213.
133 Ibid., 50.
134 Ibid., 89.
135 Ibid., 40.
136 The Society for Conservation Biology position paper on the inherent conflict between economic growth and ecological sustainability may be accessed online at www.steadystate.org.

137 R. Hudson, "Towards Sustainable Economic Practices, Flows, and Spaces: Or is the Necessary Impossible and the Impossible Necessary?" *Sustainable Development*, vol. 13, no. 4 (2005), 239–52.

138 T. W. Luke, "Neither Sustainable Nor Development: Reconsidering Sustainability in Development," *Sustainable Development*, vol. 13, no. 4 (2005), 236.

139 Richard Shearman, "The Meaning and Ethics of Sustainability," *Environmental Management*, vol. 14, no. 1 (1990), 2.

140 Herman Daly, *Steady-State Economics: Second Edition with New Essays* (Washington, D.C.: Island Press, 1991), 249.

141 The calculation from P. C. Putman is presented in Carlo Cipolla, *The Economic History of World Population* (New York: Penguin Books, 1962), 81.

142 Brown, op. cit. note 37, 19.

143 Brown, op. cit. note 1, 10.

2 The American community as a growth machine

1 Alan A. Altshuler and José A. Gómez-Ibáñez, *Regulation for Revenue: The Political Economy of Land Use Exactions* (Washington, D.C.: The Brookings Institution and Cambridge, MA: The Lincoln Institute of Land Policy, 1993), 8.

2 Harvey Molotch, "The City as a Growth Machine: Toward a Political Economy of Place," *American Journal of Sociology*, vol. 82, no. 2 (September 1976), 309–10.

3 Charles N. Glaab and A. Theodore Brown, *A History of Urban America* (New York: The Macmillan Company, 1967), 1–24.

4 Ibid., 10.

5 Ibid., 23.

6 Ibid., 15.

7 Ibid., 7.

8 Ibid., 6.

9 John R. Logan and Harvey L. Molotch, *Urban Fortunes: The Political Economy of Place* (Berkeley, California: University of California Press, 1987), 13, 52.

10 Daniel J. Boorstin, *The Americans: The National Experience* (New York: Random House, 1966), 52.

11 Ibid., 73.

12 Ibid., 74, 77.

13 Glaab and Brown, op. cit. note 3, 30.

14 Ibid., 36, 54.

15 Ibid., 31.

16 Boorstin, op. cit. note 10, 249–56.

17 Glaab and Brown, op. cit. note 3, 132.

18 Boorstin, op. cit. note 10, 252.

19 Ibid., 115–23.

20 Ibid., 116.

21 Glaab and Brown, op. cit. note 3, 113.

22 Blake McKelvey, *The Urbanization of America: 1860–1915* (New Brunswick, New Jersey: Rutgers University Press, 1963), 11.

23 As cited in Boorstin, op. cit. note 10, 117.

24 McKelvey, op. cit. note 22, 20.

25 Ibid., 12.

26 Ibid., 26.

27 John Delafons, *Land-Use Controls in the United States*. Second edition. (Cambridge, Massachusetts: The MIT Press, 1969), 17.

28 John Brinckerhoff Jackson, *American Space: The Centennial Years 1865–1876* (New York: W. W. Norton & Company, 1972), 43.

29 McKelvey, op. cit. note 22, 28.

30 Jackson, op. cit. note 28, 19.

31 Glaab and Brown, op. cit. note 3, 109, 134.

32 Ibid., 273.

33 Ibid., 281.

34 Ibid., 279.

35 George E. Mowry, *The Urban Nation: 1920–1960* (New York: Hill and Wang, 1965), 46.

36 Delafons, op. cit. note 27, 106.

37 Glaab and Brown, op. cit. note 3, 292.

38 Delafons, op. cit. note 27, 29.

39 Mel Scott, *American City Planning Since 1890* (Berkeley and Los Angeles, California: University of California Press, 1969), 161.

40 Ibid., 160.

41 Glaab and Brown, op. cit. note 3, 285.

42 Scott, op. cit. note 39, 235.

43 Ibid., 208–9.

44 Ibid., 450.

45 Ibid., 473, 504.

46 Constance Lieder, "Planning for Housing," in Frank S. So and Judith Getzels, eds., *The Practice of Local Government Planning*. Second edition. (Washington, D.C.: The International City Management Association, 1988), 365.

47 Scott, op. cit. note 39, 537.

48 Ibid., 538–39.

49 Altshuler and Gómez-Ibáñez, op. cit. note 1, 25–26.

50 Molotch, op. cit. note 2.

51 John H. Mollenkopf, *The Contested City* (Princeton, New Jersey: Princeton University Press, 1983).

52 Molotch, op. cit. note 2, 310.

53 Ibid., 310.

54 Ibid., 311.

55 Ibid., 311.

56 Ibid., 318.

57 Ibid., 320.

58 Logan and Molotch, op. cit. note 9, 13.

59 Ibid., 61.

60 Ibid., 32, 13.

61 Ibid., 24.

62 Ibid., 49.

63 Ibid., 14.

64 Ibid., 2.

65 Ibid., 32.

66 Ibid., 215.

67 Ibid., 134.

68 Ibid., 215.

69 Ibid., 296.

70 Ibid., 27.

71 Ibid., 66.

72 Ibid., 67.

73 An expressed view of Martin Melosi as cited in ibid., 52.

74 Ibid., 154.

75 Ibid., 154.

76 Ibid., 157.

77 Ibid., 178.

78 Alan S. Kravitz, "Mandarinism: Planning as the Handmaiden to Conservative Politics," in Thad L. Beyel and Gorge T. Lathrop, eds., *Planning and Politics* (New York: Odyssey Press, 1970).

79 Such a review may be found in Gabor Zovanyi, *Growth Management for a Sustainable Future: Ecological Sustainability as the New Growth Management Focus for the 21st Century* (Westport, Connecticut and London: Praeger Publishers, 1998, 2001), 61–89.

80 Herbert J. Gans, "City Planning in America: A Sociological Analysis," in Herbert J. Gans, ed., *People and Plans: Essays on Urban Problems and Solutions* (New York: Basic Books, 1968), 57.

81 Ibid., 59.

82 Kravitz, op. cit. note 78, 247.

83 An extensive treatment of the nature of urban planning during the "age of business" appears in Scott, op. cit. note 39, 183–269.

84 Kravitz, op. cit. note 78, 247.

85 Scott, op. cit. note 39, 182.

86 A detailed review of the different types of planning and their respective growth orientations appears in Zovanyi, op. cit. note 79, 67–86.

87 A treatment of the evolving nature of comprehensive plans over their history in America appears in ibid., 68–77.

88 David R. Godschalk, "Reforming New Community Planning," *Journal of the American Institute of Planners*, vol. 39, no. 5 (1973), 307.

89 Edward J. Kaiser, David R. Godschalk, and F. Stuart Chapin, Jr., *Urban Land Use Planning* (Urbana, Illinois: University of Illinois Press, 1995), 196.

90 Citations to such various "demand-based" references and alternative "supply-based" references to plan making appear in Zovanyi, op. cit. note 79, 75.

91 Kaiser *et al.*, op. cit. note 89, 172.

92 A review of the rational decision-making process as the second dominant type of planning in America appears in Zovanyi, op. cit. note 79, 77–80.

93 A survey of these alternative subtypes of planning appears in ibid., 80–84.

94 Martin Meyerson, "Building the Middle-Range Bridge for Comprehensive Planning," *Journal of the American Institute of Planners*, vol. 22, no. 3 (1956), 60–61.

95 Randall W. Scott, "Management and Control of Growth: An Introduction and Summary," in Randall W. Scott, David J. Brower, and Dallas D. Miner, eds., *Management and Control of Growth: Issues, Techniques, Problems, and Trends*, Vol. I (Washington, D.C.: The Urban Land Institute, 1975), 23.

96 Donald E. Priest, "Epilogue: Managed Growth and the Future of City Building," in Scott, Brower, and Miner, eds., *Management and Control of Growth*, Vol. III, op. cit. 95, 537.

97 See Zovanyi, op. cit. note 79, 32–38.

98 Priest, op. cit. note 96, 538.

99 References to multiple sources offering different bases for condemning growth-management programs appear in Zovanyi, op. cit. note 79, 38–39.

100 Paul L. Niebanck, "Growth Controls and the Production of Inequality," in David J. Brower, David R. Godschalk, and Douglas R. Porter, eds., *Understanding Growth Management: Critical Issues and a Research Agenda* (Washington, D.C.: The Urban Land Institute, 1989), 106.

101 Fred Bosselman, "Can the Town of Ramapo Pass a Law to Bind the Rights of the Whole World?" *Florida State University Law Review*, vol. 1, no. 3 (1973), 249.

102 Thomas I. Miller, "Must Growth Restrictions Eliminate Moderate-Priced Housing?" *American Planning Association Journal*, vol. 52, no. 3 (1986), 319.

103 A review of these different definitions of growth management appears in Zovanyi, op. cit. note 79, 40–41.

104 John M. DeGrove, "Growth Management and Governance," in *Understanding Growth Management*, op. cit. note 100, 32.

105 Citations from growth-management literature revealing the management movement's stance on growth appear in Zovanyi, op. cit. note 79, 57–59.

106 A discussion of the differences between *growth management* and *growth control* as the terms are used in the growth-management movement appears in Zovanyi, op. cit. note 79, 37–38, 40–41.

107 Madelyn Glickfeld and Ned Levine, *Growth Controls: Regional Problems—Local Responses* (Cambridge, Massachusetts: Lincoln Institute of Land Policy, 1991).
108 A review of early efforts to slow or limit future growth appears in Zovanyi, op. cit. note 79, 43–46.
109 A review of statewide growth-management laws passed through 1997 appears in Zovanyi, op. cit. note 79, 48–55.
110 Gabor Zovanyi, "The Growth Management Delusion," *NPG Forum* (Washington, D.C.: Negative Population Growth, Inc., September 1999), 3.
111 Dennis E. Gale, "Eight State-Sponsored Growth Management Programs: A Comparative Analysis," *American Planning Association Journal*, vol. 58, no. 4 (1992), 425.
112 Gabor Zovanyi, "The Role of Initial Statewide Smart-Growth Legislation in Advancing the Tenets of Smart Growth," *The Urban Lawyer*, vol. 39, no. 2 (2007), 379.
113 Ibid., 392–407.
114 Robert W. Burchell, David Listokin, and Catherine C. Galley, "Smart Growth: More Than a Ghost of Urban Policy Past, Less Than a Bold New Horizon," *Housing Policy Debate*, vol. 11 (2000), 823.
115 Zovanyi, op. cit. note 79, 164.
116 Ibid., 169.
117 Kaiser *et al.*, op. cit. note 89, 172; Arthur C. Nelson, James B. Duncan, Clancy J. Mullen, and Kirk R. Bishop, *Growth Management Principles and Practices* (Chicago, Illinois: Planners Press), xi.

3 Rationales and strategies for stopping growth in America's communities

1 Eben Fodor, *Better Not Bigger: How to Take Control of Urban Growth and Improve Your Community* (Gabriola Island, British Columbia: New Society Publishers, 1999), 110.
2 Daniel M. Warner, "'Post-Growthism': From Smart Growth to Sustainable Development," *Environmental Practice*, vol. 8, no. 3 (September 2006), 176.
3 Fodor, op. cit. note 1, 35.
4 Edwin Stennett, *In Growth We Trust: Sprawl, Smart Growth, and Rapid Population Growth* (Gaithersburg, Maryland: Growth Education Movement, Inc., July 2002), 59.
5 Fodor, op. cit. note 1, 9, 11.
6 Ibid., 34.
7 Douglas R. Porter *et al.*, *Profiles in Growth Management: An Assessment of Current Programs and Guidelines for Effective Management* (Washington, D.C.: Urban Land Institute, 1996), 6.
8 Douglas R. Porter, *Making Smart Growth Work* (Washington, D.C.: Urban Land Institute, 2002), 2.
9 Judith Perlman, *Citizen's Primer for Conservation Activism: How to Fight Development in Your Community* (Austin, Texas: University of Texas Press, 2004).
10 Ibid., 73.
11 Ibid., 95.
12 Ibid., 73.
13 Ibid., 102.
14 Ibid., 92.
15 Ibid., 141.
16 Ibid., 90–91.
17 Ibid., 6.
18 Warner, op. cit. note 2, 176.
19 Fodor, op. cit. note 1.
20 Ibid., 106–7.
21 Ibid., 15.
22 Ibid., 18, 77.

23 Ibid., 26–27.
24 Ibid., 27.
25 Ibid., 27–28.
26 Ibid., 28.
27 Ibid., 110.
28 Gabor Zovanyi, *Growth Management for a Sustainable Future: Ecological Sustainability as the New Growth Management Focus for the 21st Century* (Westport, Connecticut and London: Praeger Publishers, 1998, 2001), 165.
29 Albert A. Bartlett, "Reflections on Sustainability, Population Growth, and the Environment," in *The Carrying Capacity Briefing Book* (Washington, D.C.: Carrying Capacity Network, 1994).
30 Zovanyi, op. cit. note 28, 130.
31 Fodor, op. cit. note 1, 30.
32 Ibid., 31.
33 Stennett, op. cit. note 4, 71.
34 Daniel Quinn, *Ishmael* (New York: Bantam Books, 1995), 41, 213–14.
35 Stennett, op. cit. note 4, 103.
36 See Fodor, op. cit. note 1, for references to surveys in Seattle, Los Angeles, Colorado, and Eugene showing a preference for slowing or stopping growth over merely managing it, 18, 51, 139.
37 Quoted in Fodor, op. cit. note 1, 34.
38 Fodor, op. cit. note 1, 38–59.
39 Ibid., 42.
40 Stennett, op. cit. note 4, 108–09.
41 Perlman, op. cit. note 9, 1.
42 Warner, op. cit. note 2, 171.
43 Ibid.
44 Ibid.
45 Perlman, op. cit. note 9.
46 Ibid., 75.
47 Ibid., 17.
48 Ibid., 88, 100.
49 Stennett, op. cit. note 4, 72.
50 Ibid., 81–82.
51 Gabor Zovanyi, "Growth Management Strategies for Stopping Growth in Local Communities," *NPG Forum* (Washington, D.C.: Negative Population Growth, Inc., 2000), 5.
52 Ibid.
53 See Fodor, op. cit. note 1, for his portrayals of environmental threshold standards, quality-of-life threshold standards, level of service standards, and performance standards as alternative forms of growth threshold standards, 116–19.
54 A description of Livermore's use of facilities standards to control growth appears in Mary Cranston, Bryant Garth, Robert Plattner, and Jay Varon, *A Handbook for Controlling Local Growth* (Stanford, California: Stanford Environmental Law Society, September 1973), 90–96; California's Supreme Court upheld Livermore's initiative ordinance in *Associated Home Builders of the Greater Eastbay, Inc.* v. *Livermore*, 557 P.2d 473.
55 Porter, op. cit. note 7, 25.
56 Perlman, op. cit. note 9, 1.
57 See Stennett, op. cit. note 4, for reference to state support for development as a form of corporate welfare, 75.
58 Eben Fodor, "The Real Cost of Growth in Oregon," *Population & Environment*, vol. 18 (March 1997).
59 Eben Fodor, *The Cost of Growth in Washington State* (Bellevue, Washington: The Columbia Public Interest Policy Institute, 2000).
60 Stennett, op. cit. note 4, 79.

61 Ibid., 78.
62 Fodor, op. cit. note 1, 108.
63 Ibid., 122–23.
64 Stennett, op. cit. note 4, 72.
65 A description of economic development techniques typically utilized by local governments appears in Douglas R. Porter, *Managing Growth in America's Communities* (Washington, D.C.: Island Press), 191–94.
66 Stennett, op. cit. note 4, 77.
67 Peter E. Howard, "Report Warns of State Growth to 101 Million," *The Tampa Tribune* (Friday, April 2), A2.
68 Porter, op. cit. note 65, 80.
69 Ibid.
70 Ibid.
71 Zovanyi, op. cit. note 51, 5.
72 Ibid., 6.
73 Zovanyi, op. cit. note 28, 112–13.
74 *Golden* v. *Planning Board of the Town of Ramapo*, 285 N.E.2d 291 (1972).
75 Zovanyi, op. cit. note 51, 117.
76 Porter, op. cit. note 65, 18.
77 Ibid., 19.
78 *Hadacheck* v. *Sebastian*, 239 U.S. 394 (1915).
79 *Village of Euclid, Ohio* v. *Ambler Realty Co.*, 272 U.S. 365 (1926).
80 David L. Callies, "Property Rights: Are There Any Left?" *Urban Lawyer*, vol. 20, no. 3 (1988), 620.
81 *Lawton* v. *Steele*, 152 U.S. 133 (1894).
82 For a detailed treatment of such judicial standards used to assess the legality of land-use regulations under substantive due process challenges see David R. Godschalk, David J. Brower, Larry D. McBennett, and Barbara A. Vestal, *Constitutional Issues of Growth Management* (Chicago, Illinois: The ASPO Press, 1979), 43–48, and Zovanyi, op. cit. note 28, 97–99.
83 Ibid., 47.
84 Ibid., 48.
85 See David L. Callies, Robert H. Freilich, and Thomas E. Roberts, *Cases and Materials on Land Use*. Second edition. (Saint Paul, Minnesota: West Publishing Company, 1994), 311–12, and the 11th Circuit Court ruling in *Eide* v. *Sarasota County*, 908 F.2d 716 (1990).
86 *First English Evangelical Lutheran Church of Glendale* v. *County of Los Angeles,* 107 S.Ct. 2378 (1987).
87 See Zovanyi, op. cit. note 28, 102–3.
88 Nathaniel S. Lawrence, "Regulatory Takings: Beyond the Balancing Test," *Urban Lawyer*, vol. 20, no. 2 (1988), 432.
89 *Loretto* v. *Teleprompter Manhattan Corporation*, 458 U.S. 419 (1982), 432.
90 *Agins* v. *City of Tiburon*, 100 S.Ct. 2138 (1980).
91 *Lucas* v. *So. Carolina Coastal Commission*, 107 L.Ed.2d 798 (1992), 812–13.
92 *Penn Central Transportation Co.* v. *City of New York*, 98 S.Ct. 2646 (1978), 2659.
93 Ibid., 2659.
94 See Zovanyi, op. cit. note 28, 106.
95 *Penn Central*, op. cit. note 92, 2663.
96 Callies *et al.*, op. cit. note 85, 438.
97 See Robert H. Freilich and Elizabeth A. Garvin, "Takings after Lucas: Growth Management, Planning, and Regulatory Implementation Will Work Better," in David L. Callies, ed., *After* Lucas: *Land Use Regulation and the Taking of Property Without Compensation* (Chicago, Illinois: American Bar Association, 1993), 60, who make such a claim based on cited cases from Maryland, California, Pennsylvania, Virginia, and Oregon.
98 *Penn Central*, op. cit. note 92, 2662.

99 Godschalk *et al.*, op. cit. note 82, 93.

100 Ibid., 101.

101 Ibid., 94.

102 Ibid.

103 Ibid., 101.

104 Ibid.

105 *Associated Home Builders of the Greater Eastbay, Inc.* v. *City of Livermore*, 18 C.3d. 582, 557 P.2de 473 (1976).

106 See Zovanyi, op. cit. note 28, 128.

107 Warner, op. cit. note 2, 176–77.

108 A review of regional-welfare rulings suggesting a court-ordered mandate for ongoing growth accommodation appears in Zovanyi, op. cit. note 28, 117–24.

109 *Albano* v. *Mayor and Township Committee of the Township of Washington*, 476 A.2d 852 (1984), 857.

110 *Sturges* v. *Town of Chilmark*, 402 N.E.2d 1346 (1980), 1352.

111 *City of Boca Raton* v. *Boca Villas Corporation*, 371 So.2d 154 (1979).

112 *City of Hollywood* v. *Hollywood, Inc.*, 432 So.2d 1332 (1983), 1335–36.

113 See "Sanibel Island: A Paradise Lost and Saved," in Richard F. Babcock and Charles L. Siemon, *The Zoning Game Revisited* (Boston, Massachusetts: Oelgeschlager, Gunn & Hain, 1985), 94–118.

4 The no-growth path to sustainability

1 The James Goldsmith quotation appears in Jerry Mander, "Facing the Rising Tide," in Jerry Mander and Edward Goldsmith, eds., *The Case Against the Global Economy: And a Turn Toward the Local* (San Francisco, California: Sierra Club Books, 1996), 14.

2 Herman E. Daly, *Steady State Economics: Second Edition with New Essays* (Washington, D.C.: Island Press, 1991), 249.

3 Bill McKibben, *Deep Economy: The Wealth of Communities and the Durable Future* (New York: Holt Paperbacks, 2007), 12.

4 Gabor Zovanyi, *Growth Management for a Sustainable Future: Ecological Sustainability as the New Growth Management Focus for the 21st Century* (West Port, Connecticut: Praeger Publishers, 1998, 2001), 131.

5 McKibben, op. cit. note 3, 9.

6 Herman E. Daly, "The Steady-State Economy: Toward a Political Economy of Biophysical Equilibrium and Moral Growth," in Herman E. Daly, ed., *Toward a Steady-State Economy* (San Francisco, California: W. H. Freeman and Company, 1973), 149–51.

7 Ibid., 150.

8 Ibid., 151.

9 Brian Czech, *Shoveling Fuel for a Runaway Train: Errant Economists, Shameful Spenders, and a Plan to Stop Them All* (Berkeley, California: University of California Press, 2000), 23.

10 George Soule, *Ideas of the Great Economists* (New York: Mentor Book, 1952), 42.

11 McKibben, op. cit. note 3, 1.

12 Gary Gardner and Thomas Prugh, "Seeding the Sustainable Economy," in Worldwatch Institute, *State of the World 2008: Innovations for a Sustainable Economy* (New York: W. W. Norton, 2008), 6.

13 The noted citation attributed to Charles Schultze appears in McKibben, op. cit. note 3, 10.

14 Soule, op. cit. note 10, 41.

15 Ibid., 39.

16 Herman E. Daly and John B. Cobb, Jr., *For the Common Good: Redirecting the Economy toward Community, the Environment, and a Sustainable Future* (Boston, Massachusetts: Beacon Press, 1989), 210.

17 McKibben, op. cit. note 3, 1, 45.

18 The citation attributed to Jeremy Rifkin appears in McKibben, op. cit. note 3, 7.

19 Ibid., 1.
20 Ibid., 10, 14.
21 Daly and Cobb, op. cit. note 16, 396.
22 Soule, op. cit. note 10, 41.
23 Ibid., 44.
24 Daly and Cobb, op. cit. note 16, 11.
25 Ibid., 12–13.
26 Ibid., 13.
27 Ibid., 150.
28 Ibid., 2.
29 Ibid., 30.
30 Czech, op. cit. note 9, 28.
31 Ibid.
32 Ibid.
33 Soule, op. cit. note 10, 93.
34 The cited Mill excerpts appear in Daly, op. cit. note 6, 12–13.
35 Ibid.
36 The reference to "neoclassical growth economists" and their defense of the idea that economic growth may continue in perpetuity appears in Czech, op. cit. note 9, 44–61.
37 Ibid., 44.
38 Herman E. Daly, "Free Trade: The Perils of Deregulation," in Mander and Goldsmith, op. cit. note 1, 236.
39 Daly and Cobb, op. cit. note 16, 72.
40 Daly, op. cit. note 38, 236.
41 Czech, op. cit. note 9, 42–43.
42 Ibid., 45.
43 Mander, op. cit. note 1, 4–5.
44 David C. Korten, "The Mythic Victory of Market Capitalism," in Mander and Goldsmith, op. cit. note 1, 184.
45 Ibid., 185.
46 David C. Korten, "The Failures of Bretton Woods," in Mander and Goldsmith, op. cit. note 1, 23.
47 Ted Halstead and Clifford Cobb, "The Need for New Measures of Progress," in Mander and Goldsmith, op. cit. note 1, 199.
48 Korten, op. cit. note 44, 183.
49 Edward Goldsmith, "Global Trade and the Environment," in Mander and Goldsmith, op. cit. note 1, 79.
50 Satish Kumar, "Gandhi's *Swadeshi*: The Economics of Permanence," in Mander and Goldsmith, op. cit. note 1, 421.
51 David Morris, "Free Trade: The Great Destroyer," in Mander and Goldsmith, op. cit. note 1, 218.
52 Ibid., 219.
53 Jerry Mander, "The Rules of Corporate Behavior," in Mander and Goldsmith, op. cit. note 1, 315, 322.
54 Morris, op. cit. note 51, 219.
55 Ibid.
56 William Greider, "'Citizen' GE," in Mander and Goldsmith, op. cit. note 1, 327.
57 Ralph Nader and Lori Wallach, "GATT, NAFTA, and the Subversion of the Democratic Process," in Mander and Goldsmith, op. cit. note 1, 95.
58 Korten, op. cit. note 46, 22.
59 Jeremy Rifkin, "New Technology and the End of Jobs," in Mander and Goldsmith, op. cit. note 1, 108–21.
60 James Goldsmith, "The Winners and the Losers," in Mander and Goldsmith, op. cit. note 1, 179.

61 Korten, op. cit. note 46, 29.
62 Ibid.
63 Rifkin, op. cit. note 59, 109.
64 Ibid.
65 Korten, op. cit. note 46, 24.
66 Richard Barnet and John Cavanagh, "The Homogenization of Global Culture," in Mander and Goldsmith, op. cit. note 1, 71–77.
67 Morris, op. cit. note 51, 222.
68 Daly, op. cit. note 38, 233.
69 Ibid.
70 Edward Goldsmith, "Development as Colonialism," in Mander and Goldsmith, op. cit. note 1, 265.
71 Ibid., 264.
72 Martin Khor, "Global Economy and the Third World," in Mander and Goldsmith, op. cit. note 1, 56.
73 Carlos Heredia and Mary Purchell, "Structural Adjustments and the Polarization of Mexican Society," in Mander and Goldsmith, op. cit. note 1, 274.
74 Karen Lehman and Al Krebs, "Control of the World's Food Supply," in Mander and Goldsmith, op. cit. note 1, 123.
75 Helena Norgerg-Hodge, "The Pressure to Modernize and Globalize," in Mander and Goldsmith, op. cit. note 1, 38.
76 Goldsmith, op. cit. note 49, 86.
77 Colin Hines and Tim Lang, "In Favor of a New Protectionism," in Mander and Goldsmith, op. cit. note 1, 486.
78 Norgerg-Hodge, op. cit. note 75, 36.
79 Hines and Lang, op. cit. note 77, 486.
80 Korten, op. cit. note 46, 23.
81 Goldsmith, op. cit. note 49, 78.
82 Daly, op. cit. note 38, 235.
83 Herman E. Daly, "Sustainable Growth? No Thank You," in Mander and Goldsmith, op. cit. note 1, 194.
84 Ibid.
85 Wolfgang Sachs, "Neo-Development: 'Global Ecological Management'," in Mander and Goldsmith, op. cit. note 1, 246.
86 Robert Goodland, "Growth Has Reached Its Limits," in Mander and Goldsmith, op. cit. note 1, 217.
87 Korten, op. cit. note 46, 22–23.
88 Goodland, op. cit. note 86, 211.
89 Mander, op. cit. note 1, 4.
90 Tony Clarke, "Mechanisms of Corporate Rule," in Mander and Goldsmith, op. cit. note 1, 305.
91 Korten, op. cit. note 46, 23.
92 Goldsmith, op. cit. note 1, 502.
93 Mander, op. cit. note 1, 4.
94 Jerry Mander and Edward Goldsmith, "Engines of Globalization," in Mander and Goldsmith, op. cit. note 1, 295.
95 Jerry Mander and Edward Goldsmith, "Panaceas That Failed," in Mander and Goldsmith, op. cit. note 1, 181.
96 Mander, op. cit. note 1, 12.
97 Daly, op. cit. note 83, 192.
98 Ibid.
99 Ibid., 193.
100 Ricardo Bayon, "Banking on Biodiversity," in Worldwatch Institute, *State of the World 2008*, op. cit. note 12, 129.
101 Daly and Cobb, op. cit. note 16, 55.

102 Gardner and Prugh, op. cit. note 12, 12.

103 Sachs, op. cit. note 85, 244.

104 John Talberth, "A New Bottom Line for Progress," in Worldwatch Institute, *State of the World 2008*, op. cit. note 12, 29.

105 Robert U. Ayres, *Turning Point: An End to the Growth Paradigm* (New York: St. Martin's Press, 1998), 68.

106 Sachs, op. cit. note 85, 249.

107 Tim Jackson, "The Challenge of Sustainable Lifestyles," in Worldwatch Institute, *State of the World 2008*, op. cit. note 12, 47.

108 Sachs, op. cit. note 85, 249.

109 Daly and Cobb, op. cit. note 16, 247.

110 Richard Douthwaite, *The Growth Illusion: How Economic Growth Has Enriched the Few, Impoverished the Many, and Endangered the Planet* (Gabriola Island, British Columbia: New Society Publishers, 1992, 1999), 28.

111 McKibben, op. cit. note 3, 162.

112 Ayres, op. cit. note 105, 102.

113 Douthwaite, op. cit. note 110, 30.

114 L. Hunter Lovins, "Rethinking Production," in Worldwatch Institute, *State of the World 2008*, op. cit. note 12, 43.

115 Mander, op. cit. note 53, 316.

116 Ayres, op. cit. note 105, 104.

117 Ibid.

118 Walden Bello, "Structural Adjustment Programs: Success For Whom?" in Mander and Goldsmith, op. cit. note 1, 286.

119 Goldsmith, op. cit. note 1, 502.

120 Ibid.

121 Korten, op. cit. note 46, 23.

122 McKibben, op. cit. note 3, 230.

123 Zovanyi, op. cit. note 4, 2.

124 Daniel Quinn, *Ishmael* (New York: Bantam Books, 1995), 84.

125 Ibid., 25, 35.

126 Daly and Cobb, op. cit. note 16, 21.

127 Zovanyi, op. cit. note 4, 27.

128 Mark Halle, "New Approaches to Trade Governance," in Worldwatch Institute, *State of the World 2008*, op. cit. note 12, 205–6.

129 Douthwaite, op. cit. note 110, 336.

130 Korten, op. cit. note 44, 184.

131 Simon Singh, *Big Bang: The Origin of the Universe* (New York: Harper Perennial, 2004), 6.

132 Ibid.

133 Ibid.

134 Ibid., 7.

135 Ibid., 67.

136 Ibid., 367.

137 As cited in ibid., 367.

138 Ibid.

139 Ibid., 368.

140 Ibid., 469–70.

141 Ibid., 368, 470.

142 As cited in ibid., 75.

143 Alan A. Altshuler and José A. Gómez-Ibáñez, *Regulation for Revenue: The Political Economy of Land Use Exactions* (Washington, D.C.: The Brookings Institution and Cambridge, Massachusetts: The Lincoln Institute of Land Policy, 1993), 2.

144 Douglas R. Porter, *Managing Growth in America's Communities* (Washington, D.C.: Island Press), 190–91.

145 See Stephen B. Friedman and Alexander J. Darragh, "Economic Development," in Frank S. So and Judith Getzels, eds., *The Practice of Local Government Planning*. Second edition. (Washington, D.C.: International City Management Association, 1988), 293.

146 See reference to such a statutory requirement within the Hawaiian statute in Fred Bosselman and David Calles, *The Quiet Revolution in Land Use Control* (Washington, D.C.: Government Printing Office, 1971), 36, note 14.

147 Act 250, Chapter 151, Subchapter 3, Section 6042, 150.

148 Florida's 1985 Local Government Comprehensive Planning and Land Development Act, Chapter 163, Section 3177(6)(a), 949.

149 Oregon's Statewide Planning Goals, Land Conservation and Development Commission, Goal 14: Urbanization, 12.

150 State Planning Act of 1985, 52:18A-200(d), 15.

151 Comprehensive Planning and Land Use Regulation Act of 1988, Sections 4960(C)4C(1)(a) and 4960(C)4C(2), 15–16.

152 Rhode Island Comprehensive Planning and Land Use Act of 1988, Section 45–22.2–3(B)5, 3.

153 Georgia Planning Act of 1989, Section 2.1, 50–58-3(a)(5), 4.

154 Engrossed Substitute House Bill No. 2929 of 1990, Section 13(3), 14.

155 Maryland's Economic Growth, Resource Protection, and Planning Act of 1992, Section 1, Article 66B, 3.05(a)(1)(vi)(3), 5.

156 Tennessee's Chapter No. 1101, Senate Bill No. 3278, Section 7, (a)(1)(A), 8.

157 Forster Ndubisi and Mary Dyer, "The Role of Regional Entities in Formulating and Implementing Statewide Growth Policies," *State and Local Government Review*, vol. 24 (1992), 117–27.

158 John I. Carruthers, "Evaluating the Effectiveness of Regulatory Growth Management Programs," *Journal of Planning Education and Research*, vol. 21 (2002), 395.

159 Brief overviews of the regional initiatives addressing the California Coast and Lake Tahoe may be found in Katherine E. Stone and Philip A. Seymour, "California Land-Use Planning Law: State Preemption and Local Control," in Peter A. Buchsbaum and Larry J. Smith, eds., *State and Regional Comprehensive Planning: Implementing New Methods for Growth Management* (Chicago, Illinois: American Bar Association, 1993), 203–15; a case study of the Pinelands initiative appears in Richard F. Babcock and Charles L. Siemon, *The Zoning Game Revisited* (Boston, Massachusetts: Oelgeschlager, Gunn & Hain, Publishers, 1985), 135–57.

160 Doug Aberley, "Interpreting Bioregionalism: A Story From Many Voices," in Michael V. McGinnis, ed., *Bioregionalism* (New York: Routledge, 1999).

161 Ibid., 30.

162 Bruce E. Goldstein, "Combining Science and Place-Based Knowledge: Pragmatic and Visionary Approaches to Bioregional Understanding," in McGinnis, op. cit. note 160, 157.

163 Daniel Berthold-Bond, "The Ethics of 'Place': Reflections on Bioregionalism," *Environmental Ethics*, vol. 22 (2000), 5–24.

164 Kirkpatrick Sale, *Dwellers in the Land: The Bioregional Vision* (San Francisco, California: Sierra Club Books, 1985), 195.

165 Peter Berg, "More Than Just Saving What's Left," first published in *Raise the Stakes*, no. 8, Fall 1983, reprinted in Van Andruss, Christopher Plant, Judith Plant, and Eleanor Wright, eds., *Home! A Biological Reader* (Philadelphia, Pennsylvania: New Society Publishers, 1990), 13.

166 John Papworth, The Fourth World Declaration, first published as The Declaration of the First Assembly of the Fourth World in 1980, reprinted in Andruss *et al.*, op. cit. note 165, 148.

167 Sale, op. cit. note 164, x.

168 Andruss *et al.*, op. cit. note 165, 2.

169 Stephanie Mills, "Foreword," in Andruss *et al.*, op. cit. note 165, vii.

170 Peter Berg and Raymond F. Dasmann, "Reinhabiting California," first published in Peter Berg, ed., *Reinhabiting a Separate Country: A Bioregional Anthology of Northern California*

(San Francisco, California: Planet Drum Foundation, 1978), reprinted in Andruss *et al.*, op. cit. note 165, 35.

171 Michael V. McGinnis, "Bioregional Organization: A Constitution of Home Place," *Human Ecology Review*, vol. 2, no. 1 (1995), 72, 74.

172 Michael V. McGinnis, "A Rehearsal to Bioregionalism," in McGinnis, op. cit. note 160, 3.

173 Adrian Atkinson, "The Urban Bioregion as 'Sustainable Development' Paradigm," *Third World Planning Review*, vol. 14, no. 4 (1992), 332.

174 Aberley, op. cit. note 160, 37.

175 William E. Rees and Mathis Wackernagel, "Urban Ecological Footprints: Why Cities Cannot Be Sustainable—And Why They Are a Key to Sustainability," *Environmental Impact Assessment Review*, vol. 16 (1996), 241.

176 McGinnis, op. cit. note 172, 4.

177 Don Alexander, "Bioregionalism: The Need for a Firmer Foundation," in Jesse Vorst, Ross Dobson, and Ron Fletcher, eds., *Green on Red: Evolving Ecological Socialism* (Winnipeg/Halifax: Fernwood Publishing, 1993), 179.

178 Peter Berg, "Growing a Life-Place Politics," first published in *Raise the Stakes*, no. 11, Summer 1986, reprinted in Andruss *et al.*, op. cit. note 165, 141.

179 Aberley, op. cit. note 160, 35.

180 Andruss *et al.*, op. cit. note 165, 130.

181 McGinnis, op. cit. note 172, 5.

182 Atkinson, op. cit. note 173, 348.

183 Stephen Frenkel, "Old Theories in New Places? Environmental Determinism and Bioregionalism," *Professional Geographer*, vol. 46, no. 3 (1994), 294.

184 Christopher M. Klyza, "Bioregional Possibilities in Vermont," in McGinnis, op. cit. note 160, 82.

185 Christopher Plant, "In Pockets of Resistance: The Back-to-the-Land Movement," first published in Maria Feltes and Thomas Feltes, eds., *Kanada: Ein Express Reisehandbuch* (Germany: Mundo Verlag, 1989), reprinted in Andruss *et al.*, op. cit. note 165, 28.

186 Aberley, op. cit. note 160, 37.

187 Ibid., 37.

188 Berg, op. cit. note 178, 138.

189 Caryn Mirriam-Goldberg, "Sustaining Bioregional Groups: The KAW Experience," first published in *North American Bioregional Congress III Proceedings* (1989), reprinted in Andruss *et al.*, op. cit. note 165, 167.

190 Frenkel, op. cit. note 183, 290.

191 Helen Forsey, "Community Meeting Our Deepest Needs," first published in *Healing the Wounds: The Promise of Ecofeminism* (Philadelphia, Pennsylvania: New Society Publishers, 1989), reprinted in Andruss *et al.*, op. cit. note 165, 84.

192 McGinnis, op. cit. note 171, 74.

193 Berthold-Bond, op. cit. note 163, 13.

194 Frenkel, op. cit. note 183, 289.

195 Aberley, op. cit. note 160, 27.

196 Mills, op. cit. note 169, vii.

197 McGinnis, op. cit. note 160, 8.

198 Mitchell Thomashow, "Toward a Cosmopolitan Bioregionalism," in McGinnis, op. cit. note 160, 124.

199 Jeremiah Gorsline and L. Freeman House, "Future Primitive," first published in *Raise the Stakes*, "North Pacific Rim Alive," Bundle #3 (1994), reprinted in Andruss *et al.*, op. cit. note 165, 39.

200 Chet A. Bowers, "The Role of Education and Ideology in the Transition From a Modern to a more Bioregionally Oriented Culture," in McGinnis, op. cit. note 160, 199.

201 The North American Bioregional Congress, statement adopted at the first North American Bioregional Congress in 1983 and reaffirmed at NABC II and III, reprinted in Andruss *et al.*, op. cit. note 165, 170.

202 Aberley, op. cit. note 160, 18.

203 Berg and Dasmann, op. cit. note 170, 35.

204 Berg, op. cit. note 178, 144.

205 Jim Dodge, "Living By Life: Some Bioregional Theory and Practice," *The CoEvolution Quarterly*, vol. 32 (1981), 10.

206 Gary Snyder, "Speaking for Douglas Fir," from "Regenerate Culture!" an interview in *The New Catalyst*, no. 2, January/February (1986), reprinted in Andruss *et al.*, op. cit. note 165, 14.

207 Berg, op. cit. note 165, 15.

208 Berg and Dasmann, op. cit. note 170, 35.

209 Nancy J. Todd and John Todd, "Design Should Follow, Not Oppose, the Laws of Life," first published in *Bioshelters, Ocean Arks, City Farming: Ecology as the Basis of Design* (San Francisco, California: Sierra Club Books, 1984), reprinted in Andruss *et al.*, op. cit. note 165, 63.

210 James J. Parsons, "On 'Bioregionalism' and 'Watershed Consciousness'," *The Professional Geographer*, vol. 37, no. 1 (1985), 4.

211 Sale, op. cit. note 164, 104–5.

212 Atkinson, op. cit. note 173, 332.

213 Dodge, op. cit. note 205, 9.

214 McGinnis, op. cit. note 171, 72.

215 Todd and Todd, op. cit. note 209, 62.

216 Peter Berg, "A Green City Program for San Francisco Bay Area Cities and Towns," first published in Peter Berg, Beryl Magilavy, and Seth Zuckerman, *A Green City Program* (San Francisco, California: Planet Drum Books, 1989), reprinted in Andruss *et al.*, op. cit. note 165, 108.

217 Donald Alexander, "Bioregionalism: Science or Sensibility," *Environmental Ethics*, vol. 12, no. 2 (1990), 169.

218 Berg and Dasmann, op. cit. note 170, 36.

219 Aberley, op. cit. note 160, 26.

220 Ibid., 37.

221 Plant, op. cit. note 185, 28.

222 Sale, op. cit. note 164, 123.

223 Ibid., 46, 123, 128.

224 Atkinson, op. cit. note 173, 330.

225 McGinnis, op. cit. note 171, 73.

226 Ibid., 81.

227 Paul Lindholdt, "Literary Activism and the Bioregional Agenda," *Interdisciplinary Studies in Literature and Environment*, vol. 3, no. 2 (1996), 122.

228 Parsons, op. cit. note 210, 5.

229 Sale, op. cit. note 164, 7.

230 Berg and Dasmann, op. cit. note 170, 35.

231 Sale, op. cit. note 164, 42.

232 McGinnis, op. cit. note 172, 9.

233 Ibid., 3.

234 Aberley, op. cit. note 160, 34.

235 Mills, op. cit. note 169, vii.

236 Berg, op. cit. note 165, 14.

237 Marnie Muller, "Bioregionalism/Western Culture/Women," first published in *Raise the Stakes*, no. 10, Summer (1984), reprinted in Andruss *et al.*, op. cit. note 165, 88.

238 Judith Plant, "Growing Home: An Introduction," in Andruss *et al.*, op. cit. note 165, ix.

239 Berg and Dasmann, op. cit. note 170, 37.

240 Forsey, op. cit. note 191, 83.

241 Parsons, op. cit. note 210, 4.

242 Dan Flores, "Place: Thinking About Bioregional History," in McGinnis, op. cit. note 160, 45.

243 Parsons, op. cit. note 210, 1.

244 Aberley, op. cit. note 160, 25.

245 Alexander, op. cit. note 217, 163.

246 McGinnis, op. cit. note 171, 72.

247 Atkinson, op. cit. note 173, 338.

248 Berg, op. cit. note 178.

249 McGinnis, op. cit. note 171, 73, 77.

250 Daniel Kemmis, "Foreword," in McGinnis, op. cit. note 160, xv.

251 Alexander, op. cit. note 177, 180.

252 Atkinson, op. cit. note 173, 349.

253 Judith Plant, "Searching for Common Ground: Ecofeminism and Bioregionalism," first published in *The New Catalyst*, no. 10, Winter (1987/1988), reprinted in Andruss *et al.*, op. cit. note 165, 81.

254 Ibid.

255 Alexander, op. cit. note 217, 162.

256 Aldo Leopold, *A Sand County Almanac—And Sketches Here and There* (New York: Oxford University Press, 1949), 204.

257 Alexander, op. cit. note 217, 173.

258 Leopold, op. cit. note 256, 221.

259 Ibid., 224–25.

260 Dodge, op. cit. note 205, 9.

261 Stephanie Mills, "Planetary Passions: A Reverent Anarchy," *CoEvolutionary Quarterly*, vol. 32 (1981), 4.

262 Aberley, op. cit. note 160, 24.

263 McGinnis, op. cit. note 171, 72.

264 Frenkel, op. cit. note 183, 290.

265 Jamie Sayen, "Taking Steps Toward a Restorative Ethic," first published in *Earth First!* (May 1, 1989), reprinted in Andruss *et al.*, op. cit. note 165, 121, 124.

266 Alexander, op. cit. note 217, 163.

267 Dodge, op. cit. note 205, 11.

268 Atkinson, op. cit. note 173, 329.

269 Ibid., 330.

270 Alexander, op. cit. note 217, 163.

271 McGinnis, op. cit. note 171, 75.

272 Andruss *et al.*, op. cit. note 165, 49.

273 Aberley, op. cit. note 160, 20.

274 Lindholdt, op. cit. note 227, 125.

275 Atkinson, op. cit. note 173, 331.

276 Ibid., 331, 336.

277 Christopher Plant, "What is Bioregionalism?" The Third North American Bioregional Congress, press release (March 1, 1988). 3.

278 Sale, op. cit. note 164, 96–97.

279 Ibid., 55.

280 Atkinson, op. cit. note 173, 335, 337.

281 William E. Rees and Mathis Wackernagel, "Ecological Footprints and Appropriated Carrying Capacity: Measuring the Natural Capital Requirements of the Human Economy," in A. M. Jansson *et al.*, eds., *Investing in Natural Capital: The Ecological Economics Approach to Sustainability* (Washington, D.C.: Island Press, 1994).

282 Berg, op. cit. note 216, 104.

283 Ibid., 106.

284 Atkinson, op. cit. note 173, 348.

285 Ibid., 337.

286 Sale, op. cit. note 164, 115.

287 McGinnis, op. cit. note 171, 76.

288 Kemmis, op. cit. note 250, xvii.

289 Parsons, op. cit. note 210, 2.

290 Atkinson, op. cit. note 173, 336.

291 Parsons, op. cit. note 210, 2.

292 Kirkpatrick Sale, Interview in *The New Catalyst* (Spring 1987), reprinted in Andruss *et al.*, op. cit. note 165, 20.

293 Judith Plant, "Revaluing Home: Feminism and Bioregionalism," first published in *The New Catalyst*, no. 2 (January/February 1986), reprinted in Andruss *et al.*, op. cit. note 165, 21.

294 Gary Coates and Julie Coates, "Bioregion as Community: The Kansas Experience," first published in *The CoEvolution Quarterly* (Winter 1981), reprinted in Andruss *et al.*, op. cit. note 165, 86.

295 Kelly Booth, "How Humans Adapt," first published in *The Catalyst* (April–May 1984), reprinted in Andruss *et al.*, op. cit. note 165, 73–74.

296 Papworth, op. cit. note 166, 148.

297 Acknowledgement of 2008 as the landmark year when the majority of humans would for the first time be living in urban places appears in Christopher Flavin, "Preface," in Worldwatch Institute, *State of the World 2007: Our Urban Future* (New York: W. W. Norton, 2007), xxiii.

298 The World Resources Institute, The United Nations Environmental Program, The United Nations Development Programme, and the World Bank, *World Resources 1996–97: The Urban Environment* (New York: Oxford University Press, 1996), ix, 1.

299 Peter Hall and Ulrich Pfeiffer, *Urban Future 21: A Global Agenda for Twenty-First Century Cities* (New York: Spon Press, 2000), 13.

300 Zoë Chafe, "Reducing Natural Disaster Risk in Cities," in Worldwatch Institute, op. cit. note 297, 115.

301 From the World Resources Institute *et al.*, op. cit. note 298, 21.

302 Hall and Pfeiffer, op. cit. note 299, 3.

303 Kai N. Lee, "An Urbanizing World," in Worldwatch Institute, op. cit. note 297, 16.

304 Hall and Pfeiffer, op. cit. note 299, 110.

305 Mark Roseland and Lena Soots, "Strengthening Local Economies," in Worldwatch Institute, op. cit. note 297, 162.

306 Carolyn Stephens and Peter Stair, "Charting a New Course for Urban Public Health," in Worldwatch Institute, op. cit. note 297, 146.

307 Lee, op. cit. note 303, 21.

308 Ibid., 15.

309 Flavin, op. cit. note 297, xxv.

310 Janice E. Perlman and Molly O'Meara Sheehan, "Fighting Poverty and Environmental Injustice in Cities," in Worldwatch Institute, op. cit. note 297, 173.

311 From *World Resources 1996–97: The Urban Environment*, op. cit. note 298, xi.

312 Hall and Pfeiffer, op. cit. note 299, 15.

313 Perlman and Sheehan, op. cit. note 310, 173.

314 From the World Resources Institute, op. cit. note 298, 26.

315 Gary Gardner, Erik Assadourian, and Radhika Sarin, "The State of Consumption Today," in *State of the World 2004: The Consumer Society* (New York: W. W. Norton, 2004), 15.

316 Janet L. Sawin and Kristen Hughes, "Energizing Cities," in Worldwatch Institute, op. cit. note 297, 91.

317 David Owen, *Green Metropolis: Why Living Smaller, Living Closer, and Driving Less Are the Keys to Sustainability* (New York: Riverhead Books, 2009).

318 Douglas Rushkoff, "How Green is My City: Urban Living May be Our Best Hope for the Environment," *OnEarth Magazine*, vol 31, no. 4 (Winter 2010), 52.

319 Ibid.

320 Lester R. Brown, *Plan B 3.0: Mobilizing to Save Civilization* (New York: W. W. Norton, 2008), 115.

321 Gardner *et al.*, op. cit. note 315, 19.

322 Ibid., 17.

323 Lester R. Brown, *Plan B 4.0: Mobilizing to Save Civilization* (New York: W. W. Norton, 2009), 96.

324 Ibid.

325 Peter Neuman and Jeff Kenworthy, "Greening Urban Transportation," in Worldwatch Institute, op. cit. note 297, 67.

326 Jackson, op. cit. note 107, 59.

327 Hall and Pfeiffer, op. cit. note 299, 128.

328 Ibid., 31.

329 Lester R. Brown, *Eco-Economy: Building an Economy for the Earth* (New York: W. W. Norton, 2001), 202–3.

330 Janet L. Sawin, "Making Better Energy Choices," in *State of the World 2004*, op. cit. note 315, 28.

331 Hilary French, "Linking Globalization, Consumption, and Governance," in *State of the World 2004*, op. cit. note 315, 154.

332 Jackson, op. cit. note 107, 47.

333 Sandra Postel, "Carrying Capacity: Earth's Bottom Line," in Worldwatch Institute, *State of the World 1994: A Worldwatch Institute Report on Progress Toward a Sustainable Society* (New York: W. W. Norton, 1994), 16.

334 Lovins, op. cit. note 114, 33.

335 Albert A. Bartlett, "Reflections on Sustainability, Population Growth, and the Environment," in *The Carrying Capacity Briefing Book* (Washington, D.C.: Carrying Capacity Network, 1994).

336 A calculation carried out by the Scottish economist Malcom Slesser and cited in McKibben, op. cit. note 3, 230.

5 Envisioning no-growth communities

1 Edward Goldsmith, "The Last Word: Family, Community, Democracy," in Jerry Mander and Edward Goldsmith, eds., *The Case Against the Global Economy: And a Turn Toward the Local* (San Francisco, California: Sierra Club Books, 1996), 502.

2 James Howard Kunstler, *The Long Emergency: Surviving the End of Oil, Climate Change, and Other Converging Catastrophes of the Twenty-First Century* (New York: Grove Press, 2005), 239.

3 Michael H. Shuman, *Going Local: Creating Self-Reliant Communities in a Global Age* (New York: The Free Press, 1998), 34.

4 Herman E. Daly, "Sustainable Growth? No Thank You," in Mander and Goldsmith, op. cit. note 1, 194.

5 See "Genuine Progress Indicator: Summary of Data and Methodology," Figure 1 in Clifford Cobb, Ted Halstead, and Jonathan Rowe, *Redefining Progress* (San Francisco, CA, 1995).

6 Dennis Cauchon, "Incomes of young in 8-year nose dive – Those older than 54 increasing earnings," *USA Today* (September 18, 2009), A1.

7 See Shuman, op. cit. note 3, 20 for the cited list of social ills, and his reference to page numbers in Andrew L. Shapiro, *We're Number One* (New York: Vintage, 1992) to support the claims for each of the cited ills, note 57, 276.

8 Ibid., 38.

9 Theodore Roszak, "Introduction," in E. F. Schumacher, *Small is Beautiful: Economics as if People Mattered* (New York: Harper & Row, 1973), 3–4.

10 Shuman, op. cit. note 3, 28.

11 Schumacher, op. cit. note 9, 184.

12 See Shuman, op. cit. note 3, 46, for the claim that books on community economics converge upon the central concept of community self-reliance.

13 An example of the acceptance of community self-reliance as one of the core principles of local economic development appears in Mark Roseland and Lena Soots, "Strengthening

Local Economies," in Worldwatch Institute, *State of the World 2007: Our Urban Future* (New York: W. W. Norton, 2007), 167.

14 Colin Hines and Tim Lang, "In Favor of a New Protectionism," in Mander and Goldsmith, op. cit. note 1, 486.

15 James Goldsmith, "The Winners and the Losers," in Mander and Goldsmith, op. cit. note 1, 179.

16 See Hines and Lang, op. cit. note 14, 487–89.

17 Herman E. Daly and John B. Cobb, Jr., *For the Common Good: Redirecting the Economy toward Community, the Environment, and a Sustainable Future* (Boston, Massachusetts: Beacon Press, 1989), 363.

18 Ibid., 12.

19 Ibid., 134–35.

20 F. Stuart Chapin, Jr., *Urban Land Use Planning*. Second edition. (Urbana, Illinois: University of Illinois Press, 1965), 138.

21 See Shuman, op. cit. note 3, 52–58, and Roseland and Soots, op. cit. note 13, 154–57.

22 Shuman, op. cit. note 3, 56.

23 Ibid., 27.

24 Ibid., 77–78.

25 Ibid., 52–53.

26 Ibid., 77.

27 Daly and Cobb, op. cit. note 17, 8, citing Ulrich Duchrow.

28 Ibid., 332.

29 Ibid., 333.

30 Martin Khor, "Global Economy and the Third World," in Mander and Goldsmith, op. cit. note 1, 57.

31 Daly and Cobb, op. cit. note 17, 76, 87.

32 Ibid., 89.

33 Bill McKibben, *Deep Economy: The Wealth of Communities and the Durable Future* (New York: Holt Paperbacks, 2007), 2–3.

34 Shuman, op. cit. note 3, 6.

35 Roseland and Soots, op. cit. note 13, 152.

36 Daly and Cobb, op. cit. note 17, 311–12.

37 Kirkpatrick Sale, "Principles of Bioregionalism," in Mander and Goldsmith, op. cit. note 1, 484.

38 Ibid., 480.

39 Ibid., 484.

40 Ibid.

41 David Suzuki, *The Sacred Balance: Rediscovering Our Place in Nature* (Amherst, New York: Prometheus Books, 1998), 7.

42 Ibid., 139.

43 Ibid., 138, where Suzuki quotes Vandana Shiva to make his case for "ecosystem stability in diversity."

44 Shuman, op. cit. note 3, 48.

45 Roseland and Soots, op. cit. note 13, 154.

46 Sale, op. cit. note 37, 474.

47 Mander and Goldsmith, op. cit. note 1, 471.

48 Roseland and Soots, op. cit. note 13, 162.

49 Sale, op. cit. note 37, 480.

50 Shuman, op. cit. note 3, 49.

51 Ibid.

52 Daly and Cobb, op. cit. note 17, 59.

53 Ibid., 174.

54 Ibid., 268.

55 Ibid., 173.

56 Ibid., 268.
57 Ibid., 272.
58 Wendell Berry, "Conserving Communities," in Mander and Goldsmith, op. cit. note 1, 416.
59 Daniel Imhoff, "Community Supported Agriculture: Farming with a Face on It," in Mander and Goldsmith, op. cit. note 1, 425–26.
60 Ibid., 432.
61 Ibid., 433.
62 See McKibben, op. cit. note 33, 105, for reference to research findings by Brian Halweil published in 2004, indicating such a 10-fold increase in socialization at farmers' markets.
63 Ibid.
64 Berry, op. cit. note 58, 416.
65 Goldsmith, op. cit. note 1, 510.
66 Imhoff, op. cit. note 59, 416.
67 Ibid., 426.
68 Ibid., 428.
69 McKibben, op. cit. note 33, 64.
70 Ibid., 66.
71 Ibid., 51.
72 Ibid., 64.
73 Imhoff, op. cit. note 59, 429.
74 Ibid.
75 Helena Norgerg-Hodge, "The Pressure to Modernize and Globalize," in Mander and Goldsmith, op. cit. note 1, 396.
76 McKibben, op. cit. note 33, 66–68; Daly and Cobb, op. cit. note 17, 271–72.
77 Ibid., 280–81.
78 Ibid., citing Gever *et al.*, 281.
79 Karen Lehman and Al Krebs, "Control of the World's Food Supply," in Mander and Goldsmith, op. cit. note 1, 123.
80 Jerry Mander, "The Rules of Corporate Behavior," in Mander and Goldsmith, op. cit. note 1, 315, 322.
81 See, for example, Shuman, op. cit. note 3, 86–87.
82 Ibid., 6.
83 Ibid., 7.
84 Ibid., 6.
85 Ibid., 49.
86 Thomas Michael Power, *Environmental Protection and Economic Well-Being* (Armonk, New York: M. E. Sharp, 1996), 194.
87 Shuman, op. cit. note 3, 50.
88 Ibid.
89 Ibid., 55.
90 Daly and Cobb, op. cit. note 17, 165.
91 Ibid., 304–05.
92 Ibid., 305.
93 Ibid., 309.
94 Ibid., 310.
95 See Kai Mander and Alex Boston, "Wal-Mart: Global Retailer," in Mander and Goldsmith, op. cit. note 1, 335–43.
96 Tony Clarke, "Mechanisms of Corporate Rule," in Mander and Goldsmith, op. cit. note 1, 304.
97 See Mander and Boston, op. cit. note 95, 337.
98 Ibid., 338.
99 See McKibben, op. cit. note 33, 106.
100 Stephan J. Goetz and Hema Swaminathan, *Wal-Mart and County-Wide Poverty*, Staff Paper No. 371 (State College, Pennsylvania: Department of Agricultural Economics and Rural Sociology, Pennsylvania State University, 2004), 12.

101 Mander and Boston, op. cit. note 95, 341.
102 See Shuman, op. cit. note 3, 107.
103 Roseland and Soots, op. cit. note 13, 156.
104 Ibid., 156.
105 Ibid.
106 Ibid.
107 Ibid., 157.
108 See Shuman, op. cit. note 3, 132–38, 191–92, and McKibben, op. cit. note 33, 162–64.
109 Ibid., 162.
110 Shuman, op. cit. note 3, 133.
111 Ibid.
112 See, for example, Shuman, op. cit. note 3, 106–22.
113 Ibid., 109.
114 Ibid., 28.
115 Julia Ann Parzen and Michael Hall Kieschnick, *Credit Where It's Due* (Philadelphia, Pennsylvania: Temple University Press, 1992), 44.
116 Ibid.
117 Shuman, op. cit. note 3, 111.
118 Ibid.
119 Roseland and Soots, op. cit. note 13, 161.
120 Shuman, op. cit. note 3, 57–58.
121 Ibid., 58.
122 Ibid., 64–71.
123 Suzuki, op. cit. note 41, 216.
124 Ibid., 215.
125 Shuman, op. cit. note 3, xiv.
126 Ibid., 77.
127 Roseland and Soots, op. cit. note 13, 156.
128 Ibid.
129 Ibid., 157.
130 Michael Renner, "Moving Toward a Less Consumptive Economy," in Worldwatch Institute, *State of the World 2004: The Consumer Society* (New York: W. W. Norton, 2004), 96.
131 Tim Jackson, "The Challenge of Sustainable Lifestyles," in Worldwatch Institute, *State of the World 2008: Innovations for a Sustainable Economy* (New York: W. W. Norton, 2008), 50.
132 See McKibben, op. cit. note 33, 41 for reference to the loss of such a correlation between income and happiness at $10,000; Gary Gardner and Erik Assadourian, "Rethinking the Good Life," in Worldwatch Institute, *State of the World 2004: The Consumer Society* (New York: W. W. Norton, 2004), 166 for reference to research indicating the correlation stops at around $13,000; and Jackson, op. cit. note 131, 50 for reference to data revealing there is virtually no correlation after incomes reach $15,000.
133 Jackson, op. cit. note 131, 50.
134 Gary Gardner, "Seeding the Sustainable Economy," in Worldwatch Institute, *State of the World 2008: Innovations for a Sustainable Economy* (New York: W. W. Norton, 2008), 11.
135 Ibid.
136 John Talberth, "A New Bottom Line for Progress," in Worldwatch Institute, *State of the World 2008: Innovations for a Sustainable Economy* (New York: W. W. Norton, 2008), 21.
137 Ibid.
138 Jackson, op. cit. note 131, 50.
139 Robert D. Putnam, *Bowling Alone: The Collapse and Revival of American Community* (New York: Simon & Schuster, 2000), 332.
140 Gardner and Assadourian, op. cit. note 132, 179.
141 Suzuki, op. cit. note 41, 163.
142 Jackson, op. cit. note 131, 51.
143 Suzuki, op. cit. note 41, 216.

144 McKibben, op. cit. note 33, 113.
145 Putnam, op. cit. note 139, 287.
146 Ibid., 184.
147 Ibid., 185.
148 Ibid., 115.
149 Ibid., 98, 100, 105.
150 McKibben, op. cit. note 33, 117.
151 Ibid., 114.
152 Ibid.
153 Putnam, op. cit. note 139, 21.
154 Putnam, ibid., quoting L. J. Hanifan, 19.
155 Ibid., 22, 288.
156 Ibid., 22.
157 Ibid., 371.
158 Ibid., 335.
159 Ibid., 290.
160 Ibid.
161 Ibid., 27–28.
162 Ibid., 326.
163 Ibid., 331.
164 Ibid., 327.
165 Ibid., 367.
166 Ibid., 283–84, 367.
167 Ibid., 334.
168 Jackson, op. cit. note 131, 52.
169 McKibben, op. cit. note 33, 197.
170 Putnam, op. cit. note 139, 24.
171 Ibid.
172 Ibid., 282.
173 Ibid.
174 McKibben, op. cit. note 33, 100.
175 Ibid., 96.
176 Suzuki, op. cit. note 41, 32, 165.
177 Ibid., 20.
178 Ibid., 22.
179 McKibben, op. cit. note 33, 2.
180 Ibid., 197.
181 Ibid., 127.
182 Ibid., 153, 171.
183 Ibid., 225.
184 Suzuki, op. cit. note 41, 32, 214.
185 Ibid., 163.
186 McKibben, op. cit. note 33, 117.
187 Ibid., 156.
188 Jackson, op. cit. note 131, 58.
189 McKibben, op. cit. note 33, 214.
190 Suzuki, op. cit. note 41, 213.
191 Ibid., 174.
192 Erik Assadourian, "Engaging Communities for a Sustainable World," in Worldwatch Institute, *State of the World 2008: Innovations for a Sustainable Economy* (New York: W. W. Norton, 2008), 152.
193 Joel Kotkin, "There's No Place Like Home: Fewer Americans Are Relocating Than at any Time Since 1962," *Newsweek* (October 19, 2009), 43.
194 Jackson, op. cit. note 131, 55.

195 Suzuki, op. cit. note 41, 214.
196 Ibid., 214.
197 Renner, op. cit. note 130, 108.
198 Gardner and Assadourian, op. cit. note 132, 168.
199 Ibid., 165.
200 Shuman, op. cit. note 3, 128.
201 Ibid., 29.
202 Ibid., 123–51.
203 Ibid., 159.
204 Ibid.
205 Ibid., 183.
206 The requirement for containing future growth in urban growth areas appears in the statewide growth-management act in RCW 36.70A.110, while the requirements for maintaining rural character in rural areas appears in RCW 36.70A.011 and the conservation provisions for resource lands in RCW 36.70A.060.
207 A description of that memorandum of understanding appears in Arthur C. Nelson and James B. Duncan, *Growth Management Principles and Practices* (Chicago, Illinois: Planners Press, American Planning Association, 1995), 80.
208 Assadourian, op. cit. note 192, 152.
209 F. Kaid Benfield, Matthew D. Raimi, and Donald D. T. Chen, *Once There Were Greenfields: How Urban Sprawl is Undermining America's Environment, Economy, and Social Fabric* (Washington, D.C.: Natural Resources Defense Council, 1999), 12.
210 Douglas R. Porter, *Making Smart Growth Work* (Washington, D.C.: The Urban Land Institute, 2002), 29.
211 The noted figures come from the Natural Resources Conservation Service, *National Resources Inventory, 2001 Annual NRI: Urbanization and Development of Rural Land* (July 2003). Online. Available www.nres.usda.gov.
212 John L. Gann, "The Sound of Music: Orchestrating Growth Without Sprawl," *Planning and Zoning News*, vol. 22, no. 4 (2004), 5.
213 Gary Gardner, Erik Assadourian, and Radhika Sarin, "The State of Consumption Today," in Worldwatch Institute, *State of the World 2004: The Consumer Society* (New York: W. W. Norton, 2004), 4.
214 Benfield, Raimi, and Chen, op. cit. note 209, 32.
215 An example of the claim that the average American footprint is over 20 acres may be found in the *Living Planet Report 2006*, jointly produced by the World Wildlife Fund, the Zoological Society of London, and the Global Footprint Network, 3. Online. Available HTTP: http://assests.panda.org/downloads/living_planet_report.pdf (accessed February 20, 2012).
216 Adrian Atkinson, "The Urban Bioregion as 'Sustainable Development' Paradigm," *Third World Planning Review*, vol. 14, no. 4 (1992), 348.
217 Ibid., 336.
218 Daly and Cobb, op. cit. note 17, 176–89.
219 Hilary French, "Linking Globalization, Consumption, and Governance," in Worldwatch Institute, *State of the World 2004: The Consumer Society* (New York: W. W. Norton, 2004), 147–48.
220 Herman E. Daly, "Free Trade: The Perils of Deregulation," in Mander and Goldsmith, op. cit. note 1, 237.
221 French, op. cit. note 219, 147.
222 Lester R. Brown, *Eco-Economy: Building an Economy for the Earth* (New York: W. W. Norton, 2001), 205.
223 David Morris, "Communities: Building Authority, Responsibility, and Capacity," in Mander and Goldsmith, op. cit. note 1, 441.
224 Kunstler, op. cit. note 2, 263.
225 Morris, op. cit. note 223, 442.

226 Ibid.
227 Brian Halweil and Danielle Nierenberg, "Farming the Cities," in Worldwatch Institute, *State of the World 2007: Our Urban Future* (New York: W. W. Norton, 2007), 50.
228 Lester R. Brown, *Plan B 3.0: Mobilizing to Save Civilization* (New York: W. W. Norton, 2008), 207.
229 Kunstler, op. cit. note 2, 61–99.
230 Brown, op. cit. note 228, 44.
231 Kunstler, op. cit. note 2, 17.
232 The Wheeler citation appears in Brown, op. cit. note 228, 44.
233 *Kelo* v. *City of New London*, 545 U.S. 469 (2005).
234 Kunstler, op. cit. note 2, 261.
235 Brown, op. cit. note 222, 198.
236 Brown, op. cit. note 228, 196.
237 Kunstler, op. cit. note 2, 262.
238 Ibid., 270.
239 Ibid., 263.
240 Peter Newman and Jeff Kenworthy, "Greening Urban Transportation," in Worldwatch Institute, *State of the World 2007: Our Urban Future* (New York: W. W. Norton, 2007), 77.
241 Brown, op. cit. note 228, 195.
242 Kunstler, op. cit. note 2, 268–69.
243 Brown, op. cit. note 228, 211.
244 Erik Assadourian, "Government's Role in Design," in Worldwatch Institute, *State of the World 2010: Transforming Cultures—From Consumerism to Sustainability* (New York: W. W. Norton, 2010), 117.
245 Kunstler, op. cit. note 2, 261.
246 See Brown, op. cit. note 228, 213 and Erik Assadourian "The Rise and Fall of Consumer Cultures," in Worldwatch Institute, *State of the World 2010: Transforming Cultures—From Consumerism to Sustainability* (New York: W. W. Norton, 2010), 3.
247 Brown, op. cit. note 222, 71.
248 See Box 9–1: The Escalating Problem of Biodiversity Loss, in Ricardo Bayon, "Banking on Biodiversity," in Worldwatch Institute, *State of the World 2008: Innovations for a Sustainable Economy* (New York: W. W. Norton, 2008), 125.
249 Reference to the IUCN press release appears in the timeline of significant announcements and reports compiled by Lisa Mastny and Valentina Agostinelli, in Worldwatch Institute, *State of the World 2010: Transforming Cultures—From Consumerism to Sustainability* (New York: W. W. Norton, 2010), xxii; for additional confirmation of the role of climate change in exacerbating biodiversity loss see Thomas Lovejoy, "Climate Change's Pressures on Biodiversity," in Worldwatch Institute, *State of the World 2009: Into a Warming World* (New York: W. W. Norton, 2009), 67–70.
250 Reference to the study appears in Mastny and Agostinelli, op. cit. note 249, xxii.
251 David W. Orr, "What is Higher Education for Now?" in Worldwatch Institute, *State of the World 2010: Transforming Cultures—From Consumerism to Sustainability* (New York: W. W. Norton, 2010), 80.
252 See Mastny and Agostinelli, op. cit. note 249, xxiii.
253 Assadourian, op. cit. note 246, 5.
254 Global Footprint Network, "Earth Overshoot Day." Online. Available www.footprintnetwork.org, updated July 16, 2009.
255 Assadourian, op. cit. note 246, 4.
256 Orr, op. cit. note 251, 76.
257 Ibid.
258 Assadourian, op. cit. note 246, 4.
259 John de Graaf, "Reducing Work Time as a Path to Sustainability," in Worldwatch Institute, *State of the World 2010: Transforming Cultures—From Consumerism to Sustainability* (New York: W. W. Norton, 2010), 177.

260 Michael Maniates, "Editing Out Unsustainable Behavior," in Worldwatch Institute, *State of the World 2010: Transforming Cultures—From Consumerism to Sustainability* (New York: W. W. Norton, 2010), 126.

261 The citation attributed to Gus Speth, former dean of the Yale School of Forestry, appears in de Graaf, op. cit. note 259, 174.

262 Christopher Flavin, "Preface," in Worldwatch Institute, *State of the World 2010: Transforming Cultures—From Consumerism to Sustainability* (New York: W. W. Norton, 2010), xvii.

263 Paul R. Ehrlich and Anne H. Ehrlich, "Box 11. A New Focus for Scientists: How Cultures Change," in Worldwatch Institute, *State of the World 2010: Transforming Cultures—From Consumerism to Sustainability* (New York: W. W. Norton, 2010), 82.

264 Assadourian, op. cit. note 244, 118.

265 Robert Costanza, Joshua Farley, and Ida Kubiszewski, "Adapting Institutions for Life in a Full World," in Worldwatch Institute, *State of the World 2010: Transforming Cultures—From Consumerism to Sustainability* (New York: W. W. Norton, 2010), 85.

266 Assadourian, op. cit. note 246, 5.

267 Muhammad Yunus, "Foreword," in Worldwatch Institute, *State of the World 2010: Transforming Cultures—From Consumerism to Sustainability* (New York: W. W. Norton, 2010), xv.

268 Ibid., xvi.

269 Flavin, op. cit. note 262, xvii.

270 Assadourian, op. cit. note 246, 3.

271 Peter Newman, "Building the Cities of the Future," in Worldwatch Institute, *State of the World 2010: Transforming Cultures—From Consumerism to Sustainability* (New York: W. W. Norton, 2010), 137.

272 Ingred Pramling Samuelsson and Yoshie Kaga, "Early Childhood Education to Transform Cultures to Sustainability," in Worldwatch Institute, *State of the World 2010: Transforming Cultures—From Consumerism to Sustainability* (New York: W. W. Norton, 2010), 57.

273 Assadourian, op. cit. note 246, 16.

274 de Graaf, op. cit. note 259, 174.

275 Costanza, Farley, and Kubiszewski, op. cit. note 265, 90.

276 Jonathan Dawson, "Ecovillages and the Transformation of Values," in Worldwatch Institute, *State of the World 2010: Transforming Cultures—From Consumerism to Sustainability* (New York: W. W. Norton, 2010), 186.

277 Erik Assadourian, "Business and Economy: Management Priorities," in Worldwatch Institute, *State of the World 2010: Transforming Cultures—From Consumerism to Sustainability* (New York: W. W. Norton, 2010), 84.

278 Assadourian, op. cit. note 246, 15.

279 Øystein Dahle, "Box 12. The Folly of Infinite Growth on a Finite Planet," in Worldwatch Institute, *State of the World 2010: Transforming Cultures—From Consumerism to Sustainability* (New York: W. W. Norton, 2010), 87.

280 Cecile Andrews and Wanda Urbanska, "Inspiring People to See That Less Is More," in Worldwatch Institute, *State of the World 2010: Transforming Cultures—From Consumerism to Sustainability* (New York: W. W. Norton, 2010), 184.

281 Ibid., 183.

282 Gary Gardner, "Engaging Religions to Shape Worldviews," in Worldwatch Institute, *State of the World 2010: Transforming Cultures—From Consumerism to Sustainability* (New York: W. W. Norton, 2010), 27.

283 The cited poll by the Pew Charitable Trust appears in Brown, op. cit. note 222, 192–93.

284 Andrews and Urbanska, op. cit. note 280, 178.

285 Ibid., 179.

286 Helene Gallis, "Box 23. The Slow Food Movement," in Worldwatch Institute, *State of the World 2010: Transforming Cultures—From Consumerism to Sustainability* (New York: W. W. Norton, 2010), 182.

287 Ibid.

288 Ibid.

289 Dawson, op. cit. note 276, 185.
290 Ibid., 186.
291 de Graaf, op. cit. note 259, 174.
292 Ibid.
293 Andrews and Urbanska, op. cit. note 280, 180.
294 Serge Latouche, "Box 22. Growing a Degrowth Movement," in Worldwatch Institute, *State of the World 2010: Transforming Cultures—From Consumerism to Sustainability* (New York: W. W. Norton, 2010), 181.
295 Ibid.
296 Erik Assadourian, "The Power of Social Movements," in Worldwatch Institute, *State of the World 2010: Transforming Cultures—From Consumerism to Sustainability* (New York: W.W. Norton, 2010), 172.
297 Ibid., 171.
298 Latouche, op. cit. note 294, 181.
299 Jonah Sachs and Susan Finkelpearl, "From Selling Soap to Selling Sustainability: Social Marketing," in Worldwatch Institute, *State of the World 2010: Transforming Cultures—From Consumerism to Sustainability* (New York: W. W. Norton, 2010), 151.
300 Ibid.

Epilogue: 10 Difficult personal actions needed to save the world

1 Philip Cafaro and Winthrop Staples III, "The Environmental Argument for Reducing Immigration to the United States," *Backgrounder*, Center for Immigration Studies (June 2009), 3.
2 Leon F. Bouvier, "The Impact of Immigration on United States' Population Size: 1950 to 2050," *NPG Forum* (1998), Washington, D.C.: Negative Population Growth, Inc.
3 Cafaro and Staples, op. cit. note 1, 12.
4 Erik Assadourian and Eddie Kasner, "Box 5. Dietary Norms That Heal People and the Planet," in Worldwatch Institute, *State of the World 2010: Transforming Cultures—From Consumerism to Sustainability* (New York: W. W. Norton, 2010), 49.
5 See *Livestock's Long Shadow: Environmental Issues and Options*, 2010. Online. Available HTTP: http://ftp.fao.org/docrep/fao/010/a0701e/A0701E00.pdf (accessed May 15, 2012).
6 Bill McKibben, *Deep Economy: The Wealth of Communities and the Durable Future* (New York: Holt Paperbacks, 2007), 66.

Selected bibliography

American Academy of Arts and Sciences. 1973. The No-Growth Society. *Daedalus—Journal of the American Academy of Arts and Sciences* 102,4: 1–245.

Ayres, Robert U. 1998. *Turning Point: An End to the Growth Paradigm*. New York: St. Martin's Press.

Bartlett, Albert A. 1994. Reflections on Sustainability, Population Growth, and the Environment. In *The Carrying Capacity Briefing Book*. Washington, D.C.: Carrying Capacity Network.

Brown, Lester R. 1981. *Building a Sustainable Society*. New York: W. W. Norton.

——2001. *Eco-Economy: Building an Economy for the Earth*. New York: W. W. Norton.

——2008. *Plan B 3.0: Mobilizing to Save Civilization*. New York: W. W. Norton.

——2009. *Plan B 4.0: Mobilizing to Save Civilization*. New York: W. W. Norton.

Brown, Lester R. and Jodi L. Jacobson. 1987. *The Future of Urbanization: Facing the Ecological and Economic Constraints*, Worldwatch Paper 77. Washington, D.C.: Worldwatch Institute.

Brown, Lester R. and Hal Kane. 1994. *Full House: Reassessing the Earth's Population Carrying Capacity*. New York: W. W. Norton.

Commission on Population Growth and the American Future. 1972. *Population and the American Future*. New York: Signet.

Council on Environmental Quality and the Department of State. 1982. *The Global 2000 Report to the President: Entering the Twenty-First Century*. London, England: Penguin Books.

Cranston, Mary, Bryant Garth, Robert Plattner, and Jay Varon. 1973. *A Handbook for Controlling Local Growth*. Stanford, California: Stanford Environmental Law Society.

Czech, Brian. 2000. *Shoveling Fuel for a Runaway Train: Errant Economists, Shameful Spenders, and a Plan to Stop Them All*. Berkeley, California: University of California Press.

Daly, Herman E. 1973. The Steady-State Economy: Toward a Political Economy of Biophysical Equilibrium and Moral Growth. In *Toward a Steady-State Economy*, edited by Herman E. Daly. San Francisco, California: W. H. Freeman and Company.

——1991. Sustainable Development: From Concept and Theory Toward Operational Principles. In *Steady-State Economics: Second Edition with New Essays*. Washington, D.C.: Island Press.

——1996. *Beyond Growth: The Economics of Sustainable Development*. Boston, Massachusetts: Beacon Press.

——1996. Sustainable Growth? No Thank You. In *The Case Against the Global Economy: And a Turn Toward the Local*, edited by Jerry Mander and Edward Goldsmith. San Francisco, California: Sierra Club Books.

Daly, Herman E. and John B. Cobb, Jr. 1989. *For the Common Good: Redirecting the Economy Toward Community, the Environment, and a Sustainable Future*. Boston, Massachusetts: Beacon Press.

Douthwaite, Richard. 1992. *The Growth Illusion: How Economic Growth Has Enriched the Few, Impoverished the Many, and Endangered the Planet*. Gabriola Island, British Columbia: New Society Publishers.

Ehrlich, Paul R. 1968. *The Population Bomb*. New York: Ballantine Books.

Ehrlich, Paul R. and Anne H. Ehrlich. 1981. *Extinction*. New York: Random House.

——1990. *The Population Explosion*. New York: Simon and Schuster.

——1991. *Healing the Planet: Strategies for Resolving the Environmental Crisis*. New York: Addison-Wesley.

Finkler, Earl. 1972. *Nongrowth as a Planning Alternative: A Preliminary Examination of an Emerging Issue*, Planning Advisory Service, Report No. 283. Chicago, Illinois: American Society of Planning Officials.

——1973. *Nongrowth: A Review of the Literature*, Planning Advisory Service, Report No. 289. Chicago, Illinois: American Society of Planning Officials.

Finkler, Earl and David L. Peterson. 1974. *Nongrowth Planning Strategies: The Developing Power of Towns, Cities, and Regions*. New York: Praeger Publishers.

Finkler, Earl, William J. Toner, and Frank J. Popper. 1976. *Urban Nongrowth: City Planning for People*. New York: Praeger Publishers.

Fodor, Eben. 1999. *Better Not Bigger: How to Take Control of Urban Growth and Improve Your Community*. Gabriola Island, British Columbia: New Society Publishers.

——2000. *The Cost of Growth in Washington State*. Bellevue, Washington: The Columbia Public Interest Policy Institute.

Goldsmith, Edward, Robert Allen, Michael Allaby, John Davoll, and Sam Lawrence. 1974. *Blueprint for Survival*. New York: Signet.

Goodland, Robert. 1996. Growth Has Reached Its Limits. In *The Case Against the Global Economy: And a Turn Toward the Local*, edited by Jerry Mander and Edward Goldsmith. San Francisco, California: Sierra Club Books.

Hansen, James *et al.* 2007. Dangerous Human-Made Interference with Climate: A GISS Model Study. *Atmospheric Chemistry and Physics* 7,9: 2287–312.

Hardin, Garrett. 1968. The Tragedy of the Commons. *Science* 162: 1243–48.

——1993. *Living Within Limits: Ecology, Economics, and Population Taboos*. New York: Oxford University Press.

Heinberg, Richard. 2011. *The End of Growth: Adapting to Our New Economic Reality*. Gabriola Island, British Columbia: New Society Publishers.

Hirsch, Fred. 1976. *Social Limits to Growth*. Cambridge, Massachusetts: Harvard University Press.

Intergovernmental Panel on Climate Change. 2001. *Climate Change 2001: Third Assessment Report*. New York: Cambridge University Press.

——2007. *Climate Change 2007*. Cambridge: Cambridge University Press.

Jackson, Tim. 2009. *Prosperity Without Growth: Economics for a Finite Planet*. Sterling, Virginia: Earthscan.

Johnson, Warren A. and John Hardesty, editors. 1971. *Economic Growth vs. the Environment*. Belmont, California: Wadsworth.

Leopold, Aldo. 1949. *A Sand County Almanac—And Sketches Here and There*. New York: Oxford University Press.

Lovelock, James. 2006. The Earth is About to Catch a Morbid Fever That May Last as Long as 100,000 Years. *The Independent* January 16.

Lubchenco, Jane, Annette M. Olson, Linda B. Brubaker, Stephen R. Carpenter, Marjorie M. Holland, Stephen P. Hubbell, Simon A. Levin, James A. MacMahon, Pamela A. Matson, Jerry M. Melillo, Herold A. Mooney, Charles H. Peterson, H. Ronald Pulliam, Leslie A. Real, Philip J. Regal, and Paul G. Risser. 1991. The Sustainable Biosphere Initiative: An Ecological Research Agenda. *Ecology* 72,2: 371–412.

Mander, Jerry and Edward Goldsmith, editors. 1996. *The Case Against the Global Economy: And a Turn Toward the Local*. San Francisco, California: Sierra Club Books.

McKibben, Bill. 2007. *Deep Economy: The Wealth of Communities and the Durable Future*. New York: Holt Paperbacks.

Meadows, Donella H., Dennis L. Meadows, and Jørgen Randers. 1992. *Beyond the Limits*. Post Mills, Vermont: Chelsea Green Publishing Company.

Meadows, Donella H., Jøgen Randers, and Dennis Meadows. 2004. *Limits to Growth: The 30-Year Update*. White River Junction, Vermont: Chelsea Green Publishing Company.

Meadows, Donella H., Dennis L. Meadows, Jørgen Randers, and William W. Behrens. 1972. *The Limits to Growth*. New York: Signet.

Meyer, Judy L. and Gene S. Helfman. 1993. The Ecological Basis of Sustainability. *Ecological Applications* 3,4: 569–71.

Mill, John Stuart. 1857. *Principles of Political Economy*, Vol. II. London: John W. Parker and Son.

Millennium Ecosystem Assessment. 2005. *Ecosystems and Human Well-Being: Synthesis*. Washington, D.C.: Island Press.

Mishan, Ezra J. 1967. *The Costs of Economic Growth*. New York: Frederick A. Praeger, Publishers.

——1969. *Technology and Growth: The Price We Pay*. New York: Praeger Publishers.

——1972. Economic Growth: The Need for Skepticism. *Loyds Bank Review* (October): 1–26.

Oltmans, William L. 1974. *On Growth*. New York: Capricorn Books.

Owen, David. 2009. *Green Metropolis: Why Living Smaller, Living Closer, and Driving Less Are the Keys to Sustainability*. New York: Riverhead Books.

Perlman, Judith. 2004. *Citizen's Primer for Conservation Activism: How to Fight Development in Your Community*. Austin, Texas: University of Texas Press.

Postel, Sandra. 1994. Carrying Capacity: Earth's Bottom Line. In *State of the World 1994: A Worldwatch Institute Report on Progress Toward a Sustainable Society*. New York: W. W. Norton.

Rees, William. 1990. A Sunshine Limit to Growth. *Ecologist* 20,1: L3.

——1992. Ecological Footprints and Appropriated Carrying Capacity: What Urban Economics Leaves Out. *Environmental Urbanization* 4,2: 121–130.

——1996. Revisiting Carrying Capacity: Area-Based Indicators of Sustainability. *Popular Environment* 17,3: 195–215.

——2010. What's Blocking Sustainability? Human Nature, Cognition and Denial. *Sustainability: Science, Practice, & Policy* 6,2: 1–13.

Rees, William and Mathis Wackernagel. 1996. Urban Ecological Footprints: Why Cities Cannot Be Sustainable—and Why They Are a Key to Sustainability. *Environmental Impact Assessment Review* 16: 223–48.

Renshaw, Edward F. 1976. *The End of Progress: Adjusting to a No-Growth Economy*. North Scituate, Massachusetts: Duxbury Press.

Rockström, Johan *et al*. 2009. A Safe Operating Space for Humanity. *Nature* 461: 472–75.

Sale, Kirkpatrick. 1985. *Dwellers in the Land: The Bioregional Vision*. San Francisco, California: Sierra Club Books.

Sauvy, Alfred. 1976. *Zero Growth?* New York: Praeger Publishers.

Schumacher, E. F. 1973. *Small is Beautiful: Economics as if People Mattered*. New York: Harper & Row.

Siegel, Charles. 2006. *The End of Economic Growth*. Berkeley, California: Preservation Institute.

Stennett, Edwin. 2002. *In Growth We Trust: Sprawl, Smart Growth, and Rapid Population Growth*. Gaithersburg, Maryland: Growth Education Movement, Inc.

United States Comission on Population Growth and the American Future. 1972. *Population and the American Future*. Washington, D.C.: Government Printing Office.

Wackernagel, Mathis and William E. Rees. 1996. *Our Ecological Footprint: Reducing Human Impact on the Earth*. Gabriola Island, British Columbia: New Society Publishers.

——2002. Tracking the Ecological Overshoot of the Human Economy. *Proceedings of the National Academy of Sciences* 99,14: 266–71.

Wackernagel, Mathis, Larry Onisto, Alejandro Callejas Linares, Ina Susana López Falfán, Jesus Méndez García, Ana Isabel Suárez Guerrero, Ma. Guadalupe Suárez Guerrero. 1997. *Ecological Footprints of Nations? How Much Do They Use? How Much Do They Have?* Toronto: International Council for Local Environmental Initiatives.

Warner, Daniel M. 2006. 'Post-Growthism': From Smart Growth to Sustainable Development. *Environmental Practice* 8,3: 169–79.

Williamson, Chris. 2004. Exploring the No-Growth Option. *Planning* (November) 70,10: 34–6.

Zovanyi, Gabor. 1981. *Toward a No-Growth Urban Planning Philosophy.* Seattle, Washington: University of Washington Doctoral Dissertation.

——1998. *Growth Management for a Sustainable Future: Ecological Sustainability as the New Growth Management Focus for the 21st Century.* West Port, Connecticut: Praeger Publishers.

——1999. The Growth Management Delusion. *NPG Forum.* Washington, D.C.: Negative Population Growth, Inc.

——2000. Growth Management Strategies for Stopping Growth in Local Communities. *NPG Forum.* Washington, D.C.: Negative Population Growth, Inc.

Index

DATE D